An ATLAS of
ENDANGERED
ALPHABETS

To Saraswati, the Hindu goddess of writing

'Certainly the art of writing is the most miraculous of all things man has devised.'
Thomas Carlyle

An *ATLAS* of ENDANGERED ALPHABETS

Writing Systems on the Verge of Vanishing

TIM BROOKES

QUERCUS

CONTENTS

INTRODUCTION

History is written by the winners, and the alphabet in which it is written is the alphabet of the winners. This means that those of us in the dominant cultures of the world, especially the West, have a better chance of being able to read signage in airports and railway stations when we travel. But it puts us at three disadvantages when it comes to understanding the value and importance of writing.

First, we have no idea that script loss might even be a problem, because we've never even come close to losing our alphabet. Hint: it is. Probably 85 to 90 per cent of the world's writing systems, in particular those of Indigenous and minority communities, stand a good chance of being forced into disuse. And when that happens, and a culture's script is overrun by the Latin alphabet, or Arabic, or Cyrillic or Devanagari, then within two generations everything that culture has written in their own mother script for as much as a thousand years – collections of sacred palm-leaf manuscripts, family recipes, letters, the

deed proving ownership of the family home and land – is lost to the very people to whom it means the most.

The older generation see what is happening and feel as if they're on the edge of an eroding cliff – their history and identity, dignity and sense of purpose in the world fall away beneath their feet. The grandkids will see nothing but scrawl on paper, will call it 'the old writing', and shrug.

Moreover, we have no idea that when another culture loses their writing system, we probably caused it – just as we never hear a newscaster say, 'Today the last elephant seal died. The species is now extinct – and it's our fault.' Instead, we bleat that surely it would be more convenient if everyone in the world used the same language and the same alphabet?

Well, it would certainly be more convenient for those of us whose language and script have won out. This is a good place to say, as clearly as possible, languages and scripts do not just fade away. As you'll see in these pages, nobody loses an alphabet by accident. Every endangered alphabet is the vestige of a lost kingdom, a suffering culture. Every marginalized script is a sign of social injustice, past or present.

Second, we have no idea of the characteristics, assumptions and built-in shortcomings of our own alphabet because we can't read anyone else's. After a decade of researching endangered alphabets, I have come to see our Latin (or Roman) alphabet as pompous and unlovely, not even able to boast the minimal virtues of exactitude.

It has become the winning alphabet only by virtue of being the winner's alphabet. As you'll see in these pages, other scripts are older, more calligraphic, easier to learn, more elegant, more deeply connected to their culture's visual iconography, spiritually richer, or easier to pronounce.

Third, we use writing so much, for so many purposes, most of them functional or mundane, that we have lost sight of its extraordinary qualities – qualities we are never taught. I am all in favour of universal literacy, but teaching writing as a functional necessity and a survival skill drains it of its vitality and splendour, leaving kids no more interested in writing than they are in mathematics, another intellectual marvel.

Hardly surprising, then, that we have no academic discipline dedicated to understanding writing in all its richness – its phenomenology, the relationship between graphic/typographic design and cultural values, its spiritual potency, its ability to encode cultural values and (when handwritten) the personality of the individual, its ability to acquire iconic authority, its relationship to art and performance. A standard academic argument, even at times a linguistic orthodoxy, is that as everyone speaks but not everyone writes, writing is unworthy of serious study; that it is, at best, an artificial mechanism for representing speech.

If we in the West take writing for granted as a convenient, if slightly laborious, way of texting each other or jotting down grocery lists, other cultures are far more aware of writing as an extraordinary intellectual conception.

Many cultures have traditional tales that represent writing as a divine gift, a primordial factor in elevating humans into something approaching civilization. Zhuang mythology tells of a god who gave them two gifts: writing and fire. This is an extraordinary pairing, given that fire is often identified as the gift or discovery that enabled humans to emerge from the kingdom of the beasts. It can even be argued that the story in Exodus in which God gives Moses the Covenant, written by the finger of God on two stone tablets, is a writing-creation myth.

Yet today, we in the West have so little regard for writing that one of the standard explanations for its origins reduces it to nothing more than an accounting device – a perfect example of our inability to see the remarkable even when it is under our noses.

In Bali, the acts of writing or reading are traditionally seen as transactions between the material and immaterial worlds – by no means an absurd view when you think of an idea as something invisible and immaterial, and writing the act of capturing and gathering it into a visible, physical manifestation, a literal shaping of thought. If you consider writing with such high seriousness, and are mindful of the way it can act as the agency by which one mind may affect another, it is hardly surprising they have specific mantras that should be recited before making corrections to a manuscript and even before the opening and closing of books.   >>

>> The Balinese, and many other cultures in the region, venerate Saraswati, the Hindu goddess of knowledge, art, wisdom, nature and writing. In theory, we in the West venerate wisdom (though at times, especially during political debate, that's hard to believe), but we see writing as far too mundane an artifact to revere.

Other cultures have tales that their ancestral writing system was lost or stolen from them. The lack or loss of one's own writing system – a state that in many areas of the world is equated with being inferior, or even primitive – can be such a political and social disadvantage, such a blow to a culture's identity, that one member of the Karen people of Southeast Asia lamented, '[We] have been an ignorant people, without books, without a king, without a government of our own, subject to other kings and other governments, we have been a nation of slaves, despised and kicked about, trodden under foot by everybody like dogs.' Notice what comes first in that list of losses. Many of the scripts in this atlas have similar stories to tell.

Conversely, that lack or loss has driven, and continues to drive, people to create their own writing systems – at least a hundred that we know of. A scattered and stateless people may invent different scripts in different communities: the Hmong have, at various times in various countries, created at least nine. Their impact has often been so powerful, so galvanizing, that messianic religions have gathered around these scripts and their creators. This in turn has made

them a threat to their more powerful neighbours, and unfortunately, we know of at least four people who have been murdered for creating writing systems for their people. For this reason, this atlas includes not only endangered well-established writing systems, but also emerging ones, which are endangered in the way that fledgling birds are: all kinds of dangers lie between them and adulthood, a stable acceptance.

Writing systems are so deeply felt by their users that all around the world cultures use individual letters as cultural icons, in jewellery, on stamps, as tattoos, on coins and banknotes and on T-shirts, even if people can no longer read them.

When the Amazigh cultural revivalists in 1960s' North Africa designed a flag for their culture, which once spread from the western border of Egypt to the Canary Islands, they incorporated, right in the centre of the design, a letter. It was a brilliant conception. The letter was, and is, the *yaz* from the Amazigh writing system, found in 2,000-year-old writing etched in stones all across North Africa – a sign that they were there before the Romans, before the Arabs, before the French. That they belong.

One final acknowledgment: it can also be a sign of human-rights abuse when a culture does not have an endangered alphabet, either because it was an oral culture until a script was introduced by a colonizer or oppressor; or at some point in the past, it entirely lost its script, usually through force.

Perhaps the simplest and clearest statement of the connection between writing and

>> human rights is Article 13 of the aspirational United Nations Declaration on the Rights of Indigenous Peoples: 'Indigenous peoples have the right to revitalize, use, develop and transmit to future generations their histories, languages, oral traditions, philosophies, writing systems and literatures, and to designate and retain their own names for communities, places and persons.' This atlas aims to be one small act in support of those rights.

A Disclaimer, An Invitation

Does this atlas contain all the world's endangered alphabets? No. Our current research suggests about 300 scripts are to some extent in use, but this is a moving target: even while this book was in production, several new scripts were created in India and at least two in Africa. Some minority scripts were made official. The 'extinct' Glagolitic script began to appear on town signage in Croatia. Several scripts were welcomed into the Unicode standard and/or adapted for digital devices, making them easier to use and giving them a better chance of survival. So think of this atlas as a sampling.

In some respects, the situation is improving. Since I began the Endangered Alphabets Project in 2009, while many endangered languages have lost their last speaker, many writing systems have found a constituency, a voice, an energy and a degree of use that seemed unthinkable only a decade ago. In addition, several new writing systems have been born and are finding their feet.

Is the information in this atlas accurate? It's the best I can do. For one thing, it's impossible to prove a negative. Is it true that nobody is using the script created in 2005 by linguist Gregg Cox for the Kodava language of Karnataka? Is anyone in the remote Malian villages of Assatiémala, Dyabé, Ségala, Sérédji or Koronka still using the Masaba script? Without doing the world tour I've dreamed of, I can't be sure.

Are my sources at least reliable? Out in the world beyond the Latin alphabet, people feel passionately about writing systems, and it's possible some of my informants may not be entirely objective. Every day I correspond with a dozen or more people, trying to get a more detailed view of what is happening on the ground, where it matters most.

This is not, then, an encyclopaedia or a compendium or that holy grail, a resource. It is an invitation to travel. Fair winds and safe travels to you all, and please let me know what you find.

Tim Brookes
Burlington, Vermont

'ENDANGERED ...'

The word 'endangered' is inexact. As no census asks anyone which writing system(s) they use, we simply don't have numbers.

Most countries carry out a periodic census that includes questions about what languages people speak, so it is possible to make a fair calculation as to the number of speakers of any given one. More detailed research can identify other factors that affect its use, and thus the degree to which it is threatened.

So, as very little scholarly research examines script health or loss, describing a writing system as 'endangered' and including it in this atlas is based largely on an educated guess, using several criteria:

- Is it used as an official script for disseminating important/emergency information to the public, such as Ebola or COVID precautions? Is it used as an official script in government proceedings? For what I'm calling 'endangered' scripts, the answer to both would be 'no'.

- Is it used as the primary mode of education in government-funded schooling, with textbooks and educational materials printed in it? 'Endangered' scripts may be taught for a year or two, or as an elective, but are rarely the means by which one learns.

- Is it universally included in official signage on government buildings, schools, street signs, airports, stations? 'Endangered' scripts may in some instances be used in local signage but typically not as a clear, equal and parallel equivalent to the official national script(s).

- Does it appear regularly in multiple forms of print, in books, magazines and newspapers? 'Endangered' scripts may appear in marginal or intermittent publications but rarely make a regular or high-profile appearance.

- Does it appear in textual uses on television, such as in identification letters of stations, captions, credits or subtitles? 'Endangered' scripts typically make little or no appearance on TV, as they connote lack of sophistication and purchasing power.

- Has it been digitized, included in Unicode, and adapted with fonts and keyboards readily available? Can members of a language community text each other without having to go through one of the world's dominant writing systems, with all that entails? Some 'endangered' scripts do have an Internet presence – the Internet is the new frontier for minority cultures – but this is almost always the result of a few skilled enthusiasts rather than any official initiative either by government or major commercial interests.

The scripts in this book, then, are ones for which the answers to these questions are almost all 'no'. We simply don't have enough information yet to assign comparative levels of threat. In the end, the atlas has two related purposes: to introduce readers in the privileged world to this extraordinary field of exploration; and to let readers in Indigenous, minority or marginalized cultures know they are recognized and valued. As one user of the Sora Sompeng script of Andhra Pradesh, India, says, 'It means the world to us to know we are seen.'

' ... A L P H A B E T S '

The word 'alphabets' in the phrase 'endangered alphabets' is a kind of shorthand for familiarity's sake; a more accurate term would be 'scripts' or, most formally, 'writing systems'. An alphabet is one kind of writing system, but there are several others:

Abjad

A curious and fascinating thing: in the evolution of writing systems of Europe, North Africa and the Middle East, consonants appeared before vowels. An abjad is a writing system whose symbols represent consonants; vowels, if used, typically appear as diacritics above or below the consonants.

Alphabet

The system in which this atlas is written. In an alphabet, each symbol represents a consonant or vowel. In some languages that use alphabets, such as Czech, the one-to-one equivalence is strict; in others, such as English, the relationship is looser: some letters may be voiced in more than one way, and some sounds may need two or more letters to represent them.

Syllabic alphabets

Syllabic alphabets, also called alphasyllabaries or abugidas, have some of the qualities of alphabets, and some of those of syllabaries. They are based on the unit of the syllable, so each character represents a consonant and an implied vowel – but the actual sound of the vowel is typically indicated by a diacritic, and other modifications are used to indicate a vowel at the beginning of a word, or a word that ends in a consonant.

Syllabaries

Syllabaries are different from syllabic alphabets in that every character represents a specific consonant followed by a specific vowel. This means that syllabaries have no diacritics, but a large set of characters. Cherokee, for example, has eighty-five symbols.

Semanto-phonetic systems

Systems in which individual characters indicate both meaning and sound are richer in content than purely phonetic systems, but in order to cover all the subject matter they might want to, such systems consist of thousands or even tens of thousands of characters. They include pictograms (drawings that represent physical things), logograms (symbols that represent words) and ideograms (symbols that represent ideas). Some European road signs, then, are pictograms, some are logograms and some are ideograms.

Semanto-phonetic compounds

These compounds – Chinese characters are the best-known example – encode the greatest amount of information, each containing information about how it should be pronounced, and information about what it means.

A F R

INTRODUCTION

The continent of Africa may not have many ancient traditional writing systems on the brink of extinction, but especially in the western part of sub-Saharan Africa, from Senegal to Cameroon, it has an amazing richness of emerging scripts – far more than any comparable area apart from northeast India.

In addition to those included in this section, we know of at least twenty more that have been created in the last 200 years, some of which have been abandoned, some of which may still be in use by a handful of people.

What makes these scripts remarkable is not just the fertility of creativity and commitment to writing as a skill, an art and cultural representation – those qualities can also be seen in the recently created scripts of South Asia, for example. No, the vast majority of these emerging scripts have two qualities that together seem to be characteristically African.

One: they are graphically creative, especially in taking elements from their own culture's visual landscape as a basis for letterforms.

When creating a new writing system, unless the creator has never seen or used writing before, it's hard to avoid assumptions about what it ought to look like: that it should be consistent and simple enough to be learned and used by anyone; that it should comprise horizontal, evenly spaced, parallel lines; that the text should all be the same colour; that letterforms should all be roughly the same height and spaced more or less equidistantly from each other; and perhaps above all, that it should be based on an organized set of symbols that are recognizably different from, say, fabric patterns or designs on ceramics, or representational art.

Some African scripts follow those practices; some certainly do not.

Some, like the Nsibidi system, were never intended to be understood by everyone; they grew out of a tradition of secrecy, and are closer to what we might call a code. Some, like Mandombe, ignore standard conventions of line spacing and letter height. Some, like the Bamum script, are based on the notion that familiar symbols from art and design are easier to recognize and learn, and more clearly represent the cultural identity and experience of the people whose speech they aim to represent. Instead of practising a clear distinction between writing and design, these scripts represent a convergence of the two.

Some, in fact, extend the notion of 'writing' into such new realms that they deserve their own section ('Beyond the Alphabet', page 226).

One of the newest and most technically sophisticated scripts, Ditema tsa Dinoko (page 42), is a syllabary whose glyphs are derived from a traditional southern African art form based on decorative and symbolic patterns engraved, painted or moulded in the walls of homes. For centuries, women have combed the patterns (to imitate a ploughed field) or scratched them into the wet top layer of fresh clay-and-dung plaster of the wall and then painted them with naturally occurring pigments or, more recently, paint.

Two: a uniquely African quality of several emerging scripts is their ambition to be used continent-wide. It is remarkable in how many cases the author of a script (Adlam, Ditema tsa Dinoko, Luo Lakeside and Mandombe, for example) may have created it with one specific language in mind, but also with the explicit hope that it might be used for all African languages.

In part, this may arise from the recognition, and in some cases the frustration, that some African languages include unique sounds for which there is no equivalent in either the colonizing Latin or Arabic alphabets.

In part, the cause may be a sense of pan-African solidarity in the face of centuries, even millennia, of colonial domination and exploitation – a situation that in many places has continued into a post-colonial era. The colonial languages (English, French, Arabic) are still widely seen as the 'prestige' ones in education, administration, business and law, while Indigenous languages are seen as more vernacular. Implicit in that view is the parallel belief that Indigenous writing systems, also, are too blunt an instrument for the highest intellectual purposes.

'English, French and Arabic have been preferred over Indigenous languages,' writes Paul Sidandi, one of the authors of the Luo Lakeside script. 'In fact children in primary schools were discouraged from speaking in the native tongues, and anyone found doing so would be given a … disc, and he or she had to be on the lookout for another pupil to pass it on to. Those who received the disc got punished at the end of the day.'

(This method of passing around a physical token to crush mother-tongue usage – and getting Indigenous children to self-police and betray each other – seems to have been almost universal. In Wales, it was called the Welsh Not, in Ireland the bata scóir. In Bretagne, the token was called le symbole and was in the shape of a cow or a donkey: the pupil caught speaking Breton was given the symbol and could only get rid of it by passing it to another Breton speaker in the class saying, 'Oh la vache!' Hence the current French curse.)

Sidandi continues: 'African languages have the capability and sophistication of teaching any subject. Kiswahili is a good example. It was made popular by Mwalimu (Teacher) Julius Nyerere. It was used for teaching students up to university level. Today it is being taught in many other African countries. Setswana is also taught in many southern African countries … Our hope is that all these African languages can adopt the African Lakeside Script.'

Others working on African scripts have the same hope.

Script:
Tifinagh
—
The letter *yaz*, which has
become so iconic that it
stands at the centre of
the Amazigh flag.

TIFINAGH

Origin:
North Africa

Some of the most extraordinary writing in the world can be seen on the wall of a cave deep in the Sahara.

The site is called the Wadi Matkhandouch Prehistoric Art Gallery, near Germa in Libya. It's startling to find any evidence of human presence in such an inhospitable place, so far from what we think of as civilization. And, frankly, this doesn't look exactly like what we think of as writing. It's a meandering string of simple, bold symbols, some of which are more like mathematics than writing: is that a plus sign? A zero? A percentage sign, for heaven's sake? Is this writing from the past, or the future?

This twisting strand of language looks so old and so deep it might just be the DNA of writing. Did I mention that the symbols or letters are in such a strange and vivid red pigment that they look as if they've been written in fresh blood?

Two thousand years ago, much of North Africa – from Egypt in the east to the Canary Islands in the west, to Niger in the south – was the territory of the Amazigh people, known to them as Tamazhga. The word Amazigh means 'noble men', but the Romans gave them the condescending name *barbari*, meaning 'barbarians', from which emerged the name 'Berbers'.

The Amazigh coexisted with the Phoenicians and the Carthaginians to such an extent that the early Amazigh script, called Libyque or Libyco-Berber, overlaps

with some of the oldest alphabets of the Mediterranean and Middle East. But successive occupations by the Romans and the Arabs meant the subordination of the Amazigh, especially in terms of language. To the Arabic ear, the spoken Amazigh languages sounded barbarous, and as the sacred script of Islam scrolled across the region, Tifinagh fell mostly out of use.

In the nineteenth century, new colonial regimes emerged in the region. The official administrative language of Morocco and Algeria became French, with Arabic second and Amazigh actively, sometimes brutally, suppressed – a situation that lasted well over a century.

The Amazigh script was saved by the mountains and the desert. The colonizers' influence primarily affected the cities and larger towns. Further inland, the Touareg in particular never stopped using their traditional alphabet, which they called Tifinagh. The women, who were responsible for their children's education, not only taught the letters but incorporated them into the distinctive and complex Amazigh tattoo symbols, and into the equally distinctive jewellery, fabric and carpet designs.

As a result, for the Amazigh, as for dozens of other cultures, writing has an extraordinary depth of appeal and identification, like the head on coinage or on postage stamps, or the colours and design of a flag.

So it was in the mid-1960s that when a group of Algerian Amazigh writers, journalists and activists living in Paris formed the Amazigh Academy to re-establish the Amazigh identity and Amazigh rights in the face of centuries of repression, they decided to reinvent the Tifinagh script (technically, Neo-Tifinagh) as a specifically Amazigh form of writing – and placed one of its characters, the *yaz*, at the heart of the Amazigh flag.

Today, the status of Tifinagh varies from country to country across North Africa. As recently as 2019, Algeria has jailed Amazigh activists for flying the Amazigh flag with its Tifinagh letter. Under the Gaddafi regime prior to 2011, the Amazigh minority in Libya was ranked eleventh worldwide in terms of 'people under threat' by Minority Rights Group International.

In Morocco, where the situation is better, one of the pivotal steps in the Amazigh revival was the creation in 2001, with government funding, of the Institut Royal de la Culture Amazighe (IRCAM). Ten years before Amazigh became an official language in Morocco, IRCAM was tasked with researching and promoting Amazigh language and culture in seven areas: linguistics, didactics, translation, arts and literature, computer sciences (including the development of free Tifinagh fonts), history and the environment, and sociology and anthropology. IRCAM has published attractive and well-planned school books printed in Tifinagh, but the number of trained teachers who speak the Amazigh languages is still very small. In the post-Gaddafi era, similar schoolbooks, posters, CDs and other educational materials have been published in Libya.

So far, Tifinagh is most visible in signage – at the entrances to schools and government buildings, and outside Mohammed V International Airport. Elsewhere in the Amazigh world, more signage is appearing. Agadez, the largest city in central Niger, added signage in Tifinagh in 2016. In the past few months, the city of Agadir in Morocco and the town of Nalut district in Libya announced plans to officially include Tifinagh on street signs, and in the near future they will add signage for city and town names, tourist destinations and historic and natural sites.

Amazigh activists, meanwhile, talk of the advantages of a revived Tamazhga, a North African economic union modelled to some extent on the European Union on the far side of the Mediterranean.

Tifinagh may be the once and future alphabet.

1 **Character grid:** examples of the Tifinagh script.

2 **Sample words:** the phrase 'Thank you all', which I carved in Tifinagh script for an exhibition in 2020.

Script:
Vai
—
The syllable *ū* in the
Vai script, which would
become the inspiration
and model for other
West African syllabaries.

V A I

Origin:
Liberia

The Vai script is a rare bird indeed – an Indigenous, non-colonial script that has been accepted, adopted and used to such a degree and over such an extended history that it may be misleading to include it among other endangered writing systems. Certainly, together with N'Ko, it is one of the most successful Indigenous scripts in West Africa), both in terms of the number of current users and the availability of literature written in it.

The Vai script was created by Mɔmɔlu Duwalu Bukɛlɛ in the 1830s to represent the Vai language spoken by about 104,000 people in what is now Liberia, and about 15,000 in Sierra Leone. Tradition states that while Bukɛlɛ was working as a messenger on a Portuguese ship, he became curious about the written messages he carried. How could the recipients understand the captain's wishes without hearing his spoken words? When he returned home, he had a dream (as quoted by linguistic anthropologist Dr Piers Kelly) '… in which a tall, venerable-looking white man, in a long coat, appeared to me saying, "I am sent to you by other white men … I bring you a book …"'

(In this respect, Vai is the first of many Indigenous African scripts to have been created in response to a dream. While the figure commanding the dreamer to create a script is usually a deity, Bukɛlɛ's could be a white colonial figure, a white colonial god or a combination of the two.)

According to Bukɛlɛ, the white man revealed a written script that, on waking, Bukɛlɛ couldn't remember – hardly surprising, as he had no previous experience with the written word. Given this impetus, though, he called in a number of friends and together they created the symbols that made up the Vai syllabary.

In doing this, they may also have been influenced by non-verbal symbols already in use in Vai culture, and possibly by an unlikely transatlantic source: the newly created Cherokee syllabary (see page 212). In the late 1820s, a number of Cherokee emigrated to Liberia. One in particular, Austin Curtis, married into an influential family and became a chief himself, and he might have contributed to the creation of the Vai script and influenced its form, or simply introduced the idea of an Indigenous syllabary into the consciousness of the region.

Vai flourished for a range of reasons that show how important a written language can be, especially for an Indigenous people in a time of colonialism.

First of all, Bukɛlɛ took on the role that is crucial for any new script to catch on, or any endangered script to be revived: that of teacher. He established schools throughout the Vai-speaking region to propagate his script, which was learned so rapidly and easily (perhaps because it was based on symbols already familiar to the learners) that some scholars have suggested that the

>>

rate of literacy among the nineteenth-century Vai was, in some places, greater than in many areas of the United States and Europe.

Second, Vai played an important role in trading between the Dutch and Portuguese colonial powers and peoples from the interior of Africa. Brokering exchanges of gold, exotic woods and ivory for salt, tobacco and metals, they had a huge advantage in being able (unlike neighbouring tribes) to keep records and create written communications. The Vai syllabary may also have acted as code in the by-then illegal slave trade.

The Vai script was used continuously during each decade of the nineteenth century, but the archives held at Jondu and Bandakoro were destroyed in warfare with the neighbouring Gola tribe.

Nevertheless, during the twentieth century, the Vai syllabary was used for writing and publishing clan histories, biblical and Qur'anic translations, and the Institute of Liberian Languages has published several compilations of folk tales and history. There continues to be a market for Vai literature; it is also widely used in commerce, as well as for newspapers, tombstones and in traditional rituals.

In 1962 the script was standardized to 212 symbols, with every syllable in use being represented by a unique character. Forty or fifty of these characters are in much wider use than the others; many people find fifty characters adequate for daily use.

The script remains in use today, particularly among Vai merchants and traders. In addition to its presence in commerce, there is a growing body of literature published in Vai: the publication of some small dictionaries, an incubated Wikipedia, a copy of the Universal Declaration of Human Rights, translations of historical sources and public-health messaging about Ebola.

1 **Character grid:** examples of the Vai script.

2 **Sample words:** Article One of the Universal Declaration of Human Rights in Vai: 'All human beings are born free and equal in dignity and rights. They are endowed with reason and conscience and should act towards one another in a spirit of brotherhood.'

Script:
Bassa Vah
—
The letter *gbu* in the Bassa language written in the Vah script. This very polished character is, of course, the creation of a type designer. Traditionally the letters were written on slate using charcoal.

BASSA VAH

Origin:
Liberia

Bassa Vah raises the fascinating question of whether a writing system – or any invention – is created by one person at one time, or if it is developed by countless people over a much longer period.

Bassa is the name of a people, some 350,000 of whom currently live in Liberia; *vah* is a Bassa word derived from the word for 'sign'. Bassa Vah, then, means not so much 'the Bassa alphabet' as 'Bassa signage', especially as its symbols may pre-date the writing system, deriving from signs made using the natural environment: teeth marks in leaves, carvings in trees.

Over time, these signs developed into a more complex written language, but during the nineteenth century, the Vah fell further and further into disuse, and might have become extinct but for the efforts of a Bassa named Thomas Flo Narvin Lewis.

The story of Lewis's life reads more like a legend, and some authorities have challenged several of the details. He was born in Liberia in the late nineteenth century, and, remarkably, left the country to study chemistry at Syracuse University. At this point, he had never seen or heard of the Vah.

One account by Dr Abba G. Karnga, a Bassa linguist and author, holds that a Bassa man, Di Waḍa, first created the script and taught it to his lover, the wife of a chief, for which he was sold into slavery. In America, he taught it to his son, who met and taught Lewis. Another version says that during his pre-matriculation travels, Lewis discovered the Vah in use among ex-slaves in Brazil and the West Indies.

Determined to do his best to revive both the script and the fortunes of his people, Lewis earned a doctorate in chemistry at Syracuse University, and on his way back to Liberia stopped off in Dresden, where he ordered the first printing press specifically adapted for the Vah.

Back in Liberia, he established a school for teaching Bassa people the Vah script. Several of his students passed the Vah on, and by the 1960s an association had been formed to promote the script and a number of students in Christian schools were able to learn it.

One active Bassa user was Peter Gorwor, who learned the Bassa Vah script from his grandfather, who, in turn, learned it in a Bassa traditional school that was part of the Poro secret society – a men's secret society active in Sierra Leone, Liberia, Guinea and the Ivory Coast, introduced by the Mende people. The Poro society chose to teach the Vah script along with a number of other traditional beliefs and practices – a factor that helped the Vah survive when other Indigenous West African scripts fell into disuse.

Peter wrote to me by email: 'With my elementary graduation in 1975, I moved to Buchanan to attend the Liberia Christian High School. Here, I stayed until 1982, while working with [a Christian missionary >>

couple]; I got my high school certificate. During my senior year in high school in 1982, I got a part-time job to translate Theological Education by Extension (TEE) lessons from English to Bassa, and to duplicate tapes for TEE students. At that time I had two years' experience in Bassa writing.

'Originally, the Bassa Vah was written on slate (taken from a rubber tree, like wood but white). The students used fire coal (charcoal) to write, especially in the traditional schools. The writings were easily erased by a rough leaf that looks like sandpaper, known as *yan*. People began to use pencils on the slate in the early '40s.

'Initially, the Bassa Vah script was written from right to left then from left to right, moving right to left, left to right in parallel rows of letters … but from the 1960s the movement changed to "left to right" only, as the English.'

Bassa Vah continues to survive within its very specific community, despite being described by one authority as 'a failed script'. Efforts are under way to create a consistent, robust digital version of the script for the 650,000 Bassa speakers, and while it does not yet have full system support on Windows, there are web-based input tools and a Google Noto font that can be used on Windows and Mac. The Bassa Vah Historical Society is on Facebook, and the Christian Education Foundation of Liberia supports Bassa Vah on its website and has published a collection of Bassa proverbs written by Dr Abba G Karnga in English, Bassa Roman and Bassa Vah.

1   **Character grid**: examples of the
    Bassa Vah script.

2   **Sample words**: Article One of the
    Universal Declaration of Human Rights,
    taken from a carving I made for the first-
    ever Endangered Alphabets exhibition,
    which in turn was based on handwritten
    text sent to me from Liberia.

BAMUM

Origin:
Cameroon

Creating a new script for an Indigenous people during a colonial era is a two-edged sword.

The desire to claim and assert one's cultural identity may provide the driving force that sustains an author through the long, hard work of creating a writing system, and it may also be the force that makes the resulting script popular. The colonial authorities, though, may well not want their subjects to develop a sense of their identity and self-respect, and in that, the more successful an Indigenous script is, the more dangerous it may be.

One of the most remarkable of these creations, the Bamum alphabet, fell prey to its own success.

Starting around 1896, twenty-five-year-old King Ibrahim Njoya of the Bamum Kingdom in Cameroon invented a writing system for his people's language called *a-ka-u-ku*, after its first four characters.

It was a dream-inspired script, but one that was remarkably practical and non-ego-centric. He invited his subjects to send or give him simple signs and symbols, and he drew from them to create a system that was at first pictographic, but then, over half a dozen drafts, became increasingly rational-ized and symbolic until, by roughly 1910, it was a fully functional syllabary of eighty characters.

Using this script, he wrote a history of his people, a pharmacopoeia, a calendar,

maps, records, legal codes and a guide to good sex. He built schools, a printing press and libraries; he supported artists and in-tellectuals. This seems to have been all well and good in the eyes of the local colonial power while Cameroon was under German control, but when the French took over part of the country after the German defeat in World War I, they manoeuvred Njoya out of power, smashed his printing press, burned his libraries and books, tossed out sacred Bamum artifacts and sent him into exile, where he died.

It's a sign of how important an Indige-nously created script can be, that despite Njoya's death and the almost complete suppression of the *a-ka-u-ku* syllabary, his son and grandson held on to the script as a cultural symbol. In 2007, more than seventy years after Njoya's death, the first coordinated effort to revive it began, and today, the script is taught to students as part of their Bamum heritage, and is displayed during ceremonies and paraded on signs through the streets of Foumban.

Samuel Calvin Nbetnkom has just published a collection of poems in Bamum, possibly the first ever, and is working on a Bamum dictionary.

MEDEFAIDRIN

Origin:
Nigeria

Medefaidrin is one of several dozen examples of a 'spirit script' – that is, a writing system based on symbols or characters revealed in a dream or vision. Spirit scripts demonstrate not only the desire by a community to have its own writing system, but also the way in which letters, especially those used only in sacred activities or rituals, can be icons in themselves, glowing with numinous power.

Medefaidrin is a created language and script used by a Christian group known as the Oberi Okaime ('freely given') Christian Mission in the Ibiono and Itu Local Government Areas of Akwa Ibom State in the oil-rich Niger delta region of Nigeria.

According to the community, the written language was revealed in 1927 to one of the founders, Bishop Aikeld Ukpong (also known as Michael Ukpong) on a 'spiritual board' visible only to the initiated, after Ukpong had been taken into seclusion by the Holy Spirit. But since Ukpong himself was not literate, it fell on the secretary of the group, Prophet Jakeld Udofia, to transcribe the writing – an especially interesting and ambitious achievement, given that at the time Ibibio was not a written language.

The community continued to develop the language and script through the 1930s and then started a school in which children were instructed in Medefaidrin. British authorities closed the school within a year, but the community continued to use Medefaidrin for church activities, including liturgy and hymns, and for letters and written contracts between members. The language faded from use, but in 1986, Udofia began teaching it again in the church's Sunday school in Ididep.

The Department of Linguistics and Nigerian Languages of the University of Uyo, Nigeria is reported to be promoting and supporting the language-revitalization efforts of Medefaidrin through language-documentation projects, including scanning old handwritten texts, development of a multilingual e-dictionary and research projects by staff and graduate students of the department.

'These days,' writes Professor Eno-Abasi Urua of the University of Uyo, 'Medefaidrin is used exclusively in a religious context, with very few fluent speakers. Our role has been to try to preserve what is left of the language through digitization, especially the scripts which have been the worse for wear.'

The religious community reportedly numbers about 4,000 members, but there are said to be fewer than twenty adult speakers of Medefaidrin, of whom only a handful have mastered the script, meaning that Medefaidrin may be the world's most endangered alphabet.

Script:
Mandombe
—
The syllable *va* in the
Mandombe script, which
boldly defies letter-
height convention and the
restrictions traditionally
imposed by printing.

MANDOMBE

Origin:
Democratic
Republic of
the Congo

Among the many Indigenously created scripts of sub-Saharan Africa, several stand out for their sheer inventiveness – their out-of-the-Latin-alphabet-box thinking. One of them is Mandombe, the only writing system in the world whose visual template is a brick wall.

Like many of these African scripts, it is based on a revelatory dream – though in this case, the dream was not of a divinity but of a human prophet. The dreamer was David Wabeladio Payi (1957–2013) from the Democratic Republic of the Congo (DRC), a member of the Kimbanguist Church, who in 1978 dreamed of Simon Kimbangu, the church's prophet, telling him to create a writing system

Once given the command, Payi's eye fell on the exposed brick wall of his room, and he noticed that the mortar around the bricks could be seen as a series of patterns that, in particular, featured two geometrically opposed sacred shapes: 5 and 2.

Building on these raw materials, so to speak, he incorporated the concept that the direction in which a basic shape pointed would affect its pronunciation. He also extended the basic shapes not only left and right, but upward, defying the implicit tradition, inherited from medieval European monks, that letters should be consistently constrained by height.

He called the new script Mandombe, a word that has three possible meanings:

'For the Blacks'; 'That which has been entrusted to the Blacks'; and 'In the manner of the Blacks'.

His original intention was to use the script to write religious texts in the national languages of the Congo – Kikongo, Lingala, Tshiluba and Swahili – but as the script has steadily gained acceptance, its ambitions have grown as well, and the Mandombe Academy at the Kimbanguist *Centre de l'Écriture Négro-Africaine* (CENA) hopes it may one day be used to write all African languages.

David Wabeladio Payi was granted a patent for his script by the Ministry of Industry and Trade of the then Republic of Zaïre (now the DRC) in 1982. It was officially introduced to the public in 1994. He was given a professorship at the Kimbanguist University in Kinshasa, where he taught the script to numerous students. On 22 December 2011, he was granted the title doctor *honoris causa* at the University of Kinshasa. He died in 2013 and was buried in Nkamba, the holy city of the Kimbanguists, in the DRC.

The Mandombe script is taught in Kimbanguist church schools in Angola, the Republic of the Congo and in France and Belgium. As such, it might be considered to be emerging rather than endangered.

GARAY

Origin:
Senegal

The Garay alphabet, created by Assane Faye to write the Wolof language, which is the most widely spoken language of Senegal and also spoken in the Gambia and Mauritania, is one of many African writing systems invented as a response to colonialism.

In 1961, on the first anniversary of Senegal's independence from France, the president, Léopold Sédar Senghor, went on the radio and called on all Africans in general, and Senegalese in particular, to 'gather stones and build this new country'.

This made Faye reflect on what was missing, or on what he could do to help. The next day, as he has told the story, he went to the beach in his village, which was called 'Yen', and passed a cave named 'Garay' as the interior of the cave was white (the word means 'the whiteness of the cotton flower'). At that moment, he reported, a vision struck him and he began writing on the sand. He called to a friend to bring him something to write on, and the Garay alphabet came into existence.

The resulting script shows Arabic influence in being written from right to left. It also has its own calligraphic variant, in which every word self-underlines.

After creating the script, Faye offered lessons in it to hundreds of people over the years in a small-scale, face-to-face fashion. He translated the Qur'an using it, and had a house filled with dozens of unpublished handwritten texts, some of which had been cited in secondary sources, but with little or no bibliographic control.

Subsequently, the script seems to have moved from being a linguistic cottage industry to something more contemporary. Garay now has a font, a Facebook page and a YouTube channel with teaching videos. After his father's death, Assane's son Souleiman took over primary responsibility for teaching it.

Garay has also made a fleeting television appearance: in an episode of *Star Trek: Discovery*, the Universal Translator is infected with a virus and the computer begins to speak Wolof. At one point, the monitors on the bridge of the USS *Discovery* display the Garay script.

MWANGWEGO

Origin:
Malawi

Some scripts are like the pebbles in a stream, worn into their shapes over centuries by the collective action of millions of users.

Others are clearly the work of a single imagination, a single advocate. Such a script is Mwangwego, the product of a lifetime's labour by Nolence Moses Mwangwego of Malawi.

Born in 1951 in Zambia, at the time known as Northern Rhodesia, Mwangwego visited Paris in 1977, where he discovered the existence of other, non-Latin writing systems. He theorized that, as there were words meaning 'write' in Malawian languages, there might have been Indigenous, pre-colonial scripts. He decided to create a script himself.

'When I was creating this script,' he said, 'I was hoping and I wanted it to replace the Latin alphabet when writing Malawian Indigenous languages.'

Mwangwego was not without qualifications as a linguist, speaking and writing Chewa, Tumbuka, KyaNgonde, English, French and Portuguese.

He started his act of creation in 1979; after innumerable modifications and revisions, he considered the script finished and ready for unveiling twenty-four years later, in 2003.

The magnitude of his endeavour was recognized by the minister of youth, sports and culture, Kamangadazi Chambalo, who announced, 'Mwangwego script is in itself history in the making. Irrespective of how it is going to be received by the public nationwide, the script is bound to go into the annals of our history as a remarkable invention.'

It is one level of achievement to create a new, consistent and workable writing system; to get it adopted is an entirely different challenge. After the script was launched, Mwangwego began teaching it himself, putting on lectures and exhibitions.

In addition to his desire to create a non-Latin, non-colonial script for Malawi, Mwangwego also hoped that the combination of having a script that was specifically designed for Indigenous languages and a script that Malawians could think of as their own would encourage the development of literacy within the country.

'I was hoping,' he wrote by email, 'and I still hope, that people in my country will be encouraged to read and write.'

More than 2,000 people have been taught the script, he said, some of whom are now acting as teachers in their turn.

'The script is now being encoded and a computer font is being refined which may mean that Malawians who are proud of their languages will use it on their computers and smartphones.'

Script:
Adlam
—
The Adlam character
pronounced *ka*. At the time,
Adlam set a record by moving
from invention to digitization
in barely 25 years. Nowadays,
such swift progress is what
many script creators aim for.

ADLAM

Origin:
Guinea

Adlam is surely unique in being the only script to have been created by two brothers, the *older* of whom was barely into his teens.

Abdoulaye and Ibrahima Barry grew up in a small town in Guinea, West Africa, speaking the language generally called Fulani, though in Guinea it is called Pular.

Few people in their town could read, and their father, who could, acted as a designated reader: when people received letters they took them to him in his shop in the market, and he did his best to read them.

This was more of a challenge than it might seem, as Fulani was most often written in Arabic script whose letters gave only an inconsistent approximation of the sounds of the spoken language. In 1989, Ibrahima, then fourteen, and Abdoulaye, then ten, decided they could do better.

'After school,' Abdoulaye said, 'we would go in our room and just start randomly doodling. If we saw something that could be used as a letter, we would point it out.'

At the same time, they worked at the problem from the other direction: at school, if they heard or thought of a spoken sound that needed to be represented in writing, they made a note of it. In some cases, they came up with a symbol that looked like teeth, or a bag, 'so we represented that item with that letter'. After half a year, 'We told our dad we had worked out an alphabet – and he didn't believe us.'

Their father, however, invited an expert who tested them in the same way the Cherokee tribal council tested Sequoyah (see page 212): by giving dictation (though in this case, he especially included words whose sounds could not be written effectively in Arabic or Latin script). One brother was told to write, then the other was told to read what had been written.

The test over, the expert declared the boys had, indeed, created a functional alphabet, of twenty-seven letters – and their father made up for his earlier scepticism by teaching the script in his shop at the market.

The first iteration was cursive, but people found it hard to discern the individual letters, so in their second iteration, the brothers separated the letters.

When Ibrahima left to study at the University of Conakry, he took the script with him, and it began to be used in classes. To provide content, the brothers wrote books of practical advice, such as how to conduct a healthy pregnancy and how to filter water to make it drinkable, and a newspaper.

All the books were written by hand, Abdoulaye explained, because there were no typefaces or digital fonts. If they made a single mistake, they had to start writing the page again, aware that everything they wrote was, in effect, creating a linguistic standard that would be followed and thus needed to be accurate and consistent.

>>

By 2007, both brothers had moved to the United States and were looking for skilled help to create fonts and keyboard software. By 2016, the script had been accepted by Unicode; by 2018, Google had created a Noto Sans Adlam font and a keyboard for Android phones.

Perhaps most remarkably, the Barry brothers had effected substantial change in their own country and as many as twenty-three other countries in a west to east band across West and Central Africa where Fulani is spoken. (The Adlam script is also being adapted for neighbouring languages, such as Hausa.)

'It's about improving literacy rates generally,' Ibrahima explained. Now people had the chance of an education in their own language, more were learning to read and write. 'The people who were most excited were the women,' he went on, as it made education and literacy significantly more accessible and attainable.

As this atlas comes into being, Adlam, like Vai and N'Ko and perhaps Mandombe, is a growing new script rather than an endangered old one, and it may be moving from an Indigenous minority script to a thriving regional writing system. The purpose of the atlas, though, is not to document by categories, but to play a part in the revival of minority cultures through their writing systems, and we include Adlam here as a tale of what has been done, how it has been done and what may be done again elsewhere.

The name Adlam, by the way, is an acrostic of the first four letters of the alphabet (A, D, L, M) which represent the phrase *Alkule Dandaydhe Leñol Mulugol*: 'the alphabet which protects the people from vanishing'.

1

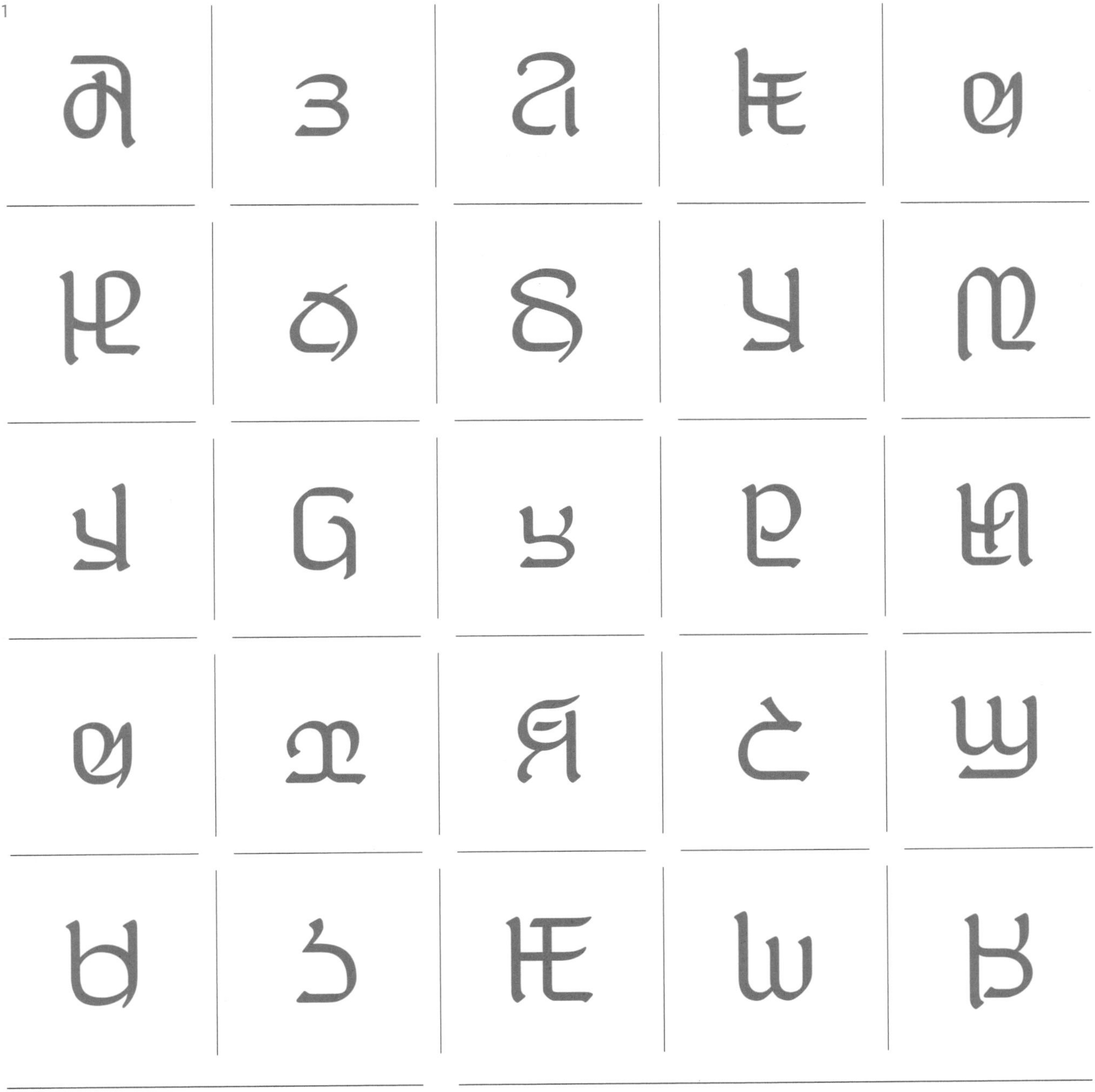

2

1 **Character grid:** examples of the Adlam script.

2 **Sample words:** the word 'Adlam' in the Adlam script.

LUO LAKESIDE SCRIPT

Origin:
Botswana; Kenya

The Luo Lakeside Script was developed by Kefa Ombewa in Kenya with help from graphic designers Will Were and Paul Sidandi of Botswana between 2009 and 2012 as a unique, non-Latin way to write the Dholuo language – so as to, in Ombewa's words, decolonize African culture: 'I was interested in making sure that African societies, and in this case particularly Luo, also have their own script.'

Creating a workable non-Latin script turned out to involve a wide range of challenges. How would the glyphs work together with a QWERTY keyboard? Would it be possible to make similar sounds look the same when written?

These questions go to the heart of writing. What is functional in terms of symbol-to-sound correspondence? What is functional in terms of the human body itself, and the physical act of writing? How do these fundamentals combine with what one's culture sees as attractive, as *writing-like*, whatever that is?

'Through trial and error, samples of simple abstract strokes and curves were used,' Ombewa said. 'Further modifications were done in order to fit specifications of font creator softwares.'

Developing a new script in an era of digitization presents opportunities as well as problems. Dozens of newly created scripts around the world are in a kind of pre-digital limbo, waiting for someone with a new and unusual combination of skills – linguist, typographer, coder – to take them along the tedious and arduous road into Unicode. Interestingly, many newly developed scripts still use features of handwriting. The guiding principle for Luo, Ombewa explained, was to develop a cursive script with a central connection, having ascenders and descenders.

At the same time, Paul Sidandi, working independently from Francistown in Botswana, was developing an African number system, then known as Luo Numbers. (It was later changed to Lwo Numerals to avoid confusion with Chinese, who also have Luo Numbers.)

'Africans generally learn to write letters in the air, then on the ground,' Paul Sidandi explains. 'This is the logic for the horizontal line which can be seen running through the letters and numbers when written sequentially.'

As always, the challenge facing a new script was partly invention, but mostly acceptance and implementation. It was publicly launched by Kefa Ombewa in an interview on the Kenya Television Network in 2014, after which an implementation team was set up with representatives from Botswana, Kenya, Australia, the United Kingdom, Tanzania and Uganda.

In Botswana, graphics designer Taolo Dipatane of Lobatse was tasked with producing infographics and designs for posters, clocks and T-shirts. The team pitched the script to local chiefs, magistrates, academics, youth groups, museums, schools and sign-language interpreters.

The script has been tested in several primary and junior secondary schools around Botswana; and in Kenya, an academy that opened in 2020 has made a commitment for the script to be taught at the school. The script has also been presented at the museums of Botswana, University of Botswana Mathematics Department and the Botswana International University of Science and Technology.

Maureen Oyuga's book of Luo words, written in the Lakeside script and translated into English, has sold nearly a thousand copies. But, as with many recently created Indigenous African scripts, the aim is to make it continental rather than national, and keyboard developments mean that the script can now be used by any African language, ranging from Akan of Ghana to Zulu of South Africa.

'I want to make it an African script,' Ombewa said. 'If the Luo want to enjoy the script and own it, I don't mind, but it is an African script. I envision an Africa that is de-latinized all the way from West Africa to East Africa.'

Script:
Luo Lakeside
—
The letter *ba* in the Luo Lakeside Script for the Dholuo language. The script's refusal to imitate the Latin colonial script is entirely intentional.

N ' K O

Origin:
Guinea

N'Ko is one of a startling number of Indigenous scripts from West Africa, and (along with Vai) one of the most successful. It was created around 1949, by Solomana Kanté of Kankan, Guinea, in order to write the Mandenkan languages of Mali, Guinea, the Gambia, Ivory Coast, Burkina Faso, Senegal, Liberia, Guinea-Bissau and Sierra Leone.

Kanté reportedly created the script in a defiant spirit – in response to a newspaper article reflecting the colonial misconception that Africans were culturally inferior due to their lack of Indigenous writing systems.

N'Ko – which means 'I say' in all of the Manding languages – was invented in Bingerville, Côte d'Ivoire, then brought to Kanté's natal region of Kankan, Guinea, before being disseminated into other Manding-speaking parts of West Africa, where Kanté committed himself to helping the speakers of Mande languages achieve literacy in his writing system. As a result, he authored works on many subjects – the history of the Mande people, science, healing arts, mathematics and religion – writing the books himself, by hand.

Since its invention, the alphabet has acquired a life of its own. A grassroots movement promoting literacy by using the N'Ko alphabet has blossomed across West Africa from the Gambia to Nigeria, wherever there are speakers of Mande languages, despite the fact that these countries use French and English as official languages.

'It is slowly growing here in West Africa,' suggested Dwayne Rainwater, a Bible translator: 'There are even N'Ko schools (complete with some books written in N'Ko). We are also putting our translations into N'Ko as there is a significant portion of the population that can already read and write N'Ko. There are several books written in N'ko including a good-sized dictionary which I use all the time in my work.'

Publications include a translation of the Qur'an, a variety of textbooks on subjects such as physics and geography, poetic and philosophical works, descriptions of traditional medicine, a dictionary and several local newspapers. In a slightly adapted form, N'Ko has also been used for traditional religious publications in the Yoruba and Fon languages of Benin and southwest Nigeria.

The script is now included in the Unicode standard, and can be used on most computers and phones. N'Ko is even celebrated on its own Alphabet Day, 14th April – the date in 1949 when the script is believed to have been finalized. And Baba Diané, a linguist based in Egypt, has written a book about Indigenous African writing systems in N'Ko – possibly the first example of a book about endangered alphabets written in an endangered alphabet.

BERIA

Origin:
Sudan

One of the main values of an Indigenously created script is that it reflects something specific and unique about its culture of origin. As such, one of the most distinctively Indigenous scripts is Beria, created to write the Zaghawa language of Chad and Darfur, in western Sudan. The script is based on one of the culture's most iconic figures: the camel.

In the 1950s, a Sudanese Zaghawa schoolteacher named Adam Tajir created an alphabet for his people's language whose characters were derived from the clan brands used for camels and other livestock. Its name is Beria, or sometimes the Beria Branding Script.

Beria has the two ideal qualities of Indigenous alphabets: it looks like nobody else's script, and it gives hints of its own origins. Handwritten scripts tend to show the lateral flow of the hand, the turn of the wrist; Beria, however – crisp, uniform, slightly industrial, almost geometrical – looks like a series of symbols to be stamped rather than written.

This script, though innovative and Indigenous in the best sense, turned out not to be ideal for representing the sounds of the Zaghawa language, as it was based on the Arabic script. Under the circumstances, perhaps it's not surprising that the person who remedied its shortcomings was a vet. In 2000, a Zaghawa veterinarian named Siddick Adam Issa created a modified version of the Beria script, which he called Beria Giray Erfe ('Writing Marks').

Even though the Zaghawa inhabit one of the driest and poorest areas in the world, ravaged by decades of civil war, supporters of the script created a YouTube channel for reading and writing lessons in Beria. AlSadig Sadig, a native of Darfur, became possibly the first person to try to digitize an emerging script by crowdfunding: 'I was born in … a small village in the Darfur region of Sudan, in 1987. As children, me and my friends were beaten just for speaking our own language. Since then, it has been a dream that I share with many others, to make it possible for us not only to speak Beria freely, but also to be able to read and write it!'

The first schoolbook in Beria has just been published. The *Beria-English Dictionary*, though it does not use the Beria script, is full of culturally rich translations, such as *dabara*: a blister, especially on a camel's back after a long day racing; *dabo*: the season between November and January, when the herds are dispersed to pastures toward the northeast, the grain is beaten and stored and the markets are more intensely frequented; and *dabûrû*: a camel that has not given birth.

Script:
Ditema tsa Dinoko
—
The letter *zwi*. The
architectural nature of the
Ditema characters is almost
literal: each syllable is built
up from elements indicating
how it is to be pronounced,
such as the directionality
of the triangle or chevron
denoting its core vowel.

DITEMA TSA DINOKO

Origin:
South Africa

African writing systems created over the past 200 years have a rich tradition of going beyond the Western convention that a letter is an arbitrary, abstract symbol whose purpose is to denote a spoken sound.

In some cases, the connection between visual symbol and meaning is so strong it draws writing into a range of symbols and practices that are deeply spiritual in nature and pre-date the act of writing – so a new script that is inspired by these images can also seem as ancient as civilization.

The Ditema tsa Dinoko script, also known as Isibheqe Sohlamvu, is the most stunning example of this tradition. It is possibly the most exact and illustrative writing system in the world, but at first glance, it doesn't look like writing at all.

Pule kaJanolintshi, one of the designers involved in the development of the script, explains: 'The script is based on the traditional symbologies of southern Africa, which are still used today in certain contexts, such as in Sesotho litema or IsiNdebele amagwalo murals, the knowledge of which is traditionally kept by women.'

Litema, based on the Sesotho word that means, fascinatingly, both 'text' and 'ploughed land', is an art form based on decorative and symbolic patterns engraved, painted or moulded in the walls of homes. For centuries, women have combed the patterns (to imitate a ploughed field) or

scratched them into the wet top layer of fresh clay-and-dung plaster of the wall and then painted them with naturally occurring pigments or, more recently, paint. Litema are not intended to be permanent, and usually dry or are washed off by the next rain. (Interestingly, a similar tradition exists in South Asia, called *rangoli* or *kolam*.)

IsiNdebele murals, vivid and often geometrical designs using coloured clay and cow dung that often decorate Ndebele homes, seem both ancient and hypermodern – so much so that they have been used to paint a BMW for the company's Art Car series, and the tail of a British Airways jumbo jet. Other symbols for the script were drawn from basketry, beadwork and pottery traditions, and symbols used by traditional healers.

Not surprisingly, the Ditema tsa Dinoko script that draws on these traditions is easily one of the most vivid and extraordinary writing systems in the world. It was developed between 2010 and 2015 by a group of linguists and designers to write southern Ntu languages such as IsiZulu, IsiXhosa, TshiVenḓa, XiTsonga, SeSotho, SiSwati and SeTswana, including the marginalized languages such as Khelobedu, SiPhuthi, IsiBhaca, IsiMpondo, Sepulana and SiLala.

The script is amazingly detailed and specific, almost a blueprint as opposed to an alphabet. For example, it is one of only a handful of scripts in which the direction a glyph faces is significant. A triangle   >>

pointing upward indicates one vowel (i), while one facing downward indicates another (a).

There's also an element of diagramming involved to show where and how a sound is voiced. Labials and nasals are positioned outside the triangle at the apex; dentals are indicated by two lines across the triangle from side to side, parallel to each other.

Shape is central, and vital. Curved lines, for example, indicate fricatives. Their straight-line counterparts in the same positions indicate plosives.

Additional elements indicate sounds not found in English. Clicks are a bottomless hourglass shape. Syllabic laterals and trills are represented with duplication of the ordinary lateral and trill graphemes.

The writer has other opportunities usually associated with artists – the assignment of colours, for example. Drawing on traditions in the visual arts such as beadwork, colour may have an associated mood or non-linguistic meaning: green may connote contentment, for example, but used negatively may imply discord or illness. Certain colours may have spiritual, ethnic or regional associations.

There's no telling how widely adopted the script will become, of course, and as with all constructed scripts, we're left holding our breath. But in one respect, the script has already started putting down new roots of its own. Unknown Union, a South African-based clothing company, has started incorporating features from Ditema and other African writing systems in its clothing designs, thus completing the circle from art/craft to writing and back again.

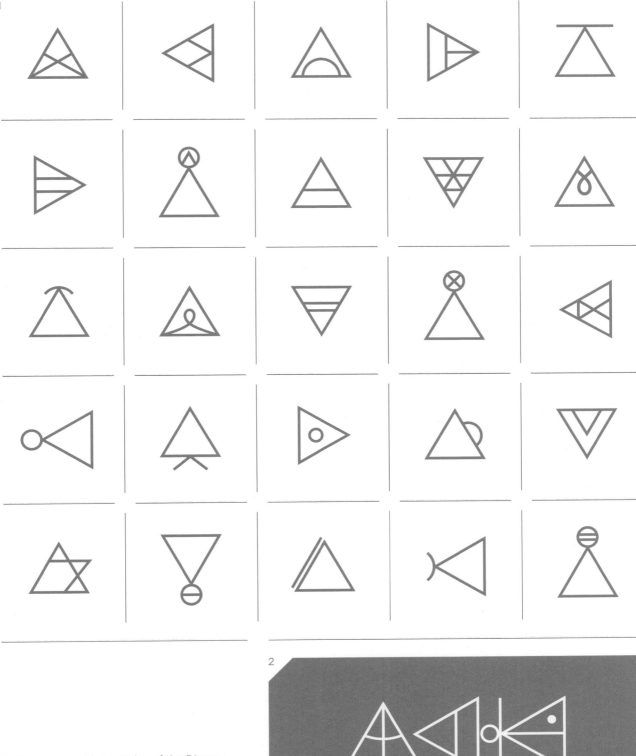

1 **Character grid:** examples of the Ditema tsa Dinoko script.

2 **Sample words:** 'Believe in yourself', using Ditema text provided by Pule kaJanolintshi.

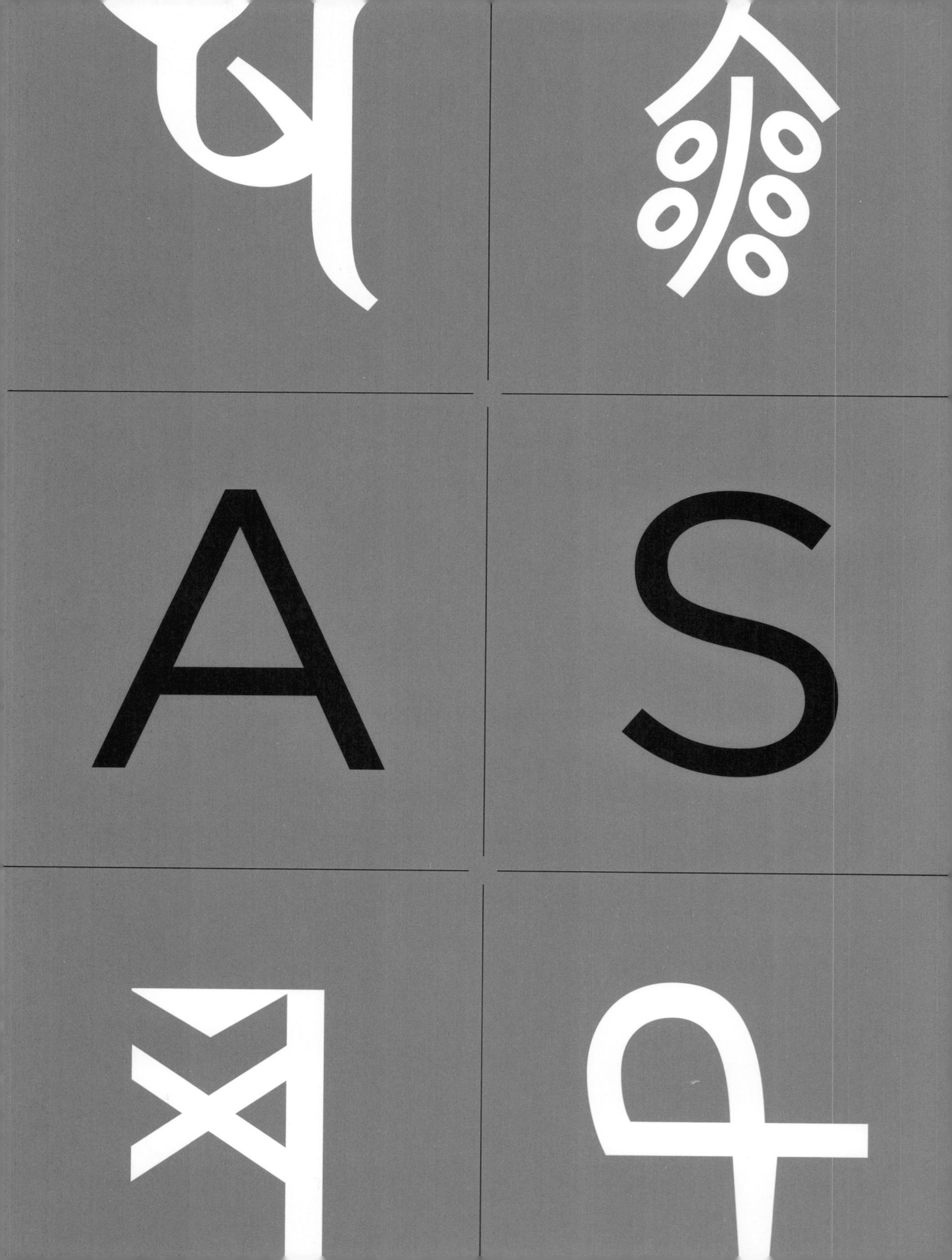
A
S

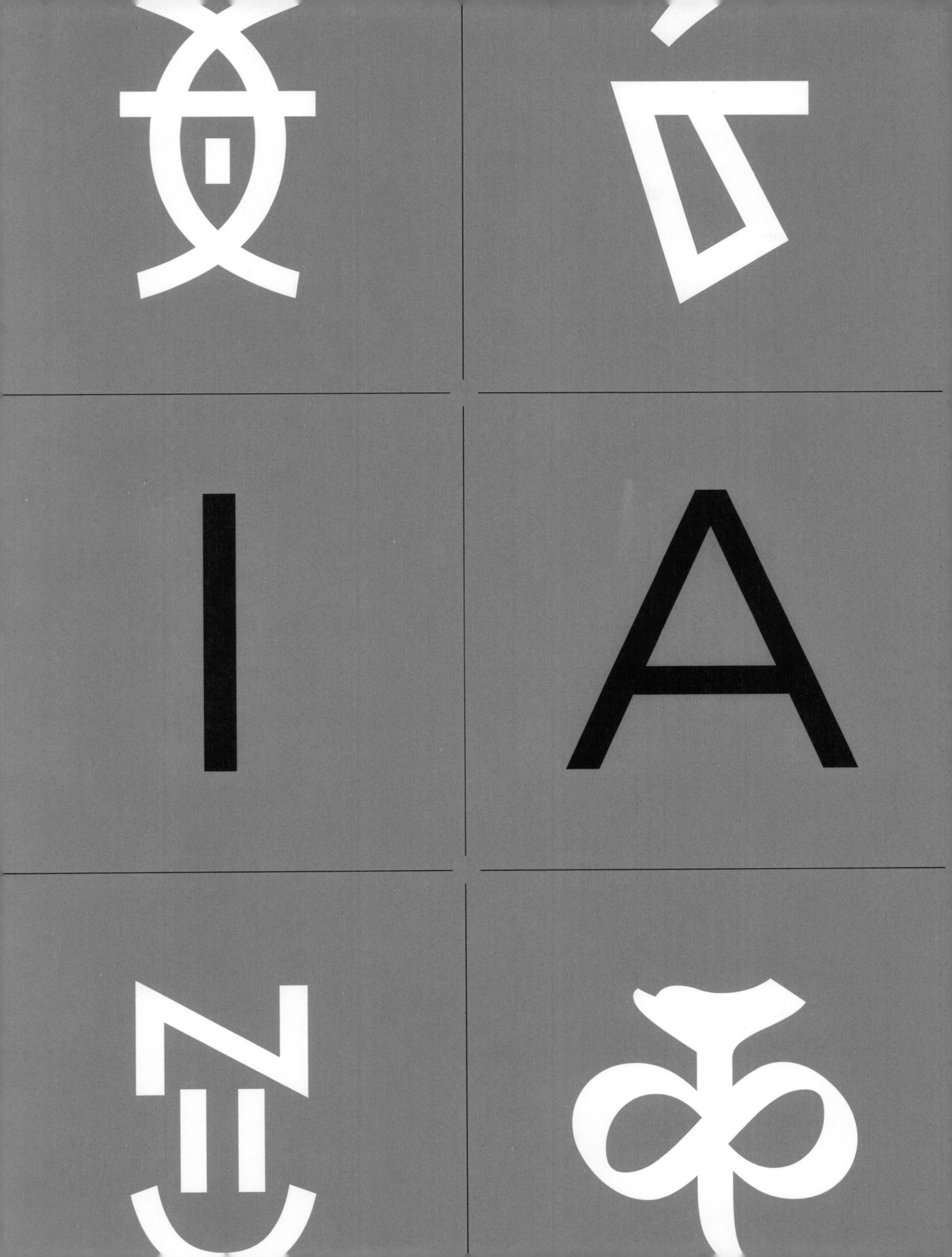
I
A

INTRODUCTION

In many regions of the world, writing is equated with civilization – that is, the birth of writing is seen as being an essential feature of the birth of an orderly human society, and vice versa. This is especially true in Asia.

Many cultures have creation myths; cultures that are deeply wedded to their writing often have writing-creation myths. These are often fascinating for what they tell us about the way that culture sees writing – not just its origins, but its value.

The Zhuang, for example, are an ethnic minority of southern China. Their creation epic tells the story of how a primordial god named Baeu Rodo brought the Zhuang people not one script but two: Sawgoek, or 'root script', and Sawva, or 'insect script'. It was a particularly rich gift, consisting of 4,000 glyphs, which suggests that these were pictographic, meaning-based writing systems, rather than phonetic ones in which a letter corresponded to a sound. He also gave them the gift of fire.

As with many gifts from the gods, according to the epic, these novelties proved to be too much, too soon. The Zhuang, not understanding fire, stored both fire and writing together – under a thatched roof. The building burned down, and with it the Zhuang lost the knowledge of writing.

This may seem fanciful, but in fact, recent archaeological finds in southern China suggest that there may be some historical basis to the myth – they reveal two ancient writing systems or styles, both of which were gradually replaced by the Han Chinese character script over the course of several generations.

One is more angular (possibly Sawva, the insect script), the other more curvy (perhaps Sawgoek, the root script).

Interestingly, the angular/Sawva signs resemble the Chinese minority Yi script, and the curvy/Sawgoek ones are not unlike the Shui script.

For me, the most interesting aspect of this cluster of information and possibility has less to do with the origin of writing, which is fascinating, of course, but at the moment, we just don't have the evidence to do more than speculate. No, it's that in this epic, writing is seen not only as a divine gift, but one that is on a par with fire – an extraordinary status. We think of the invention/discovery/use of fire as being – along with the use of tools – the vital evolutionary step that distinguished us from the great apes or the proto-hominids. But the Baeu-Rodo narrative implies that those who thought of the story as important enough to remember and pass on considered writing not only to have a divine genesis – other cultures share this view – but to be as essential to their creation and survival as fire.

More than in any other continent, Asian minority scripts show that the roots of writing are far deeper than we in the twenty-first-century West tend to believe, and more intimately entwined among our beliefs about what it means to be civilized, to be human.

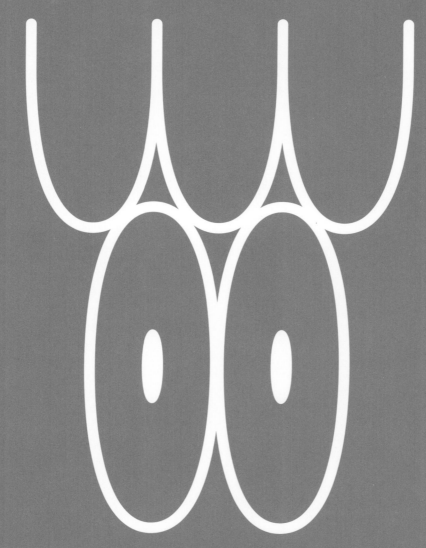

Script:
Yi
—

The reformed Yi syllabary has
several thousand characters,
but these have been designed
rather than evolving through
use, and consequently they
have a unique feature. Every
one is made from two or more
of five basic strokes: dot,
horizontal line, vertical line,
arch and circle. This is *gōt*.

Y I

Origin:
China

Yi is perhaps the most elastic writing system in the world.

The Yi are a minority nationality of China, some 7–8 million in number, who – until 1,500 years ago – had their own dynastic homeland in southwest China around Kunming, but were defeated and dispersed around the region, with small numbers settling in Vietnam and Laos.

With diaspora comes fragmentation, and with fragmentation comes linguistic variation and language loss: of the sixty or more languages that now comprise the Yi language family, most are endangered and some are in the process of disappearing. This process has accelerated since 1950, thanks to the official Chinese process of trying to 'standardize' Indigenous and minority languages and scripts.

Even without this external influence, though, the Yi script always had its own reasons for, and means of, varying.

Originally, written Yi, which might better be called the Yi script family, was ideographic, and existed as several overlapping but distinct regional scripts: Nosu, Nisu, Nasu and Sani.

The Yi are animists, with elements of Taoism, shamanism and fetishism. Shamans/medicine men are known as *bimo* or *pimu*. *Bimo* officiate at births, funerals and weddings. They are often seen in the street consulting ancient scripts. As animists, Yi worship the spirits of ancestors, hills, trees, rocks, water, earth, sky, wind and forests. Magic plays a major role in daily life through healing, exorcism, asking for rain, cursing enemies, blessing, divination and analysis of one's relationship with the spirits. They believe dragons protect villages against bad spirits, and demons cause diseases. After someone dies, they sacrifice a pig or sheep at the doorway to maintain a relationship with the deceased spirit.

Writing was, and is, central to this world view, used almost exclusively by *bimo* for life-cycle, divination and healing rituals, and keeping historical and genealogical records. Books were handwritten on handmade paper, bound with handmade hemp covers, and rolled up for storage. Traditionally, each shaman would train a son or nephew to succeed him, a process that involved copying all his mentor's books, plus as many other books as he could find. (All literate shamans were men; female religious-healing practitioners did not use writing.)

The word 'copy' should not imply that each manuscript was identical to its original, however. The representation of one word by a single character is a modern innovation, based on the Chinese governmental desire for standardization. In traditional materials, a single word or idea might be written in many different ways. The most extreme example is the character meaning 'not' in Nisu, of which no fewer than 103 versions have been found.

>>

One shaman used twenty-two alternative forms in a single text, possibly as a series of stylistic flourishes, possibly as a means of disguise.

With such latitude for individual expression, it's hardly surprising that over time the collective written Yi vocabulary became larger and larger. Originally the Yi script family is said to have consisted of 1,840 characters, but there are now as many as 90,000 recorded glyphs, including some 40 different ways of writing the word 'stomach'.

The various members of the Yi written family even use different kinds of punctuation. Nisu and Nasu manuscripts insert a comma equivalent to indicate pauses in chanting. The Nisu version is an equilateral triangle resting on one base, often coloured red, with a horizontal line going to the left from the top. The Nasu 'comma' is a small circle at the bottom right or left of the last character in the chanted line.

Yi even refused to be restrained by geometry. At first – perhaps 1,400 years ago – all the written Yi variants were arranged, like Chinese, from top to bottom and right to left. At some point, though, the Nosu version got rotated 90 degrees clockwise, and was read from left to right, starting at the top.

In 1974, the Sichuan government, following standard Chinese 'one nationality, one language, one script' policy, set about to convert and consolidate the Yi scripts into the largest syllabary ever to be (to some extent) standardized.

This is the version of Yi displayed in this atlas, which has a unique quality that might be called distributive design: every syllabic Yi character is made, like linguistic DNA, from a different combination of five basic strokes: dot, horizontal line, vertical line, arch and circle.

Yi was not to be so easily reined in, however. Three other provinces – Yunnan, Guizhou and Guangxi – still use the ideographic form of Yi (interestingly, showing the limits of the Chinese policy, whatever the official aims), and other dialects of Yi do not yet have a standardized script. There are 756 basic glyphs based on the Liangshan dialect, plus 63 for syllables only used for words borrowed from Chinese.

Chinese legislation states that standardized Yi is written horizontally, from left to right. The traditional form used in southern Sichuan, however, is still written in vertical columns from top to bottom and right to left, then rotated 90 degrees anticlockwise for reading, so that it is read in horizontal lines from left to right.

As with the more than fifty other official Chinese minority languages, the Yi group is suffering from attrition, marginalization and neglect. When it comes to written Yi, though, it's hard not to believe that this ancient and profoundly nonconformist writing system continues to resist.

1   **Character grid:** examples of the Yi script.

2   **Sample words:** Article One of the Universal Declaration of Human Rights in the reformed Yi syllabary.

MANCHU

Origin:
China

An endangered alphabet is usually the sign of a fallen kingdom. Manchu is perhaps the only example of an imperial script that fell from grace – indeed, fell almost into extinction – even while its empire continued to flourish.

The striking vertical Manchu alphabet was proposed in 1599 when the Manchu leader Nurhachi ordered his secretary, Erdeni Baksi, and his prime minister, Gagai, to adapt the traditional Mongol script – already identified with the epic military conquests of Genghis Khan – for use with the Manchu language.

Gagai protested that the conversion would be extremely difficult, but he was soon put to death for an unrelated offence, and the task was completed by Erdeni.

It was a natural transition. Nurhachi already employed scribes who were literate in Mongolian and kept records in Mongolian, and Manchu leadership modelled itself in a number of respects on its Mongolian predecessors: language and literary forms, horse-raising and hunting on horseback (necessary for the development of a swift and efficient cavalry, as important to the conquest of China as it had been to the Mongol conquests), the use of slave and serf labour and some elements of military organization and civil administration.

By 1636, the Manchus proclaimed the last great dynasty, the Qing, which ruled China proper from 1644 until 1911.

During the first decades of the Qing dynasty, Manchus were required to learn Chinese, and Chinese were encouraged to learn Manchu. For a variety of reasons, though, it was not a happy marriage, and a slow, reverse linguistic conquest took place. By the mid-century, Chinese was overtaking Manchu: the emperor ordered the teaching of Chinese to be abandoned, and instead established schools to teach Manchu. By the early eighteenth century, however, many high officials could not read Manchu, and by the end of the century, even the palace household staff could not speak Manchu with the emperor. Officially, Manchu was the language of government and scholarship – in the Beijing First Historical Archives the catalogue of Manchu documents takes up 107 volumes listing over 1,500,000 documents in Manchu – but in everyday terms, Chinese became dominant.

By the start of the twentieth century, a French observer wrote: 'This language is still in theory the National Language of the Chinese Empire, but in reality it is disappearing day by day in face of the rapid invasion of the language of the Chinese. Manchu is no longer used at court, except in a minor way. In the streets of Peking … one almost never hears people speaking this language.'

The anti-Manchu nationalist revolution of 1911 ended the dynasty and Manchu identity, linguistic and cultural, became a negative.

By the 1950s, it was observed that only five people in Beijing knew Manchu well, and they were the curators of the Manchu archives. At the end of the twentieth century, the Manchu fall from grace was so complete that only a handful of elderly people in Heilongjiang still spoke Manchu natively, along with a variety of Manchu, Sibe, which is spoken in Xinjiang.

As elsewhere in China, there seems to be a paradoxical official attitude toward Manchu: interest in Manchu culture seems to be on the increase – the 1980s and 1990s saw a resurgence in Manchu as a subject for study, with translations, dictionaries and professional journals appearing – but as a mother tongue and mother script, Manchu continues to decline.

Script:
Manchu
—

'Mother tongue' in Manchu, based on a carving I made for an exhibition on International Mother Language Day, which is held on 21st February each year.

就 佈 由 样 理

SAWNDIP

Origin:
China

The Sawndip or Old Zhuang script is one of a number of ancestral scripts, probably more than a thousand years old, that survive in China – and the fact that it still exists and is used by a minority is a sign of the degree to which China, no matter how much it presents a unified front to outsiders, is actually a fascinating mix of cultures and traditions.

The Zhuang are an ethnic group who mostly live in the Guangxi Zhuang Autonomous Region in southern China. They form one of the fifty-six ethnic groups officially recognized by the People's Republic of China. Their population, estimated at 18 million, makes them the largest minority in China.

Zhuang is one of the array of northern Tai languages, and Sawndip is the Zhuang name for their own script, even though, curiously, it means 'raw characters'. The script is not only used by the Zhuang, but also by the closely related Buyei in Guizhou, China, Tay in Vietnam and Nung in Yunnan, China and Vietnam.

Sawndip, which is probably about 600 years old, is made up of a combination of Chinese characters, Chinese-like characters and other symbols. Like Chinese, it can be written horizontally from left to right, or vertically from right to left. The script has never been standardized; some characters have as many as a dozen variants.

The script has been used mainly by Zhuang singers and ritual specialists, to record poems, scriptures, folk tales, myths, songs and play scripts. Traditional songs, or stories, are often adapted over time, and new works continue to be written to this day.

After the Chinese Revolution in 1949, even communist revolutionary propaganda was written using Sawndip.

In 1957, the Chinese government introduced an official, alphabet-based script, and that became the standard for official documents, laws and newspapers, but, at least at the time, it was largely ignored by the Zhuang themselves because it was based on a single dialect, not widely spoken.

The current Chinese government policy is to standardize language usage and reduce the range and variation of minority spoken and written forms. After five years in preparation, a *Dictionary of Ancient Zhuang Characters* was published in 1989 with 4,900 entries and over 10,000 characters – the first and only dictionary of Zhuang characters published to date; but the official position seems to be that Sawndip is 'historical' and its usage is largely local, vernacular, unsupported by local and regional governments.

SOYOMBO

Origin:
Mongolia

The Soyombo script may be the only writing system in the world that is endangered in the sense that virtually nobody uses it, yet everyone in its home culture recognizes one of its letterforms and sees it virtually every day.

Soyombo – the name means 'self-developed holy letters' – is one of at least five scripts that have been used to write Mongolian. It is said to have been designed in 1686 by Bogdo Zanabazar (1635–1723), the first spiritual leader of Tibetan Buddhism in Mongolia, who according to tradition, saw the letterforms appear in the night sky. (He also developed a Horizonal Square script, known as Zanabazar Square.)

Zanabazar created the script for the translation of Buddhist texts from Sanskrit or Tibetan, and both he and his students used it extensively for that purpose, but it was too ornate and complex to be written hastily or used for everyday purposes.

It continued to be a familiar sight in temples, on official seals and on prayer wheels, though, and in time, this ceremonial and decorative use translated into the secular realm: the script, and especially the character for Soyombo itself, became so central to Mongol identity that in 1921 it appeared on the national flag.

In a sense, the very fact that it was no longer in general use meant it could take on a purely iconic value. In 1960, the Soyombo symbol was included as part of the Emblem of Mongolia, and has also been used on the country's postage stamps and money. It has become so associated with the national character that it is, in essence, a brand; so it is not surprising that it has become the name and logo for a premium vodka.

To Mongolians, it has made the transition from letter to rich, complex visual symbol. One interpretation sees it in five vertically stacked elements. The top part, the flame, is seen as a symbol of prosperity, the three branches of the flame standing for past, present and future. The sun and moon stand for the sky, a central feature of Mongolian spiritual beliefs. The two triangles represent a spear and an arrow, traditional Mongol weapons. The circle, an unstable form, is stabilized between two guardian rectangles. The round yin/yang-style form stands for two fishes, who never close their eyes and represent watchfulness – and in being male and female, they stand for fertility.

The situation may change if and when Soyombo is included in the Unicode standard, but given that there are so few practitioners left, it may become the only alphabet in the world to have dwindled to a single letter, the Soyombo symbol.

Script:
Mongolian bichig
—
The Mongolian script has
three different versions of
each letter, depending on
whether it occurs at the
beginning, middle or end
of the word. This is the final
version of *wa*, which like many
finals consists of a glorious
swoosh, making the Mongol
script inherently calligraphic.

MONGOLIAN

Origin:
Mongolia

Classical Mongolian is one of the great imperial scripts – the script of an empire that once stretched from the Pacific to the Mediterranean, the largest contiguous land empire in history. By the end of World War II, though, it was no longer used officially even in Mongolia.

It had its roots, aptly enough, in a military victory (or, to look at it another way, a military defeat) in 1203, when Chinggiss (or Genghis) Khan defeated the Naimans (a group of Turkic tribes living in Central Asia) and captured their scribe, Tatar-Tonga. Tatar-Tonga was induced to create a script for the great Khan, and to do so, he adapted a script with a fascinating history: the Old Uyghur alphabet.

Let's go still further back into history – to biblical times, in fact. The *lingua franca* of what we now call the Middle East was Aramaic. At the eastern borders of Aramaic, in modern Iran, the script evolved into Sogdian, a script that first appeared around the fourth century and was initially used to write letters and inscriptions. A cursive form of Sogdian was used in secular documents, royal proclamations and Buddhist and Manichaean manuscripts.

Over time, and still further east, Sogdian morphed into the Old Uyghur alphabet, but something fascinating happened in the process – something that fundamentally defines the Mongolian script: it turned through 90 degrees.

Sogdian was written from right to left in horizontal lines, but its offspring, the Old Uyghur alphabet, was written from left to right in vertical columns. We don't know why this happened, any more than we know why the Phoenician alphabet turned through 90 degrees when adopted by the ancient Greeks. It may have been to imitate Chinese writing; it may have been to pay homage to Tengri, the sky god; it may have had something to do with some aspect of convenience that no longer occurs to us, accustomed as we are to writing on flat, level surfaces or geometrical screens. But the result of this twist, and the Mongol victory over the Naimans, was that soon the whole of Asia would see a vertical script, the Classical Mongol script, known in Mongolian as *bichig*.

One of the many fascinating features of *bichig* is that it has what might be thought of as a built-in calligraphic quality. Each letter has three forms: initial (used when it comes at the beginning of a word), medial (used when it comes in the middle of the word) and final (I'll leave you to guess what that means). In almost every case, both the initial and final forms have a certain flourish, while the medial tends to be simpler and more contained. The effect is to allow the writer to start each word with a kind of fanfare, and to sign off with a swoosh. We'll come back to this in a minute.

Over the centuries, of course, the Mongol empire was eroded by civil war

>>

and division. By 1400 both China and the territories in the west had largely been lost, and the Mongols retreated to Mongolia. In the seventeenth century, the country was overtaken by the Manchu-founded Qing dynasty, which ruled Mongolia until the collapse of that dynasty in the early twentieth century. No sooner had Mongolia achieved independence, however, than it came under the influence of the Soviet Union, which imposed the Cyrillic script on all its domains. By the time a peaceful revolution took place in 1990, the traditional *bichig* script had been all but forgotten, though it had survived to some extent in what had become the Inner Mongolia Autonomous Region of China.

It is a testimony to the striking graphic qualities of the Mongolian script that its revival is being led by artists, designers, calligraphers and poets. Mongolian calligraphy in particular is gaining respect and visibility in the global landscape of calligraphy, especially since 2013, when the art form was inscribed on the UNESCO List of Intangible Cultural Heritage in Need of Urgent Safeguarding. Individual works of calligraphy are increasingly being used in fashion design, interior design and tattooing.

The Mongolian script is still used, to some extent, in outposts of Mongol culture, such as two of the Russian federal republics: Buryatia, on the shores of Lake Baikal and sharing a border with Mongolia, and Kalmykia, on the shores of the Caspian Sea. The Kalmyks suffered dreadfully in World War II: the killing of a large fraction of the Kalmyk population and the destruction of their society as consequence of deportation, along with the subsequent imposition of Russian as the sole official language, have meant that only the elderly have a fluent command of Kalmyk, and still fewer use the traditional bichig script.

In breaking news, though, the Mongolian Ministry of Education, Culture, Science and Sports recently announced that the traditional vertical script would return to use by 2025. In the 'comprehensive restoration' of the alphabet, scientific, literary and state registry offices have been asked to establish a system for Mongolian names; information and communication technologies are required to adapt traditional Mongolian to the 'electronic environment', schools must allow more time to teach the script and cultural centres will be set up to promote the Mongolian written heritage.

This move is in sharp contrast to the situation in Inner Mongolia, where the Chinese government has announced that the Chinese language and script will replace the traditional Mongolian language and script – an edict that, to the Mongols, amounts to nothing less than a programme of cultural genocide.

2

1 **Character grid:** examples of the
Mongolian script.

2 **Sample word:** *Bayarlalaa*, or 'Thank you',
in calligraphy by Oyunaa Oyuntungalag.

Script:
Mongolian
—
'To love love' in calligraphy
by Tamir Samandbadraa
Purev, one of the
greatest living Mongolian
calligraphers and co-
founder of the Erdenesiin
Khuree centre for the
promotion and teaching
of Mongolian calligraphy.

Script:
Siddham
—
In Shingon Buddhism, each Siddham syllable has a spiritual meaning of its own – to such an extent that they are sometimes depicted rising above a lotus. This is *vamh*.

Script:
Siddham
—
One of the glories of the
Siddham script is that its
forms retain the movement
of the brush, which in itself
is characteristic of a sacred
script and a devotional
attitude by the writer.

SIDDHAM

Origin:
Southern India

Siddham is an example of how a script can become more and more narrowly used to the point where, instead of being considered on the verge of extinction, its specialized use has given it historical identity and even spiritual value.

Siddham flourished between 600 and 1200, originating somewhere in southern India to write Sanskrit, but spreading along the Silk Road to China, Japan and Korea in the form of Buddhist texts. The script is still used today in this highly specific context wherever Shingon and Tendai Buddhism are practised, and indeed it has spread far further now. The Reverend Eijun Bill Eidson explained: 'My wife and I are Koyasan Shingon priests with temples in Fresno, California, and Nara, Japan. We actively teach Siddham meditations for use in life.

'Most priests learn Siddham as a part of the licensing procedure. It is taught as calligraphy to both priests and lay people. Our students include priests but mostly lay people. We have about 250 teachers who are authorized to teach our system. We developed it based on texts from ancient Japan … We have translated 62,000 pages of Chinese/Japanese text, including 600 pages on the esoteric meanings of Siddham letters. Last week we taught a class on the three universal truths from the perspective of Siddham and next week we are teaching a three-day class for becoming a Siddham teacher. Next weekend we are teaching a

class on Kaji (healing) using Siddham syllables from the Mahāvairocana Sutra.'

He has written in detail about the healing power of meditation on Siddham letters or syllables: 'In the practice of Shingon Buddhism, developed by its Japanese founder Kukai (Kobo Daishi) in the early ninth century, one slowly awakens to the realization that one is not separate from anything in either the phenomenal or non-phenomenal universes. The means of achieving this realization are available to the practitioner, who is generally referred to as a priest, in the form of several thousand highly structured individual practices. Shingon, which means "true word" or "mantra", uses practices involving hundreds of mantras, mudras and visualizations at deepening levels that are revealed as one's practice matures. At the heart of all of these is the notion of Honzon Kaji, becoming one with the main deity.'

Kaji is also held to have healing qualities. In both ancient and modern times, kaji healing has been performed to assist a person who is ill, by positively affecting their energy system.

Perhaps the most fascinating linkage between language and spiritual beliefs is the Buddhist/Hindu concept of 'seed syllables' – that a single syllable is a metaphor for the origin or cause of all things, and, planted in the mind, can be a seed out of which enlightenment may flourish.

Script:
Nüshu
—
The tall, narrow strokes of
the Nüshu script led even its
users to refer to it as 'mosquito
writing'. This is the word *Nüshu*.

NÜSHU

Origin:
China

Nüshu is one of the very few scripts we know about that was created by a woman – or women – and used exclusively by women.

It is not known when or how Nüshu (the word means 'women's writing') came into being (certainly no earlier than 900), but it seems to have reached its peak during the latter part of the Qing Dynasty (1644–1911). The characters, adapted from standard Chinese ones, were used exclusively among women in Jiangyong County in Hunan province of southern China.

Unlike Chinese, Nüshu writers valued characters written with very fine, almost threadlike, lines as a mark of fine penmanship. The writing was sometimes modified to fit an embroidery pattern or the individual panels of a fan: concealment was part of its very identity.

This fact underlies almost every aspect of Nüshu – not just because women were not permitted to learn to read and write, but because it was used to capture and communicate aspects of women's lives that were also personal, private or secret. It is little exaggeration to say that Nüshu represents, both metaphorically and literally, the world of women at a time and in a place when that world was largely invisible to men, and was neither understood nor respected.

One glimpse into this culture is offered by Tan Dun's multimedia performance work *Nu Shu: The Secret Songs of Women*, inspired by Jiangyong's folk songs, mainly the minority (Yao ethnic) music and Sinicized Yao women's bridal laments.

Tan Dun, who scored the movie *Crouching Tiger, Hidden Dragon*, spent several years in a remote village in his native province of Hunan recording over 200 hours of audio and video, and created a work for orchestra incorporating recorded voices and projected images.

Nu Shu: The Secret Songs of Women consists of thirteen movements: 'Secret Fan'; 'Mother's Song'; 'Dressing for the Wedding'; 'Cry-Singing for Marriage'; 'Nu Shu Village'; 'Longing for Her Sister'; 'A Road Without End'; 'Forever Sisters'; 'Daughter's River'; 'Grandma's Echo'; 'The Book of Tears'; 'Soul Bridge'; and 'Living in the Dream'.

The featured solo instrument is the harp; the instrumentation is predominantly strings, flute, oboe and percussion, with additional handmade sound effects: water trickling into a bowl, the string players' bows rapping on their instruments to imitate the snapping of fans.

The music is by turns dramatic, plaintive, reflective, melancholy and grief-stricken, but it is the video images of the (mostly elderly) women singing in Nüshu and the circumstances of their singing that demonstrate its social context, meaning and poignancy.

'Dressing for the Wedding', for example, sounds like a joyful title until it becomes

>>

clear that the wedding would have been arranged, the daughter no more than fifteen years old and the wedding itself possibly the last time the mother and daughter would ever see each other.

Nüshu was developed to express emotions that were inconvenient or even unacceptable to the orderly regulation of human life, and as such, these songs represent an entire panorama of concealed emotion. Mothers losing daughters, daughters losing mothers, sisters losing each other – a social web so torn, so desperate, it needed a secret language to bear such emotional weight.

The apparently tranquil, even transcendent 'Soul Bridge', which shows a young woman walking thoughtfully across an ornate bridge, has a sadder undercurrent: this is a bridge where she walks to remember her mother, who might be dead or simply not seen for decades.

The final movement, celebrating the working community of women, provides a cheerful ending, but this, in turn, implies how much that community was needed when those women were routinely separated, sundered, left devastated and facing despair.

After the Communist Revolution of 1949, Nüshu slowly fell out of use as women were granted equal access to state-sponsored public education. At the same time, Nüshu was condemned as a 'witch's script' during the Cultural Revolution, and many texts and artifacts were burned. Yang Huanyi, the last native writer and speaker of Nüshu, died in 2004.

On a more optimistic note, efforts to revive the script are currently being carried out by a few scholars in both China and the West. In 2002, Nüshu was added to the Chinese National Register of Documentary Heritage. A Nüshu museum was built in Puwei Island, Jiangyong County, in May 2007, and at least two typographers have recently created Nüshu fonts. Both are women.

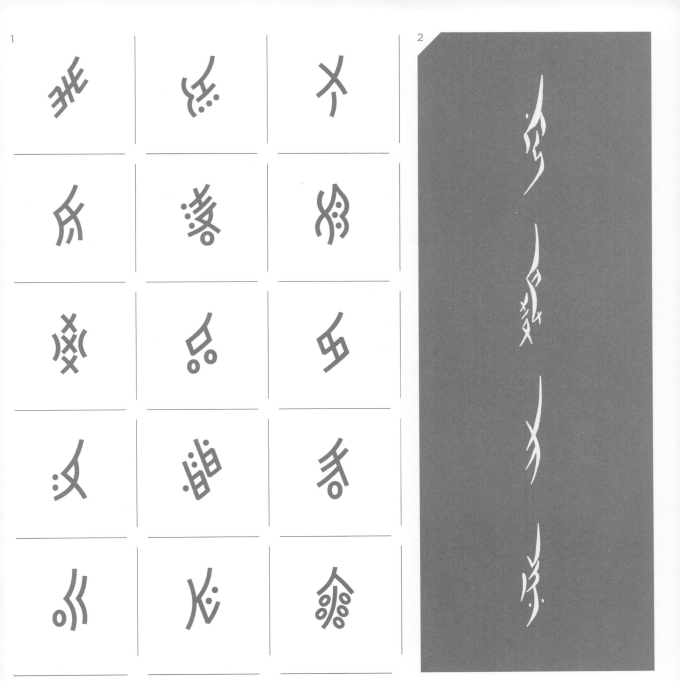

1   **Character grid:** examples of the
     Nüshu script.

2   **Sample words:** in Nüshu, another of the
     carvings from my 'Thank you all' series.

EURO
AND
MIDD
EAST

PE
THE
LE

INTRODUCTION

Europe has far more endangered and minority languages than you might expect (Italy alone has more than thirty living minority languages and dialects), but her handful of writing systems have been well entrenched for some time, largely thanks to the Roman empire and the spread of Christianity.

The Irish script Ogham can be found in thousand-year-old stone inscriptions, and the Dalecarlian Runes of Sweden survived locally into the twentieth century, used to write the hyper-local, charmingly named Elfdalian language, but in general, the continent has achieved a remarkable, possibly depressing, uniformity.

The Middle East, thought to be one of the few places where writing itself was born, is another story. Regional and local cultures have survived the rise and fall of empires and centuries of feuding with neighbours, and though the advance of Islam propagated the Perso-Arabic script in the same way

that the expansion of the Church of Rome spread the Latin alphabet, its dominance was by no means total.

The endangered writing systems from this region, in fact, are all closely associated with religions, whose adherents have travelled far across the globe.

The relationship between a religion and its writing system is a fascinating one. In the shamanic religions, written or painted symbols might serve to remind the shaman of the content and sequence of a ritual, but in some cases, the symbol itself might be a way of capturing and harnessing the spiritual power of the object, acting as a kind of bridge or portal between the material world and the spiritual. If writing can take something invisible and immaterial – a thought, an idea – and make it physical and visible, in some respects it imitates *the divine act of creation itself*.

Likewise, when a traditionally oral culture encountered representatives of a different culture that offered them not only a new religion but the new medium of writing, it's hardly surprising that writing would take on a numinous aura, like the runes engraved on Beowulf's sword.

Even when a religion was well established within a culture, often the only people who could read and write were priests or scholars who studied religious texts. Thus the awe and mystery of the religion were given visible expression in, among other iconic displays, the writing.

The region we now think of as Europe and the Middle East, then, has been both a cradle and an exporter of religions, and thus a nurturer and exporter of scripts. Zoroastrians brought the Avestan script not only to India but China; the East Syriac Rite flourished among Christians in Mongolia.

In several cases, though, this means a religion becomes a time capsule. Just as spoken Latin survives almost exclusively in Catholic church services, so several of the scripts in this section of the atlas have outlived their day-to-day secular usage. Conversely, attacks on religions often include, or are expressed as, attacks on their scripts. To defend one's belief system, then, may involve defending one's writing system, and religious endangered alphabets are often the most fiercely protected of all.

Script:
Mandaic
—
The Mandaic letter *asz*. It
seems almost sacrilegious
to separate out one letter,
given the Mandaeans' view of
their mystical alphabet as an
'indivisible republic of letters'.

MANDAIC

Origin:
Lower
Mesopotamia

Mandaeans may have the most fascinating alphabet in the world, a mystical system in which every letter has its own secret meaning and is part of a larger sacred whole.

Until recently, the greatest single concentration of Mandaeans, a non-Arab people whose lineage may go back to ancient Babylon, was located to the south and east of Baghdad. This group faced varying degrees of isolation and harassment under the regime of Saddam Hussein, and many left for other countries in the region (and, to a lesser extent, Sweden, Australia and the United States).

The US-led invasion of Iraq in 2003, however, served only to make their situation much worse. As law and order broke down, Mandaeans (along with other minority groups such as Assyrians and Armenians) suffered at the hands of both Shiite and Sunni groups, reporting murders, rapes and kidnappings – the last an especially common form of violation because Mandaeans are renowned goldsmiths.

In the face of these assaults (against which Mandaeans were powerless, being forbidden by their faith to carry weapons), nearly all of the 60,000 Mandaeans living in Iraq have fled into a global diaspora.

This grim story is all the sadder because of the extraordinary nature of Mandaean culture and the Mandaic script.

The Mandaeans consider their script to be as sacred as their literature. Like several other cultures, they see writing as such an exceptional gift that it could not have been invented by mere humans – it must have been divinely created and given to them. This, in turn, means that writing – the script itself – is divine, and its forms and practices need to be preserved as they are and always have been.

In a writing-creation myth, the divine creator himself, known as the Light King, sees writing for the first time and is so impressed and astonished he utters: 'Who created these [letters]? I did not, therefore there must be one mightier than I!' In other words, writing must have been created by a divinity mightier than the one who created the world itself.

The fact that the script of the modern manuscripts is not appreciably different from that of the earliest manuscripts illustrates how faithfully the Mandaeans have transmitted their sacred literature across the centuries.

Given that the earliest Mandaean writings are perhaps 1,500 years old, that's amazing. In English, handwritten manuscripts even 200 years old are noticeably different from today's writing; anything 400 years old (say, from Shakespeare's time) is very hard to read.

This faithfulness is also an indication of the Mandaeans' sense of the importance, even sacredness, of the written word per se. >>

In Mandaic, each individual letter has its own mystical meaning. Moreover, the alphabet consists of Mandaean versions of the twenty-two separate functional letters of the Aramaic alphabet; but it then adds on another two letters to make the total up to twenty-four – the number of hours from sunset to sunset and, therefore, a mystical number. One of the added letters is a ligature of two characters, something like an ampersand in English; the final letter is simply the first letter, repeated, to give the impression that the alphabet is not linear and finite but, like the day, repeats every twenty-fourth time. A mandala of an alphabet.

The Mandaean text *The Thousand and Twelve Questions* tells us that each letter of the alphabet emanated from the last, starting with the circular A, the wellspring (*aynā*) from which all the letters emerged, to the letter B, and from the letter B to the letter G, and so forth, until twenty-three came into existence. Each praised and worshiped its predecessor, until they formed a new kind of structure – a wall spreading out to the left and the right from the L, the middle letter, because the L is the builder's clay (or *lebnā*) that holds the left wing and the right wing of the wall together. Unfortunately, this wall stood only for itself, and could not support anything else, because the right and the left stood apart from one another.

They soon realized that if they were to clasp their hands together and form four corners joining back to the letter A, they could build a solid foundation. Thus, A became both the wellspring from which they emerged and the crown atop their heads. Only then did it become possible to name all things and speak every mystery, because language is not possible without this indivisible republic of letters.

This indivisible republic of letters – an astonishingly rich phrase – shows us how much we take writing for granted and fail to give it its due. The Mandaic alphabet invites us to think of writing as a miraculous transaction, analogous to the act of creation itself. In creating the physical universe, according to many traditions, the creator took a thought, something invisible and insubstantial, and made it visible, solid, habitable. Likewise, the act of writing takes an invisible, insubstantial thought and makes it visible, available to all – in a sense, habitable.

The point, then, is not that Mandaic writing, surviving as well as it can scattered across the world in small, dedicated pockets, is a vehicle for transmitting information that can lead to enlightenment – it's that each word, each letter, is in itself charged and radiant with enlightenment.

1

1 **Character grid:** examples of the
   Mandaic script.

2 **Sample word:** my carving of the Mandaic
   word for 'word' – which takes on
   astonishing depth of meaning when you
   consider the Mandaean saying, 'I am a
   word from words. I came for the name of
   Life', means something like 'I am a spirit
   from among spirits'.

2

Script:
Samaritan
—
One of the fascinating
features of the Samaritan
script is that it does not
follow the convention that
the letters should rest on an
invisible horizontal line. This
letter, *it*, seems, like much of
the alphabet, to be dancing.

SAMARITAN

Origin:
the Kingdom
of Israel

Some writing systems are thriving, some are extinct, some are newly created, some seem to be falling into disuse.

One language and its alphabet defy all these categories. Two thousand years ago it was the mother tongue of as many as a million people, but by the end of the nineteenth century it had dwindled to the point where it was used by only four families. Yet it has survived defiantly, like a desert plant. It is Samaritan.

The Samaritan family tree is very old, and has deep roots. Perhaps the first writing system to see widespread usage around the Mediterranean was the Phoenician alphabet, the script of a great trading empire. Phoenician was adopted (and adapted) by the ancient Greeks, and as such, is ultimately the ancestor of the Latin alphabet in which this atlas is typed. Another variant, perhaps 3,000 years old, has been dubbed the 'Paleo-Hebrew' alphabet. But while the Jews migrated to writing with the Aramaic alphabet (the second great international script) around 2,500 years ago, their neighbours the Samaritans did not.

One theory is that the destruction of the First Temple and the exile of educated Hebrew speakers to Babylon led to Hebrew commingling with Babylonian; another suggests that when they returned to Judah they found it a Persian province where Aramaic was the official script. The Samaritans, having suffered no such exile, regard

themselves as the true descendants of the sons of Israel, and their alphabet as the ancestral Hebrew script – a contentious position, given the power of writing as an iconic system.

By the time of Christ, the two neighbours loathed each other. The entire point of the parable of the Good Samaritan is that it's not the priest or the Levite, both representatives of the Jewish religious hierarchy, who help the mugged man – it's the hated and despised Samaritan who gives first aid and puts the victim up at the nearest inn. 'Which of these three was his neighbour?' Jesus asks, neatly making a point about both spiritual integrity and local hostility.

Despite Christ's endorsement, the next 2,000 years were not kind to Samaritans. Disliked by Jews, Christians and Muslims, they suffered massacres under the Christian Byzantine Emperor Zeno, were slaughtered or forced to convert to Islam by the Ottoman Pasha Mardam Bey (in 1625) and by the beginning of the twentieth century consisted of only four families, numbering perhaps 120 individuals.

Samaritans are not a weak-willed people, though, and their devotion to survival is as strong as their devotion to their language. If anything, they may have become more devoted to their script. Nowadays, the Samaritan population, restricted to two settlements in Nablus (a Palestinian city in the West Bank) and Holon (near Tel Aviv), has >>

clawed its way back up to roughly a thousand, and is as proud of its language, both spoken and written, as ever.

As Binyamin Tsedaka, the official Samaritan librarian, translator and scribe, writes: 'It is not by any means in a process of extinction, but [is] in daily use by the Samaritans teaching their children and boys and girls between the ages 5–15, and an integral part of the "A.B. – The Samaritan News" fortnightly magazine since its establishment in 1969 which contains a constant ancient Hebrew section alongside new compositions by today's Samaritan writers of all ages.'

But Samaritan has one more unique feature: it's part of the secret iconography of Freemasonry. Freemasons revere the Emerald Tablet of Hermes, also known as the Smaragdine Tablet, or Tabula Smaragdina, as the most ancient witness to their Craft, perceiving within it the name of Hiram, the hero of Masonic legend.

This text is one of the foundations of European alchemy and a sacred text of the Hermetic tradition, so named after Hermes Trismegistus, the Greek equivalent of the Egyptian Thoth. The earliest surviving version of this text is Arabic, but its most iconic version is German esotericist Wilhelm Christoph Kriegsmann's 1657 'Phoenician' reconstruction, which is actually written in Samaritan letters, albeit modified to accommodate the rectilinear aesthetics of the Latin alphabet.

It was his often-reproduced depiction that brought the Samaritan script furthest away from its home territories: a mountain in the American state of New Mexico. There, a copy of the Ten Commandments appears, inscribed upon a boulder in Kriegsmann's characteristic hand. The date and origins of this inscription are unknown, although scholars have variously attributed it to Freemasons, Mormons and Samaritans alike.

1 **Character grid:** examples of the Samaritan script.

2 **Sample words:** Article One of the Universal Declaration of Human Rights in Samaritan. You can see clearly the refusal of this ancient script to conform to modern typographic conventions and sit on a straight line.

S Y R I A C

Origin:
Syria

It is hard to think of another endangered alphabet that has been used to write as many languages, and over as wide a geographical area, as Syriac.

The Syriac language is a literary variety of Aramaic, the *lingua franca* of much of the Near East from about seventh century BC until the seventh century AD. Aramaic was thus also the language spoken by Jesus, and as the Syriac script superseded the Aramaic script over the first four or five centuries AD, versions of Syriac became the official scripts of Christianity wherever Aramaic was spoken.

As Eastern Christianity expanded, it took the Syriac script eastward, establishing communities in India (the Saint Thomas Christians), among the Mongols in Central Asia and in China, which became home to a thriving community under the Tang dynasty from the seventh to the ninth century. Between the ninth and fourteenth centuries, the Church of the East was, in terms of sheer acreage, the world's largest Christian church, and the Syriac script appears in an astonishing number and variety of documents of the time.

As the de-facto script of learning, Syriac was used for many of the documents of early Christianity and many translations of works from Arabic, in addition to Christian hagiographies, chronicles and numerous theological works. But having a script whose fate is tied to a religion is both a

strength and a potential weakness. The rise of Islam saw Syriac replaced by Arabic in much of the Middle East, and when the Ming Dynasty overthrew the Mongols, Christians were expelled from China.

Today, then, the Syriac script is in an ambiguous position. It is still the active liturgical script of many minority communities in the Middle East, southeast India, and wherever Syrians have established religious communities overseas, especially in Europe, Australia and the Americas. As such, it enjoys a protected status within the church, and moreover, the wealth of historical documents in Syriac makes them an important field of study – so, unlike other endangered alphabets, the cultural freight of Syriac is unlikely to be lost.

Yet very few Syrian speakers use the script on a day-to-day basis, and it is very seldom taught. The future of the Syriac script, like the future of Syria itself, remains uncertain. It's worth noting, though, that a number of organizations in Syria have included Syriac script on their signage, another illustration of the way in which a script can have an iconic richness that transcends the meanings of words.

GLAGOLITIC

Origin:
Moravia

Here and there in Central and Eastern Europe, the visitor can see, carved into the walls of churches and cathedrals, fascinating panels of mysterious writing – ornate and yet apparently as old as stone itself. That writing is in Europe's only endangered alphabet: Glagolitic.

The oldest-known Slavic alphabet, Glagolitic was probably created in the ninth century by Saint Cyril, a Byzantine monk from Thessaloniki. He and his brother, Saint Methodius, were sent to spread Christianity among the West Slavs in Moravia.

The Slavs already had scripts of their own, but the missionaries dismissed them as 'mere dots and lines'. The brothers decided to translate liturgical books into the Old Slavonic language that was understandable to the general population, but as the words of that language could not be easily written using either the Greek or Latin alphabets, Cyril decided to invent a new script, called Glagolitic (possibly from the Slavonic word *glagolŭ*, meaning 'utterance').

Not long afterwards, followers of Cyril and Methodius developed a second liturgical alphabet, named Cyrillic in Cyril's honour.

As the centuries passed, the Cyrillic script, which was more flexible and frankly easier to write, became used more and more, and Glagolitic began a long, slow fade. As the second millennium drew to a close, Cyrillic had, ironically, become the totemic script of the atheistic Soviet Union, but the only people who still read and wrote Glagolitic were priests.

Yet the script somehow refused to die, especially in Croatia and Bulgaria, where its historical roots were too deep for it simply to be pulled up.

Glagolitic had moved to the position of many ancient scripts (such as runic alphabets, or Ogham in Ireland): the fact that it is not readily read and understood makes it all the more mysterious and alluring.

It's also fascinating that in the aftermath of the terrible Yugoslav civil war throughout the 1990s, the newly minted countries needed to give themselves a fresh identity that conveyed historical legitimacy – and Croatia began including Glagolitic script on its tourist literature.

Meanwhile, the sculptor Želimir Janeš created a series of giant Glagolitic letters along the road between Roč and Hum in Croatia, and other Glagolitic signage has sprung up since.

Perhaps that is the best way to view Glagolitic: visually striking, sculptural and culturally emblematic, rather than functional.

Script:
Avestan
—
The Avestan letter *tte*, part
of an alphabet that has
the extraordinary distinction
of having been moribund, but
then revived specifically to write
texts to help a religion survive.

AVESTAN

Origin:
Iran

One sign of the importance of writing in the spread of religion – and vice versa – can be seen in the phrase 'People of the Book', an early term of respect for members of faiths that had written scriptures.

The Avestan script may have been created so a religion that had no book might better compete with those that did.

It may also be the only script (perhaps with the exception of Vedic Sanskrit) ever to have been created to write a language no longer in everyday use at the time it was devised.

Zoroastrianism is one of the world's oldest continuously practised religions. Possibly as much as 3,500 years old and traditionally based on the teachings of Zoroaster (or Zarathushtra), Zoroastrianism was the state religion of a succession of Iranian empires for more than a thousand years, from around 600 BC until the Muslim conquest.

The languages used in the early practice of Zoroastrianism were Old and Young Avestan, a pair of related regional Indo-Iranian languages. This pair has so completely died out, though, that all we know of them is what survived in Zoroastrian liturgical use. This hyper-narrowing led to a remarkable situation in which this pair of languages were named *retrospectively*: the Avesta is the primary collection of religious texts of Zoroastrianism, so the languages have come to be called Avestan – even though they were functionally extinct,

in a daily-use sense, by the time the Avestan texts were written!

The development of the Avestan alphabet, starting around the fifth or sixth century AD, may have been the result of the religion's desire to compete with Buddhists, Christians and Manicheans, each of which were, in their own ways and before the Islamic phrase had been coined, 'People of the Book'. The Zoroastrian religion, until that point, had been based on oral tradition – a recitation of prayers in specific cadence and inflection, passed down from teacher-priests to their pupils, accompanied by rituals in which a text would have been an encumbrance and a distraction. A phonetic written form would allow for a greater exactness of pronunciation, and a more coherent body of wisdom.

The right-to-left script devised to write the Avesta ultimately consisted of fifty-three characters –the majority derived from Pahlavi which, in turn, was derived from Aramaic, some seemingly adapted from Greek, and a few invented specifically for the purpose. It was a full alphabet, with characters for vowels, and it came with a unique system of punctuation.

All languages and scripts associated with religions, however, are both protected and vulnerable as the fortunes of the religion rise and fall, and Avestan, being functionally extinct outside the Zoroastrian setting, was especially vulnerable. Once the Sasanian Empire had fallen to the Arabs by >>

651 AD, Zoroastrianism began to decline. It survived mainly in what nowadays may seem an unusual context: India.

Over the next several centuries, many Persian Zoroastrians decided to escape persecution and preserve their religious traditions by fleeing eastward into Sindh and Gujarat, where they were known as Parsis, meaning 'Persians'. They were granted permission to stay by the local ruler, Jadi Rana, on the condition that they adopt the local language, Gujarati, and that their women adopt local dress (the sari).

Parsis developed a substantial Zoroastrian community in India, especially in Gujarat, and many of the religion's surviving documents originate in India. But the everyday language of the community steadily changed to Gujarati, with Sindhi, Marathi, Hindi, Bengali or other regional languages used for trade and mercantile reasons and interacting with domestic help. Many of the ancient texts were preserved in translation, especially into Persian and Gujarati, using the Persian and Gujarati scripts.

From the nineteenth century onward, Parsis gained a reputation for their education and widespread influence in all aspects of society. They played an instrumental role in the economic development of the region over many decades; several of the best-known business conglomerates of India such as the Godrej and Tata groups were founded by Parsis.

At the request of the government of Tajikistan, UNESCO declared 2003 a year to celebrate the '3,000th anniversary of Zoroastrian culture', and in 2011, it was announced that for the first time in the history of modern Iran and of the modern Zoroastrian communities worldwide, women had been ordained in Iran and North America as *mobedyars*, or assistant clergy,

authorized to perform secondary religious functions and initiate people into the religion (though this step is highly contentious, largely supported by the Iranian Zoroastrians but not the vast majority of Parsis).

Today, the world population of Zoroastrians is perhaps a little more than 100,000 (the greatest population centre being around Mumbai, with smaller groups elsewhere in the region, and the world), and is shrinking.

Yet even though the Avestan script remains at the core of Zoroastrian worship, only a few hundred scholars and priests can read it, and for the devout faithful it survives as a series of symbols with spiritual weight rather than literal meaning or phonetic value, representing a language that died more than 2,000 years ago.

1 **Character grid:** examples of the Avestan script.

2 **Sample words:** detail from a lithographed facsimile of the key manuscript on which Anquetil-Duperron based his Zend-Avesta, a key Zoroastrian text, published in Paris in 1771. Photo courtesy of the Incunabula Library.

Script:
Coptic
—
Many of the Coptic letters
look very much like Greek
letters of the time – which
is hardly surprising as
the Copts were Christian
Greeks living in Egypt. Some,
however, like this *ksi*, have
entirely their own character.

C O P T I C

Origin:
Egypt

Nowadays, we have almost forgotten the Greeks in Egypt. We know the Pharaohs and the pyramids; we know the Arabs and Islam; but it's a telling omission that we tend to assume the one just ran into the other, and the fact we do so says a great deal about the sad fate of the Copts and their language and alphabet.

The word 'Copt' derives from the Greek word for 'Egyptian', and Greeks have been in Egypt since the seventh century BC – as visitors, as mercenaries, then, under Alexander the Great, as conquerors. Alexander proclaimed himself Pharaoh, and established the city-port of Alexandria. One of his generals, Ptolemy, made Alexandria an international centre of commerce, art, science and learning, with the greatest library in the world at the time. The last Pharaoh was a Greek princess named Cleopatra.

By then, the seeds of the Coptic alphabet had been sown – a version of the Greek alphabet, with several additional letters from the older Demotic Egyptian script.

Even after the battle of Actium in 31 BC, when Ptolemaic Egypt fell under Roman rule, Egypt was still home to a large Greek-speaking population, so it's hardly surprising that Greek Christianity should reach Egypt early, in the person, according to tradition, of Saint Mark. When the sectarian disputes common in the early Christian Church led to a split between the Coptic Orthodox Church and the Byzantine Orthodox Church, Egyptian Christians wanted a visible symbol of their new faith, and in the third century, the Bible was translated into the Coptic language and script. (The astonishing Gnostic codices found at Nag Hammadi were written in Coptic.)

By the year 600, then, Coptic was an official language of Egypt, well established in both home and church. It had (and still has) a number of regional variants, but a substantial number of fine manuscripts demonstrated a characteristic and handsome calligraphy. Coptic was even recognized across the border in the three newly Christian kingdoms of Nubia.

The rise of Islam and the Arab conquest of Egypt began a gradual decline in Coptic fortunes. At times tolerated, at times actively persecuted, the Copts became a religious minority in the twelfth century, and during the fourteenth and fifteenth centuries lost a cross-border ally when Nubian Christianity was supplanted by Islam. While still using Coptic as their liturgical language and script, Copts had fewer and fewer opportunities to use their language in any other situations – a problem that still exists today.

Meanwhile, the Jesuit polymath Athanasius Kircher, sometime owner of the infamous *Voynich* manuscript, published the first grammar of the Coptic language in 1639. In this work, Kircher was the first scholar to acknowledge that Coptic is none other than the latest stage of the

>>

Egyptian language. A few decades later, in 1678, the German traveller J. M. Wansleben encountered an elderly gentleman whom he identified as the last living speaker of Coptic, although reports persist of individuals and families who use colloquial forms of Coptic in daily life, even in the present day.

In the early twentieth century, Egyptologist Claudius Labib made a determined effort to revive Coptic as a spoken language, teaching it, publishing a Coptic periodical on a printing press he had imported from Germany and compiling the first five volumes of a Coptic–Arabic dictionary (he died before it was finished).

Even in the last half-century or so, things have deteriorated for the Copts, many of whom were forced to leave Egypt after Gamal Abdel Nasser's coup of 1952; and the Arab Spring of 2011 led to an increase in religious discrimination and violence against the estimated 6–25 million who remain. According to Human Rights Watch and the Egyptian Initiative for Personal Rights, in one province alone, seventy-seven sectarian attacks were documented between 2011 and 2017, including abductions and disappearances of Coptic women and girls.

'In Egypt,' wrote one first-hand observer, 'there is more than a small discomfort with public expressions of Coptic identity. Churches cannot ring their bells. Houses of prayer are sometimes sacked for putting up a cross. Those Copts who achieve public prominence are expected to play down their identity.'

As in neighbouring Sudan, though, there are signs of a grassroots movement toward cultural revival. One Coptic nationalist writes: 'Coptic Nationalists work for a civilian, secular democratic Egypt for all Egyptians regardless of religion, sex, colour or nationality … We believe that Egypt is formed of three nations,

Arabs, Copts and Nuba. We work also for the collective rights of the Copts within a multinational Egypt.'

Today, the Coptic language is the mother tongue of only about 300 people worldwide. It survives, along with its script, as the liturgical language of the Coptic Catholic Church and the Coptic Orthodox Church (in Egypt, Sudan, Libya and overseas), and to a small extent online, where you can follow @copticcomedy on Instagram.

And though it is rare to see or hear Coptic outside a church setting (or on Twitter), during the African soccer tournament in June 2019, a stadium crowd in Cairo displayed a banner, nearly 10 metres wide, in the red, white and black tricolours of the Egyptian flag. On each colour band was the same message: 'We Love Egypt' in Arabic, English and Coptic.

ϻ	ⲇ	ⲏ	ϥ	ⲱ
ⲗ	ⳙ	ⲩ	ⳁ	ⲧ
ⲑ	ⲥ	ⳉ	ⳅ	ⲡ
ⳛ	ⲍ	ϭ	ⲃ	ⲫ
ⲉ	ⲕ	ⲯ	ⲭ	ⲅ

1 **Character grid:** examples of the Coptic script.

2 **Sample words:** 'In the beginning was the Word', carved in Coptic – always a profound idea to meditate on, especially in this context.

ϩⲛ ⲧⲉϩⲟⲩⲉⲓⲧⲉ ⲛⲉϥϣⲟⲟⲡ
ⲛϭⲓ ⲡϣⲁⲇⲉ

N U B I A N

Origin:
the Kingdom
of Nubia

The ancient Nubian script is the product of not one but two great, thousand-year-long kingdoms in the cradle of the upper Nile valley. Yet Nubia is now almost forgotten, its land area divided between Egypt and Sudan, its language and cultural traditions marginalized. Its script, however, gives clear hints of a Nubian past and perhaps a Nubia to come.

By 800 BC, the first major Nubian kingdom, the Kingdom of Kush, was established, with its capital at Meroe. The Kushites preserved numerous ancient Egyptian customs but were unique in many respects, not least for their place in the history of writing. They developed their own writing system, known as Meroitic – one of the first true alphabets, a script with twenty-three phonetic symbols.

The Kingdom of Kush disintegrated in the fourth century AD after more than a thousand years of existence, and in its place three smaller Nubian kingdoms arose: Nobatia in the north, Maqurrah in the centre and Alwah in the south. We don't know much about their early days, including how they converted to Christianity – which, according to one account, was the result of a bizarre contest between the orthodox Byzantine Emperor Justinian and his wife Theodora, both of whom sent competing priests and bishops racing across the desert, helped or hindered by the local authorities.

Whatever the case, the three kingdoms were Christianized, and the result can be seen in their writing. Nobatia and Maqurrah adopted the Coptic alphabet being used by Egyptian Christians, but incorporated three Meroitic letters that expressed sounds not represented in Coptic. The Alwan kingdom seems to have developed its own alphabet that combined Greek and Meroitic letters with glyphs of local invention. Over the next 200 years, especially when Maqurrah conquered Nobatia, the Old Nubian alphabet and language were gradually adopted throughout the unified kingdom.

Again, it's important to stress how deep these roots go: Old Nubian writing is perhaps as old as the earliest written English, and arguably older than written French and written German. Unlike Egypt, Nubia was strong enough to resist the rise of Islam, though the price for peace was a treaty by which the Nubians would supply 360 slaves a year in exchange for a shipment of Egyptian grain. The Nubian language was increasingly supplanted by Arabic, which was more international and therefore more widely used in commerce. Eventually, in the sixteenth century, the northern part of Nubia was conquered by the Ottomans, while the southern section was swallowed by the Sennar sultanate of Sudan/Eritrea/Ethiopia. Nubia would never be whole again, and like other subjugated cultures, it lost control of its language, its religion, its land and its destiny.

The conversion of Nubians to Islam accelerated the process of Arabization, and as Arabic was a language of high importance in both Sudan and Egypt, the Nubian language, spoken and written, became largely confined to Nubian homes. Of the roughly 600,000 Nubians in Egypt and Sudan today who speak a cluster of related Nubian languages, the vast majority cannot read the Nubian script and most likely do not even know it exists.

In the past few years, though, scholarship in Old Nubian has seen a revival, and the Taras Press has published four delightful illustrated children's books for learning the Nubian script: *Nabra's Nubian Numbers*, *This is How We Read Nubian*, *This is How We Write Nubian* and *The Miracle of Amanirenas*. One other odd ancestral quality makes the Nubian script unique. When the Coptic alphabet was adapted for writing Old Nubian, for some long-lost reason the invariably upright Coptic letters were written, by Nubian scribes, on a slant. This means that in a sense Old Nubian is *the only alphabet in the world to be written entirely in italics.*

Script:
Nubian
—
If this letter *a* looks familiar, it is because the Greek alpha migrated both southwards through Coptic into Nubia, but also west and north throughout the Roman empire as part of the Latin alphabet.

SOU

ASI

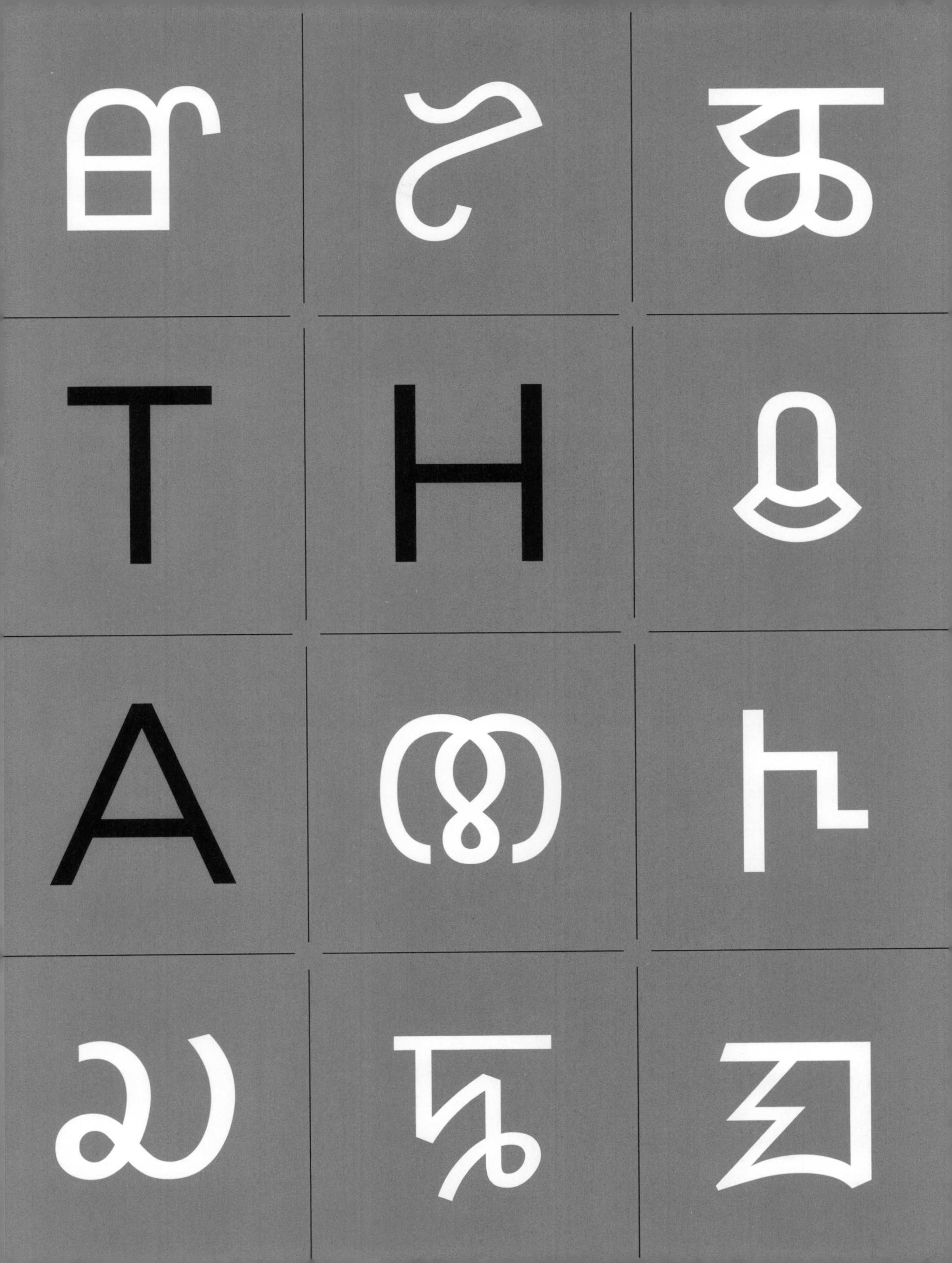
T
H
A

INTRODUCTION

Everyone who lives in South Asia, and everyone who has visited South Asia, will tell you that their dominant impression is one of almost overwhelming variety. The same holds true for languages and scripts.

When the British administrator George Abraham Grierson undertook to survey and record every language in India (which at the time encompassed more or less all of South Asia) it took him over thirty years, and the final result, published in 1928, encompassed eleven volumes and included no fewer than 364 languages and dialects.

Even so, a range of voices complained that Grierson's *Linguistic Survey of India* was incomplete – but the sheer effort involved in updating it has defeated everyone. A revision started by the Language Division of the Office of the Registrar General & Census Commissioner of India in 1984 was still only 40 per cent completed after twenty-six years. A 1991 census found 1,576 'mother tongues'. And that's just contemporary India: it doesn't include the rich linguistic stew to be found in Pakistan, Bangladesh, Sri Lanka and the Himalayan region.

The official census (like all censuses, mystifyingly) did not inquire about writing systems, but even a cursory pencil-and-paper list identifies at least fifty scripts in use in South Asia – some new, some ancient, some widespread, some extremely local.

Any country faces the tension between trying to sustain a national sense of identity and purpose, and respecting local cultures and their traditions, beliefs and languages.

The countries of South Asia face that problem on as many levels as in a video game.

Not surprisingly, then, history has seen a number of bureaucratic efforts to simplify the linguistic picture, most of which have failed to satisfy everyone. For example, after Partition in 1947, the new nation of Pakistan declared that Urdu was to be the country's official language, even though only a minority spoke it – an issue that would cause not only bureaucratic difficulties but outright bloodshed.

(As a side note: Urdu is written right to left in a version of the Persian script – itself a version of Arabic – and is associated with the nasta'līq style of Persian calligraphy. nasta'līq is notoriously difficult to typeset, so Urdu newspapers were handwritten by master-calligraphers until the late 1980s. One handwritten Urdu newspaper, in fact, is still published daily in Chennai.)

Language, written and spoken, has been and remains extremely politically sensitive. Hindi, written in the Devanagari script, has been closely identified with Hindu nationalism, and the rising movement to rid India of the British (and, later, the country's Muslim population) led to a corresponding rise in the script's use, at the expense of many previously healthy regional writing systems.

It's not surprising, then, that South Asia should be the world leader in endangered alphabets. What may be unexpected is that it is also remarkably rich in emerging scripts – some of them newly minted, some revitalized versions of ones that fell out of use decades, even centuries ago. And while many Indigenous African scripts have been created as a response to, even in defiance of, a colonial authority, the enemy in South Asia is more likely to be one's own neighbour – hence the fact that I don't know of a single newly created South Asian script that aims to be pan-Indian. Why is that?

There has long been an equation in India (and elsewhere) between civilization and writing – an equation that leads to an implied superiority by cultures that have their own writing system. This may be all well and good, but it has a darker underside: a view that any community without its own writing system (or worse, an oral culture that does not use writing) is 'tribal' and 'backward', even if its history can be traced over centuries. Script creation, then, may help to reduce social and intellectual stigma. Moreover, having one's own script may, under the right circumstances, be a political advantage, or make a people eligible for government subsidies.

Finally, there are many ethnic communities, sometimes numbering in the millions, who were not granted their own state after Partition and are now starting to demand recognition – and having a unique script is one immediate way of being recognized.

A strong incentive exists, then, for Indigenous and minority groups to develop their own writing systems. More often than not, the author is a single individual, almost always a man. He is a linguist by passion rather than profession, who hopes that after the years of hard work involved in developing a symbol system that matches the full range of sounds of his language, and – just as importantly – is easy to learn, his community will embrace his script. Sooner or later, the local newspaper hears of his labours and dispatches a reporter, who writes an article that is generally respectful of the effort expended in the name of the community and its identity.

In some cases, the official attitude toward these scripts is one of acceptance, or even encouragement, especially in multi-ethnic states like Sikkim; in others, the reception is frosty, and enthusiasts take to the Internet to plead their cause, and to YouTube to teach the emerging alphabet.

The Internet, in fact, is the new frontier for South Asian writing systems. Getting a new script recognized by local government may well stir up old animosities and inflame old prejudices; having it adopted in schools may take years of debate, and considerable expense in printing textbooks. Going online is the youthful alternative in an ancient region.

Facebook and Twitter are alive with communities celebrating their culture or arguing their cause, and as a wider range of scripts is digitized, these discussions are more likely to fly their own scripts, ancient or modern, like flags.

CHAKMA

Origin:
India

Some 300,000 Chakma live in the Chittagong Hill Tracts of Bangladesh, making them the largest ethnic community in the region. Others live elsewhere in Bangladesh, and a further 175,000 live across the border in India.

The Chakma had, and have, their own language and script, which derived from the Brahmi script of ancient India via Burmese, and like most Burmese-derived scripts, it has a familiar concatenation of circles and part-circles.

For roughly 500 years, the Chakma people and their king were treated with respect by the Arakanese, the Mughals and the East India Company; even when the Chakma were defeated, they retained a great deal of autonomy, and, as the British Governor of Chittagong said, 'We recognized no right on our part to interfere with their internal arrangements'. As such, the Chakma script was used for all official documentation and a wide variety of private publications.

When Bengali Muslims tried to seize territory in the Chittagong Hill Tracts – a theme that will return shortly – the Chakma and other ethnic groups living in the area appealed to the British for protection, given that they and the Bengalis did not share a religion, language or ethnicity. Under British India, in fact, the Hill Tracts were a separate administrative area that enjoyed a considerable degree of self-rule.

In the event of Indian independence, they were assured, the Chittagong Hill Tracts would be split off separately. This did not turn out to be the case. Even though the people of the Hill Tracts were 98 per cent non-Muslim, the region was given to Pakistan (which, at the time, incorporated what is now the separate nation of Bangladesh) – a decision that was disastrous for the Chakma and other ethnic groups of the Hill Tracts. After the bloody civil war that led to the birth of Bangladesh, the new Bangladeshi constitution denied full citizenship to any non-Bengalis and insisted on a one-language policy that made Bangla the sole spoken language and script.

Many Chakma had already migrated to India, especially after the Kaptai Dam project flooded 54,000 acres and displaced 100,000 Indigenous people, some 70 per cent of whom were Chakmas. This displacement continued when the Bangladeshi government began a policy of granting tracts of land traditionally farmed by the Indigenous inhabitants of the region to Bengali settlers.

The result was an exodus of tens of thousands to India and Myanmar and a 22-year-long series of violent and armed confrontations between the Bangladesh government and Indigenous residents of the Hill Tracts. Even following the cease-fire in 1997, the area remains a militarized region, with access denied to journalists and human-rights workers. Regular massacres, rapes, murders and destruction of villages have been documented.

Official education in the Hill Tracts is in Bangla, a language spoken by few of the region's Indigenous peoples, and steady cultural erosion is the result. Few Chakma can still read their own script. In the midst of all this, the work of Bivuti Chakma – writer, teacher, typographer, coder – to create viable digital fonts and keyboards for the Chakma script shines like a small, unwavering light.

In 2015, Bangladesh's first Chakma-language film, *My Bicycle*, was shown at several international film festivals – but it was banned in Bangladesh for promoting the issue of Indigenous languages and for its unfavourable portrayal of the police and military forces in the Chittagong Hill Tracts.

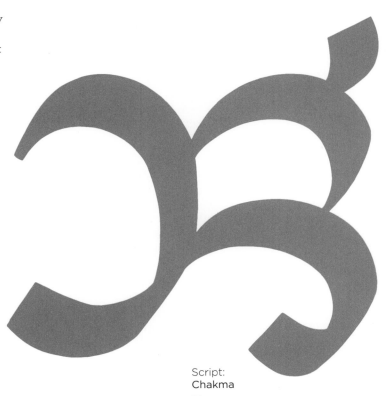

Script:
Chakma
—

The Chakma script is being hauled back into use almost singlehandedly by Bivuti Chakma of Bangladesh, a font developer, keyboard layout creator, author of *Chakma Mini Grammar* and other Chakma books.

GRANTHA

Origin:
India

Like almost all traditional South Asian scripts, Grantha is based on the Brahmi alphabet. Its first appearances are in cave inscriptions in southern India. Historically, it was used for writing texts in the Sanskrit language. The word *grantha* in Sanskrit means 'knot', suggesting that the script was originally used in palm-leaf manuscripts held together by knotted string.

Grantha was a major southern Indian script until World War II, but after independence in 1947, Hindi was promoted as the national language (as Gandhi had recommended) and in parallel, the standard Devanagari script started receiving more attention and usage, even in South India. More and more Sanskrit books were printed in Devanagari by publishers desiring to cater to a nationwide audience, and thus the usage of Grantha for the purpose decreased.

The rise of the pro-Tamil movement, too, in the second half of the twentieth century, further eroded the use of Grantha in Tamil Nadu, one of the strongholds of the script. Until World War II, books in Maṇipravāḷam (a language mixing Tamil and Sanskrit) were written alternating Tamil script (for Tamil verbs and endings) and Grantha script (for Sanskrit roots and nouns). By contrast, currently, books printed in Tamil Nadu and mixing Sanskrit and Tamil words are printed either in Tamil script with Devanagari insertions or purely in Tamil script.

If this sounds confusing, bear in mind that Japanese script combines no fewer than three types of characters: hiragana (a syllabary developed from Chinese characters, originally used mainly by women), katakana (a syllabary developed from simplified Chinese characters used by Buddhist monks, originally used mainly by men) and kanji (a Chinese-based character set of thousands of characters). Nowadays, sometimes even Latin letters are used.

Even if the Grantha script may no longer be in widespread general use, scholars and priests use it daily to write and read Sanskrit texts, and a large number of other people interested in Sanskrit and Vedic have learned the script to varying extents and use it occasionally. Grantha is used in religious almanacs, and also by Tamil-speaking Hindus to write a child's name for the first time during the naming ceremony, the Sanskrit portion of wedding invitations and announcements of a person's last rites.

One final note: like many South Asian scripts, including Tamil, Grantha has its own number system, unusual in the way it writes fractions. These are written using distinct symbols representing fractions of 320. So what is written in the Latin script as 1/4, for example, is written in Grantha/Tamil using a single symbol read as 80/320. Distinct symbols only exist for some fractions, but composites can be created; one symbol represents 8/320 and another represents 1/320, so 9/320 is written using both.

SIRIJANGA

Origin:
Limbuwan

The Sirijanga script, used for writing the Limbu language of Nepal and northern India, has a remarkable creation myth, in which a fragmented and warring kingdom is unified and saved by the creation of an alphabet.

Although Limbuwan is now a state of Nepal, for centuries it was an independent nation. Historically, it was made up of ten Limbu kingdoms, each of which had its own territory, its own king and its own fort. Late in the ninth century, King Sirijanga Hang of Yangwarok kingdom rose to power, subduing all the independent rulers and taking over as the new supreme ruler of Limbuwan. He built two big forts, one of which still stands.

According to tradition, he was also responsible for another construction that stood the test of time and unified all ten Limbus: the Kirat-Sirijanga script. Limbu folklore has it that he prayed to the goddess Saraswati for wisdom as to how to devise a script for his people, and in response she revealed the story of creation to him, written in the script.

The archetypical quality of this story is reinforced by the fact that, having apparently done its job, the script vanished. But its disappearance seems to have had an Arthurian waiting-to-return quality, for some 800 years later, during a time of tension and upheaval in Sikkim – in other words, just when it was needed – it was

reintroduced by the Limbu scholar Te-ongsi Sirijanga, believed to be the reincarnation of King Sirijanga.

He researched, revived and taught the Kirat-Sirijanga script, collecting, copying and composing Limbu literature, teaching Limbu language and the importance of Limbu history and cultural traditions, while at the same time preaching openness to other cultures and knowledge.

This work made him a cultural hero. But cultural heroes are also often threats. The Sikkimese Bhutia rulers ordered that he be tied to a tree and shot to death with arrows – possibly a cruel irony, as *limbu* means 'archer'.

In 1925, Iman Singh Chemjong, a Limbu scholar, named the script after Sirijanga, who laid down his life for its preservation and promotion.

Today Sirijanga is an active but vulnerable minority script. Since the late 1970s, it has been offered in the state schools of Sikkim as a vernacular language subject in areas populated by Limbus, and up to Master's level at university. Over 4,000 pupils study Limbu for one hour daily, taught by more than 300 teachers. Course books are available for classes one to twelve. In Nepal, the script is taught more sporadically as a private initiative. A Limbu newspaper has been published somewhat irregularly in Kathmandu since 1995.

Script:
Ranjana
—
The Nepali family of scripts
are closely related, ranging
from the most vernacular,
Prachalit, to the most formal
and regal, Ranjana.

NEPAL LIPI

Origin:
Nepal

Nepal has traditionally been a rich and complex linguistic culture. The Newa language, or Nepal Bhasa, has been written for a thousand years in a total of nine closely related scripts: Ranjana, Bhujinmol, Kunmol, Kwenmol, Golmol, Pachumol, Hinmol, Litumol and Prachalit Nepal. Collectively, these scripts are called Nepal Lipi.

Ranjana, whose name is derived from the Sanskrit word meaning 'joyful', is the boldest and most widely visible, seen in almost every temple, stupa or monastery in Nepal, and still used for reciting sutras and mantras. It has also been seen as a holy text that will bring good fortune to the home and protect it from negative energies. An inherently calligraphic script, it is written with a clear stroke form, angled at 25 to 30 degrees, and each letter is seen as consisting of a head, a backbone, a tail and, in many cases, a hand or torso. Ranjana can be written in both horizontal and vertical (or 'monogram') forms. The latter is called *kutakshar*, or 'secret writing', and was traditionally used to write sutras or to send secret messages; presumably because each word is so highly condensed and interwoven it is harder to decipher.

'You can see Ranjana script in every Buddhist monument you visit in Tibet,' Padhmadhar Tuladhar, a member of the Asa Safoo Kuthi, told the *Kathmandu Post*. 'Tibetans believe that Ranjana is the script of their guru, Manjushree, and therefore treat the scripts with utmost reverence. That's why the script is used so much in Tibet. You will see it everywhere, particularly on ceilings, because you always keep things that you respect at the top of your head.'

Use of the Nepal scripts began to decline when Prithvi Narayan Shah defeated King Jaya Prakash Malla of Kathmandu in 1769, leading to the Gorkhali conquest of the Nepal Mandala. He began to eliminate the use of Nepalese scripts in administration and trade. Once the Rana dynasty came to power, the scripts of Nepal Lipi were completely replaced. Nepal Bhasa was removed from education, and the government abolished the use of textbooks and documents written in Nepal Lipi in favour of Devanagari.

In 1912, Rana Prime Minister Chandra Shumsher officially nullified all property-ownership documents and deeds written in any language other than Gorkhali (Gorkha Bhasa), and any script other than Devanagari. The assault on the script continued for decades: in 1941, all writers and poets using it were thrown in jail and their property confiscated.

'Books were seized and burned, but many Newa families hid their books in their *dhukoos*, secret wardrobes, while others, to save their ancestral texts, cast them afloat in rivers,' said Niranjan Tamrakar, current president of the Nepal Lipi Guthi, or Institute of Nepalese Epigraphy.

>>

Even after the fall of the Rana dynasty in 1951, King Mahendra introduced a policy of 'one country, one language, one script' in the 1960s. Devanagari was enforced. 'An entire generation never learned their traditional script and languages, pushing many languages and scripts to the verge of extinction,' explained language activist Sunita Dangol.

'Even after the transition to democracy, people were still not learning Ranjana, claiming that it is too difficult, impractical and—' she paused, ironically, 'out of use.'

'That's when the Nepal Lipi Guthi came into the picture,' said Sharad Kasa, librarian at the Asa Safoo Kuthi, a public library of Nepali manuscripts and a teacher of the Nepal scripts. 'In 1980, Bikash Man Sheshya started the institution and played a significant role in spreading awareness about the importance of Nepal Bhasa and the history it carries. Today, the institution continues to teach people how to write in Nepal scripts under the leadership of its various guthi members,' said Kasa.

More recently, the cause of Nepalese scripts has been taken up by Callijatra, a youthful group consisting of artists, architects, engineers, photographers, calligraphers, designers and app developers. Callijatra has taken Nepal Lipi back to the streets, running workshops and demonstrations of writing, calligraphy and type design, often in markets and open public spaces in and around the Nepa (Kathmandu) Valley.

Apps and interactive video tutorials have been developed to teach both Ranjana and Nepal Lipi, a Newa font is now available for Android and local governments in the Kathmandu Valley have shown signs of interest in bringing Ranjana and Nepal Lipi into school curricula.

In Tibet, the Ranjana script is called Lanydza or Lantsa, and it is frequently used on the title pages of Tibetan texts, on temple walls, on prayer wheels and in mandalas.

This usage gave the script a place of honour in Tibetan society, but that, in turn, made it a target: many original Sanskrit manuscripts written in Lanydza, which had been preserved in monasteries, were destroyed following the Chinese invasion of Tibet.

य ङ त क्क ह्न

न ॐ व ल ।

का ह्म ङ म य

द ह्व f ह्म न

द ह्व ग न व

1 **Character grid:** examples of the Ranjana script.

2 **Sample words:** this Ranjana text translates into English as 'Thank you all'. It is the work of the type designer Ananda K. Maharjan, who is reviving the script by teaching it in typography courses in Kathmandu.

2

TAKRI

Origin:
India

To talk about 'the rise and fall' of languages (and scripts) makes it sound like a natural phenomenon, as though languages or scripts – or cultures – just get old and die. Such is not the case. The enemy is not age but policy.

Take Takri, a script that was widely used in several northern princely Indian states from the sixteenth century. It was patronized by Dogra rulers of Jammu and Kashmir in the seventeenth century and employed extensively by them for official purposes, developing several regional variants and coexisting with the Persian script, used to write Urdu, and the Devanagari script.

In 1944, though, Devanagari was chosen as the official script for Dogri and many other languages, and Takri fell almost completely into disuse.

What saved Takri from oblivion was the fact that it had been used for so long, so widely, and for both official and everyday purposes. Takri was used for keeping business records and writing administrative documents, such as letters, copperplate land grants and official decrees. It appeared on postage stamps and postmarks from Jammu and Kashmir in the nineteenth century, and in temple inscriptions. Translations of Sanskrit texts into the Dogri language printed in the Dogra version of Takri, called Dogra Akkhar, were commissioned by Maharaja Ranbir Singh.

Perhaps uniquely, Takri also survived because it had been used in art. One of the distinctive features of Pahari miniature paintings, a form that developed in northern India between the seventeenth and nineteenth centuries and defined a new genre in Indian art, is the practice of including titular inscriptions or commentary along one border in Takri script.

Revival efforts have been under way in both Himachal Pradesh and Jammu since the official recognition of Dogri as a scheduled language by the government of India in 2004, guaranteeing a degree of official recognition and support.

In February 2006, a workshop was held in Kullu, Himachal Pradesh, to provide training in the Takri script that was used for writing Kulvi. In January 2009, the government of Himachal Pradesh established a programme in association with Indira Gandhi National Open University to train specialists in Takri under the guidance of the National Manuscripts Mission.

In 2015, after two years of research into inscriptions, account books and letters preserved in museums, a team of enthusiasts produced two Takri fonts, and now Noto Sans Dogra has been released.

The Dogra Art Museum in Jammu features signs in Takri, and most recently, so does the Jammu railway station. 'Set on top of the signage,' writes Dogra blogger Jammu Virasat, 'it is enough to fill any Dogra heart with pride and a sense of relief.'

শ ঙ রঁ জা ঠ

TIRHUTA

Origin:
India

Tirhuta, also called Mithilakshar, is one of many Indian scripts that have a long, rich history but have been edged out of their language communities by the increased use, starting around the middle of the twentieth century, of the Devanagari script.

The script, which is at least 700 years old, derives its name from Tirhut or Tirabhukti, which means the 'land of riverbanks' – in this case, the region of Bihar, north of the Ganges river.

Tirhuta was originally used to write Sanskrit and Maithili language in the state of Bihar in India and in the Terai region of Nepal. There are inscriptional records found on temples in Bihar and Nepal dating back to the tenth century AD.

The Maithil Brahmin and Kayasth communities have used the script for maintaining *pañjī*, or genealogical records, from at least the fourteenth century. Tirhuta also has a delightful character that is often used as a kind of prefatory insignia before the beginning of a piece of writing: the sign *āñjī*, which is said to represent the tusk of the deity Gaṇeśa, patron of learning.

Currently, only the Devanagari script is officially recognized to write Maithili, but Tirhuta shows signs of life. In 2014 it was added to the Unicode standard, and at least one font has been developed for the script and a video teaching the letters is available online. Moreover, a traditional usage has persisted: Tirhuta is the script of choice for formal invitation and announcement cards called *paataa*.

Tirhuta is also reportedly used for other purposes, such as in signage in Darbhanga and other districts of north Bihar, and as an optional script for writing the civil-services examination in Bihar.

It has even reached the big screen, according to a 2016 post by Mithila cultural blogger Alma Rosina: '*Mithila Makhan*, a Maithili film by director Nitin Chandra on the backdrop of the 2008 Kosi deluge, captures the plight of those who faced the river's wrath, losing lives, land and livelihood to it. Use of Mithilakshar in credits of the movie by Nitin certainly needs to be appreciated. The film brought us a National Award for best film in Maithili. The film was one among the three films that had a world premiere at the recently concluded International Film Festival of South Asia (IFFSA) in Toronto.'

Script:
Sylheti Nagri
—
The distinction between
a language and a dialect may
not seem very important, but
in fact one way to delegitimize
a language (especially common
in South Asia but also found
in, say, Italy) is to dismiss it
as a dialect of some more
established language. Some
claim that Sylheti is merely a
dialect of Bengali. Sylhetis tend
to vehemently disagree.

SYLHETI NAGRI

Origin:
Bangladesh

Sylheti (or Syloti) Nagri may have the extraordinary quality of being a script that is highly endangered in its homeland but is being revived in a different country halfway around the world.

Most of Sylhet (also written as Sylot) is now a division of Bangladesh. The traditional story of the origin of the Sylheti Nagri alphabet – that is, the script used for the Sylheti language – is that it was developed around the beginning of the fourteenth century by Saint Shah Jalal and his 360 saintly companions, most of whom were Arabic speakers. In the late seventeenth century, Persian became the official language of the Delhi Sultanate and the Perso-Arabic script was used in all official documents, but the Sylheti language and alphabet continued to be used by ordinary people for everyday purposes.

Sylheti Nagri enjoyed relatively good health under British rule in India. The first Sylheti Nagri print font was made in woodblock in about 1870 by Abdul Karim, who learned the printing trade in Europe in the 1860s. Later, metal typefaces were made using the same design. At least seven presses flourished in Sylhet, Sunamganj, Shillong and Calcutta (now Kolkata), printing books and at least one newspaper.

Sylheti Nagri was taught in schools in Sylhet until its incorporation into the new nation of Pakistan in 1947, when Urdu was imposed as the new national language.

The right to use one's mother tongue was a major driving force behind the bloody civil war that led to the emergence of the new nation of Bangladesh in 1971–2, but by a bitter irony, the new government established Bangla (Bengali) as the national language, refusing to recognize the mother tongues of the country's non-Bengali residents.

'Sylhetis fully supported liberation from Pakistan,' writes one Sylheti publisher. 'The general who led the liberation army was, interestingly, a Sylheti. The Bengali nationalism suppressed all other languages in Bangladesh including Sylheti. It became embarrassing to use Sylheti in formal situations. Bangla was considered to be the proper language and the attitude was that Sylheti was nothing more than an illiterate person's Bangla.'

By the turn of the century, one scholar estimated: 'Literacy [among the nearly 7 million inhabitants] in Sylhet Division of Bangladesh was recorded at 28.2 per cent in the 1991 census. Currently, of those who are literate, the vast majority are literate in Bengali script; there are probably no more than a few thousand who are literate in Syloti Nagri.'

But if the Sylheti language and its script were declining alarmingly in its homeland and among the Sylheti populations in nearby Assam, Meghalaya, Tripura and Manipur, the émigré Sylheti population in the United Kingdom, numbering perhaps

500,000, began supporting cultural revival projects on an impressive scale.

Projects in London and Birmingham published reading primers in Sylheti Nagri and trained teachers. After an invitation from the director of the Surma Community Centre, Camden, London, the School of Oriental and African Studies (SOAS) founded the SOAS Sylheti Project, which has compiled a dictionary for an app, published a storybook in Sylheti and held an academic conference.

Perhaps by osmosis, there seem to be the early beginnings of a revival of interest in the script in Sylhet, even though it is still not taught in schools. The Ragib Rabeya Nagri Institute (a private institution where the script is taught) reports seeing increased enrolment – perhaps a hundred students a year – and some research and publishing activity.

Like several other language cultures, Sylheti Nagri also has its own number system, which is not only endangered, but is apparently the target of what might be called an active endangerment programme.

Marie Thaut of the internationally renowned SOAS, an expert and impeccable witness, discovered that the original numbers, and references to them, have been deleted in several Internet locations. They have been replaced with text saying that Sylheti Nagri uses a different set of numerals called Purbi Nagri, which are associated with Bangla, the official language of Bangladesh.

'The original numbers', Thaut writes, 'do exist and shouldn't be erased from history.'

1

ল ব দ্দ ট ন

ন জ হ ঞ গ

ড দ্দ ঢ দ্ব ও

ঞ ঐ ণ দ দ্দ

ব স দ্ব র ল

2

1 **Character grid:** examples of the Sylheti
   Nagri script.

2 **Sample words:** 'Mother tongue' in
   Sylheti Nagri. It's a cruel irony that the
   Mother Tongue movement began in
   Bangladesh, yet the Sylheti Nagri script,
   like other Indigenous and ethic scripts,
   is significantly underrepresented.

KHOJKI

Origin:
Pakistan

The Khojki script developed as a kind of bridge between the Muslim and Hindu faiths, flourishing while those two faiths coexisted in the northern part of the Indian subcontinent.

The Khojas are an ethnic group in India and Pakistan, formerly a Hindu trading caste, and followers of the Agha Khan, the spiritual leader of the Ismaili sect. Khojki comes from the Sindhi word *khojā*, literally meaning 'of the master'. According to tradition, Khojki was created by Pir Sadruddin, an Ismaili missionary who was sent by the Ismaili imam of the time to spread the Ismaili Muslim faith among the Hindu Lohana community of Sind during the fifteenth century. (*Pir* refers to a Muslim saint or holy man.) He did this by singing and teaching Ismaili Muslim *ginans* (literally 'knowledge'), which he then wrote down in Khojki.

Early Khojki manuscripts expound on mystical, mythological, didactic, cosmological and eschatological themes, and some contain accounts of Ismaili saints. The printing of Khojki books flourished in the nineteenth century at the Khoja Sindhi Printing Press in Mumbai.

Until 1947, Khojki was a visible manifestation of religious tolerance. With Partition, the era when Muslims and Hindus coexisted in Sindh and Gujarat came to a violent end, and as elsewhere in India, writing became a touchpoint for sectarian conflict. Khojki, it was claimed, was used for political purposes or to hide or spread secret literature. In the new climate, Khojki was too Muslim for Hindus, and not Muslim enough during a time of increased Islamization.

Khojas gradually stopped using the Khojki script as it was too strongly identified with the Indian part of their roots, yet in being subsumed into a broader narrative of Islam, they were stripped of an element that was an essential part of their identity. They absorbed the Arabic script for liturgy and adopted English and French as the global languages of the community.

All the same, the resilience of the script was remarkable. Ismailis had always responded to cultural diversity by being tolerant. They were particularly skilled in adapting to different contexts, adjusting to the ever-changing political and social environment.

The depth of connection between the Khojki script and Nizari Ismaili Muslim religious practice can be seen in the fact that even though members of the religious community have been scattered by the forces of the twentieth century, Khojki primers continue to be published in Pakistan for teaching the script and Khojki is still used ceremonially wherever Nizari Ismaili Muslims of South Asian origin live: Pakistan, India, Canada, the United States, the United Kingdom, Kenya, Tanzania and Uganda.

TIGALARI / TULU

Origin:
India

The Tigalari script, also known nowadays as Tulu Lipi, or 'the script for the Tulu language', is in the unusual position of having been used to write one language, falling into almost complete disuse, and now being used to revive a different language.

For centuries, sacred Sanskrit documents, typically palm-leaf manuscripts, in southwest India were written in the Tigalari script. Indeed, in the Karnataka/Kerala region, it was mandated by religious leaders. With the advent of printing, though, Tigalari, which was exclusively a handwritten script, fell into disuse, apart from for ritual purposes like writing birth charts, creating charms and mandalas.

In the past twenty years, though, the Tigalari script has re-emerged wearing, as it were, a different hat: an endangered-language hat. It's an unfamiliar twist on a familiar situation – the importance of a culture having its own writing system as a symbol of its unique identity.

The Tulu people, or Tuluvas, are an ethnic community of southwest India, speakers of the Tulu language and inhabitants of Tulu Nadu or Tulunad, a region of southern Karnataka and northern Kerala.

When India achieved independence, the Tuluvas demanded national status for the Tulu language, and a state of their own. That demand has been growing steadily stronger in the past twenty years, and partly as a result, the state of Karnataka founded the Tulu Sahitya Academy in 1994. The Academy introduced the Tuḷu language and the Tigalari-Tulu script in schools across the Mangalore and Udupi districts.

The Academy's mission statement says: 'Never in the past the people of Tulunadu had unitedly waged a struggle for preserving and fostering Tulu, an important language belonging to the Dravidian family of languages. Tulunadu being an abode of many languages and cultures and due to lack of encouragement from the administrative system, and due to the blind fascination of people toward English, Tulu faced the danger of losing identity in its own land.'

Tigalari scholars are not altogether happy about an ancestral script, in which hundreds of manuscripts survive, being repurposed to write a different and traditionally oral language.

Proponents of Tulu culture, though, are delighted they now have a script that can be seen as a visible manifestation of the Tulu language and identity. The Tulu script is becoming more popular day by day, and is used everywhere in Tulunad, including sign boards, marriage invitations, house names, flex boards, Tulu movies and signage. The state of Kerala opened its own Tulu Academy in 2007, and a number of Tulu organizations are offering free classes in person and, increasingly during the COVID-19 pandemic, via WhatsApp.

Script:
Sharada
—
When a script is used for
sacred purposes, it acquires
a natural constituency of usage
and respect. But if the religion
that uses it becomes a target,
the script, too, is targeted.

ध म्र ट्र ङ क

S H A R A D A

Origin:
India

The Sharada script (the word Sharada is one name of Mata Saraswati, Hindu goddess of knowledge and wisdom) was once widely used in the northern Himalayan regions, mostly for writing Sanskrit texts as well as Kashmiri and other languages of northern South Asia, first as inscriptions on stone and copper. Even when its range shrank, it was still a significant means of inspirational and literary writing in Kashmir until the late nineteenth or early twentieth century.

The history of Kashmir in recent years, though, has been divided, disastrous and bloody, and the decline of the Sharada script is just one symptom of that history.

The script's marginalization began in the nineteenth century with the rise of a variant of the Perso-Arabic script called Nastaliq. The script accepted for writing Kashmiri in the Eighth Schedule to the Constitution of India and the Jammu and Kashmir State Constitution is 'Kashmiri written in Nastaliq', so all official Kashmiri publications are in the Nastaliq script. Meanwhile, almost all the new generation of Kashmiri writers who come from Hindu backgrounds write Kashmiri in Devanagari. By the end of the twentieth century, the only people still writing in Sharada were Kashmiri Pandits – a Saraswat Brahmin Hindu community who were the original inhabitants of the Kashmir Valley, who used it for religious and ceremonial purposes.

Sectarian violence, which had riven Kashmir since Partition, returned in force in the late 1980s. Perhaps 20 per cent of the Kashmiri Pandits had left Kashmir after the 1950 land reforms, but an estimated 140,000 had stayed. Though they comprised fewer than 10 per cent of the population of Kashmir, they were in general highly educated and literate, and socially elite.

They were increasingly the targets of threats and persecution by radical Islamists: on 19 January 1990, for example, mosques issued declarations that all male Kashmiri Pandits had to quit Kashmir (leaving their women behind), convert to Islam or be killed. Kashmiri Muslims were instructed to identify Pandit homes so they could be targeted for conversion or killing.

Estimates of the number of Pandits who left the valley during the decade start at 100,000. The BBC World Service reported in 2013 that many of the 250,000 refugee Kashmiri Pandits were living in pitiable conditions in camps in Jammu, a Hindu-majority region south of the Kashmir Valley.

The vast majority of Kashmiri Pandits remain in exile. Some, while vociferously advocating for their right to return in safety to Kashmir, teach Sharada online. On International Mother Language Day 2020, a petition on behalf of the Sharada script was presented at the House of Commons, including a poem by Koshur Atom in Kashmiri, written in Sharada script.

ऋ घो ४ ओे छ

M O D I

Origin:
India

Sometimes, the sheer weight of history can drag a script back from the edge of extinction.

The Modi, or Mudiya, script is some 700 years old (there are not only theories but even sub-theories about its date and manner of origin), and for much of that time was the primary script used to write Marathi, the primary language of the state of Maharashtra in western India.

It was even used for other regional languages such as Hindi, Gujarati, Kannada, Konkani, Persian, Tamil and Telugu — yet it became a casualty in the perennial battle between linguistic uniformity and linguistic pluralism. In part, it was about the British desire for the administrative convenience of using a single script throughout British India; in part, it was about the British fear of nationalist efforts in western India; in part, it was a fear of regionalism and fragmentation under the new nationalist independent republic. The outcome was that in the 1950s, the Devanagari script replaced Modi as the officially sanctioned script for Marathi, and the use of Modi nosedived until it became almost extinct.

What has saved Modi is not the present, but the past – thousands of Modi documents were preserved in Maharashtra, with smaller collections in Denmark and other countries, owing to the presence of Europeans in Tanjore, Pondicherry (now Puducherry) and other regions in South

Asia through the nineteenth century. While the majority of Modi documents are official letters, land records and other administrative documents, the script was also used in education, journalism and other routine activities before the 1950s.

In short, the collective cultural identity of Maharashtra was encoded in Modi, and Modi needed to be encoded in the Unicode standard for it to be rediscovered, studied and shared. And to digitize Modi, researchers and digital-font developers had to learn Modi.

Will digitization serve only to make historic documents accessible, or will it revive Modi to the point where it is put to everyday use to write Marathi?

As with even the most robust revival efforts, there are no guarantees. Instead, we're left looking for individual signs and guessing whether they are portents. Driven by enthusiasts, Modi is starting to appear on social media, and in 2017, the *Indian Express* reported that *Vasundhara Vrutta*, the only newspaper published in the Modi script, would undergo a radical transformation: thanks to a font developed by the Centre for Development of Advanced Computing, the monthly Pune-based newspaper, would, for the first time in its four-year history, be printed. Until then, every issue had been written by hand.

MEITEI MAYEK

Origin:
India

If there is such a thing as a formerly endangered alphabet, it might be Meitei (or Meetei) Mayek, used for writing the Manipuri language in the Indian state of Manipur. It is, to a remarkable extent, a rebound script, and as such perhaps a sign of hope for the global movement toward reclaiming cultural heritage and traditional languages, spoken and written.

Nobody knows how old the Meitei Mayek script is. Estimates range from several hundred years to more than 3,000, but we know exactly when and why it died.

The script was lost to the speakers of the language when Shantidas Gosai, a Hindu missionary, spread Vaishnavism in the region in 1709. The king, who converted, decreed that Meitei Mayek should be replaced by the Bengali script. According to the sole surviving account, books and documents in Manipuri were burned – such a traumatic event in Manipuri history that even today, events and marches are held to commemorate this destruction.

After World War II and the tumult of Partition, Meitei scholars began campaigning to bring back the Meitei alphabet. At a writers' conference in 1976, scholars finally agreed on a reconstructed version of the alphabet with additional letters to represent sounds absent in Meitei when the script was first developed.

When the government dragged its feet, activists adopted extreme methods.

Signboards without the Manipuri script were defaced with tar. A plaque at a city flyover was vandalized and the government library in Imphal, which housed a considerable number of books in Bengali, was burned down one night by unidentified protesters.

These guerrilla tactics succeeded: Manipuri-language newspapers now have to publish at least one news item in the traditional script on their front pages. Hoardings, billboards and other material for public events must also be in the script. Vehicle owners must display their registration numbers in the Manipuri script.

Publishers with a longer-term view of the market began printing newspapers in the Manipuri tradition, and in English. Most writers have stopped using the Bengali script, while others have rewritten their old books using the traditional alphabet, and one copy of the State Assembly proceedings is recorded in the Manipuri script.

Since 2006, students have been taught in Meitei Mayek, creating a new generation of educated Manipuris.

Perhaps part of its success is that the Meitei Mayek script has a unique built-in learning device through the use of body parts in naming the letters: every letter is named after a human body part in the Meitei language. The first letter, 'kok', means 'head', for example; the second letter, 'sam', means 'hair'; the third letter, 'lai', means 'forehead'.

THAANA

Origin:
Maldives

Thaana, the script of the Maldives in the Indian Ocean, is the only script in the world to have been ousted in a linguistic coup, only to return in triumph after two years out of favour, but now to be endangered by global warming.

The earliest existing records of Thaana date from 1705. According to oral tradition in the Maldives, the script was introduced to the islands by a chief and his companions who came from the north, indicating that it was the national hero Muhammad Thakurufaanu (Bodu Thakurufaanu) who introduced this script in the sixteenth century. But there is no factual evidence supporting this tradition, and it is more likely that Thaana was developed late in the seventeenth century.

The origin of the name Thaana is unclear. The late Maldivian historian Mohamed Ibrahim Luthufee, Special Advisor to the National Centre for Linguistic and Historical Research, concluded that one of the following derivations might be possible:
Tana (Sanskrit), meaning 'offspring' or 'posterity'
Tanah (Indonesian), meaning 'land' or 'country'
Tan (Maldivian), meaning 'place'
Tana Akuru would then mean 'script of the country' or 'script of the people'.

Thaana is unique in other respects, too. For one thing, its letters are based on numbers – but numbers from two different number systems. The first nine letters (h–v) are derived from the Arabic numerals, whereas the next nine (m–d) were the local Indic numerals. The remaining letters for loanwords (z–ch) and Arabic transliteration are adapted from native consonants, except for y (the letter Y in Dhivehi, the language of the Maldives, looks exactly like the letter 'shaviyani' but with a short line downward at the start), which is of unknown origin.

The Thaana alphabet doesn't follow the alphabetical order of other Indic scripts or of the Arabic script. There is no apparent logic to the order; it has even been suggested this was an attempt to keep it secret.

The script was originally used primarily to write magical incantations, including Arabic quotations, written from right to left. It's presumed that learned Maldivians, all well versed in sorcery, saw the advantages of writing in this simplified hidden script, and Thaana was gradually adopted for everyday use. Thaana grew in popularity also because of the support of Sultan Muhammad Thakurufaanu, who is credited with emancipating the country from Portuguese rule. Thaana became the visual embodiment of a nationalistic reform movement determined that the country should not be subject to foreign occupation again.

Modern invasions and occupations, however, tend to be economic and technological, and can be just as lethal. When telex machines were introduced to the

islands in the 1970s, they operated in the Latin alphabet. A hasty Latinization was created, approved and implemented in 1976 during the tenure of President Ibrahim Nasir, even though the Latin alphabet ignored many features of Maldivian spoken language. Booklets were printed and dispatched to all atoll and island offices, as well as schools and merchant liners. The Thaana script, it seemed, was doomed.

Yet when the new president, Maumoon Abdul Gayoom, took office in 1978, Thaana was welcomed back, and according to one source, literacy in the script is now above 95 per cent.

The very fact that the islands' government could unilaterally implement a Latin script, plus the fact that Thaana is anything but international, makes Thaana simultaneously a) the standard usage of 300,000 people in the Maldives and b) a potentially endangered alphabet – not least because the islands themselves are endangered. In 2009, the then president of Maldives, Mohamed Nasheed, held a cabinet meeting underwater in scuba gear to raise awareness of rising sea levels.

Script:
Thaana
—
One fascinating feature of the Thaana script is it shows the islands' history as a crossing of trade routes. In some respects, it's like a true alphabet from the northwest; in others, it's more like Arabic, or like an abugida from the East. The result is that virtually every letter comes with its own diacritic, like a script written on both treble and bass clefs.

Script:
Saurashtra
—
Saurashtrans have their own
beautiful and systematic script,
the origin of which is not known.

SAURASHTRA

Origin:
India

The story of the Saurashtra (or Sourashtra) script begins, in a sense, in Japan. In the 1980s, Norihiko Ucida, a Japanese scholar, went to Madurai, in southern India, to research Saurashtran – something of an island of a language as the Saurashtrians originated in Gujarat but migrated to the Madurai area, in Tamil Nadu, where (not surprisingly) they were surrounded by Tamils, whose languages derive from an entirely different language family.

Ucida learned Saurashtran well enough to compile the first Saurashtra–English dictionary, published in 1990. The Saurashtrans, he wrote, had their own 'beautiful and systematic' script, the origin of which was unknown. At the end of the nineteenth century, T. M. Rama Ra[i] had reformed the script, designed and cast metal type for it, and published many books in Saurashtran. Over time he tweaked and improved the script until, by common consent, it became the Saurashtran standard.

Alas, Rama Ra[i]'s good work was undone. When Mahatma Gandhi argued that Indians needed to unite to drive out the British, this included agreeing on a common language and script – a cry that is periodically echoed to this day by Hindu nationalists. Part of the Saurashtran community decided to abandon their own script in favour of Devanagari, the script associated with Hindi and the Hindu identity, and they destroyed the matrix designed by Rama Ra[i]. (Rama Ra[i]'s achievement was held in such regard that even today the Saurashtra script is sometimes called Ramarai in his honour.)

The move toward centralization and unification of languages in India, which to some extent had begun under colonial rule, gathered force immediately before and after independence. Between the world wars, a resolution was passed to adopt the Devanagari script for the Saurashtra language. When the case for teaching Saurashtran in schools was presented to the state's Commissioner for Linguistic Minorities in 1964, who had been sent a copy of a book in Saurashtran, the Commissioner seems to have come up with a catch-22 argument: as he had been sent only one book for scrutiny, there was no point in examining the merits of the issue. The question of printing textbooks in Saurashtran would have to wait until a large number of books was available for examination.

The point was, Saurashtra did not fit in. Devanagari needed at least seven extra characters to represent the full range of the Saurashtran spoken language, and for some it also epitomized the authority of the voice of government up in Delhi. Tamil (which most Saurashtrans speak to a virtually bilingual degree) worked up to a point, but only when a number of superscript marks were added.

With the new millennium, though, the tide changed. Even though, as is the case   >>

with language communities all over the world, the Saurashtra community is conflicted (Devanagari or Tamil or Saurashtran? Ancient or modern? Global or local?), a series of journals and other publications have appeared in the script.

In 2007 a former Sanskrit Professor of Saurashtra College in Madurai, T. R. Damodaran, won the Sahitya Akademi's Bhasha Samman Award for Saurashtra language for his book *Jiva Sabda Kosam*, a compilation of 1,333 Saurashtra words with English and Tamil meanings, compiled with help from the Central Institute of Indian Languages. S. Saroja Sundararajan was named co-winner of the award for her poetry and translations, and won a special prize for 'the contribution of authors writing in unrecognized languages of India'.

Even though Saurashtra is an unofficial script, not taught in schools by the government of Tamil Nadu, it seems to be gaining traction through independent channels. Groups such as Saurashtra Vidya Peetam are teaching Saurashtra through Facebook, and an online newspaper appears in Saurashtra and Tamil. Most recently, digitized fonts and mobile-friendly applications have been created locally.

Local institutions in Madurai and Tanjore teach Saurashtra in Saurashtri script, as well as a teacher training centre – an essential ingredient for reviving and perpetuating a script. A certificate course, taught by Saurashtra University, graduated 115 students in 2023.

The script, then, is in an interesting and profoundly democratic situation: if it were officially adopted it would acquire a utilitarian, quotidian quality that would, in a way, make it less special, in the same way that the Latin alphabet feels ordinary because it is used by so many different countries and cultures.

Instead, it is in a very Indian situation in that it is being used and promoted by those who love it, believe in it and feel its special connection to their culture.

1 **Character grid:** examples of the Sourashtra script.

2 **Sample word:** the word 'Saurashtra' in the unique Saurashtran script.

KHUDABADI

Origin:
Pakistan

Khudabadi (also Khudawadi or Khudavadi) may be the only script to take its name from its city of origin – Khudabad, a city in Sindh (now in Pakistan), which for a time in the mid-eighteenth century was capital of the Kalhora dynasty.

It is also a script that was intended *not* to be read. A modern view of writing is that its purpose is to communicate information; likewise, one theory of the origin of writing is that it was needed to keep accounts and record transactions. But writing was also used to keep information secret – indeed, a number of famous people (including Leonardo da Vinci, who invented a special shorthand and wrote backwards) devised their own scripts for just this purpose.

In pre-Arabic times, the Sindhi language was written in a script simply called Sindhi Lipi, or 'Sindhi writing'. When the Perso-Arabic script became official, Sindhi Lipi took on a new and more specialized role: it was used by merchants to keep accounts that government officials could not read. Its name changed, too: it became known as Hatvaniki, from *hat*, meaning 'shop', and *vaniki*, meaning 'merchants', thus 'script of traders and shopkeepers'.

Sindhi traders and merchants started keeping their business documents in the new script to make them secret from competitors, foreigners and any government officials who wanted to inspect their affairs.

Though widely used in Sindh, Khudabadi was by no means the only writing system in the region. It's a sign of the degree to which different communities developed or adopted different alphabets that Sindhi was written in at least eight scripts.

This linguistic diversity was not at all to the liking of the British colonial administration that took over the region in the mid-nineteenth century. They found the Pandits writing Sindhi in Devanagari, government servants using the Perso-Arabic script and traders keeping their business records in Khudabadi, which was completely unknown to the British at the time.

The Court of Directors of the British East India Company directed that Sindhi should be written in Arabic script for government office use, on the grounds that Muslim names could not be written in Devanagari, that Muslim schools should teach in the Arabic script and Hindi schools should teach in Khudabadi. It was also used for book printing and court records.

That was the script's last hurrah. It was gradually usurped by Devanagari, becoming more and more exclusively a mercantile script. After Partition, when Sindh became part of Pakistan and Urdu was declared to be the new official language, the use of Khudabadi declined even further. A small colony of Sindhis migrated to Hyderabad in South India, though, and for now, the script, always a traveller, lives on.

RONG

Origin:
India

The *Sikkim Herald*, a state-run weekly news bulletin in the Indian state of Sikkim, is a model of linguistic pluralism. It is published in thirteen languages: Bhutia, English, Gurung, Limboo, Mangar, Mukhia, Nepali, Newar, Rai, Sherpa, Tamang, Tibetan and Lepcha, making use of no fewer than eight scripts.

Lepcha, the most commonly used name for the script, is perhaps more accurately called Rong. (The English name 'Lepcha' derives from a Nepali insult meaning 'inarticulate speech'.) The Rong people make up a minority, fewer than 50,000, of the population of modern Sikkim, which has been flooded by immigrants from Nepal. Their own word for themselves is Róngkup, or 'children of the Róng', and their language, Róngríng, 'language of the Róng', is the oldest language in Sikkim, pre-dating the arrival of the Tibetan and Nepali languages. The Rong themselves are thought to be the original inhabitants of Sikkim.

The Rong language is spoken in Sikkim, West Bengal in India, parts of Nepal and in a few villages in southwestern Bhutan – a tribal homeland they refer to as 'hidden paradise' or 'land of eternal purity'.

According to tradition, the Rong script was adapted from Tibetan in the seventeenth century by the scholar Thikúng Men Salóng, or at the beginning of the eighteenth century by prince Chakdor Namgyal of the Tibetan dynasty in Sikkim.

Early Lepcha manuscripts were written vertically – a sign of Chinese influence. When they were later written horizontally, the letters remained in their new orientations, rotated 90 degrees.

The Rong may be a minority, but they are not an abandoned minority. Like the *Sikkim Herald*, the state of Sikkim is unusually pluralistic. Lepcha is taught in schools, there is a textbook department that develops official learning materials, and the government radio station broadcasts news bulletins and cultural programmes in the Lepcha language. There is even a Rong cultural-conservation area at Dzongu in North Sikkim, where few outsiders have been allowed to settle.

All the same, the *Telegraph of India* reported in 2008 that Rong culture is endangered: 'The Lepchas are nature-worshippers and it is often claimed that their language has names for all the birds, plants, butterflies, animals and other insects as well as the hills and rivers in their native habitat. This knowledge, which is mostly passed orally, is disappearing fast as the community grapples with modernity.

'It is this vast but dying knowledge base that has been attracting researchers and academicians to Dzongu, the last bastion of Lepchas in the remote parts of North Sikkim, for conservation and documentation works.'

Script:
Gunjala Gondi
—
The three minority Gondi scripts
could not be more different.

G O N D I

Origin:
India

Gondi sets the record for the South Asian language with the most endangered alphabets – no fewer than three.

The Gonds are among the largest Indigenous groups in South Asia, living all over India's southern Deccan Peninsula. Most describe themselves as Gonds (hill people) or as Koi or Koitur. Scholars believe Gonds settled in Gondwana, now known as eastern Madhya Pradesh, between the ninth and thirteenth centuries AD.

For a while, they were a significant, even a dominant culture. Gond dynasties ruled in four kingdoms in central India between the sixteenth and mid-eighteenth centuries.

According to traditional bards and storytellers, it is said that when Gond gods were born, their mother abandoned them. The goddess Parvati rescued them, but her consort Sri Shambhu Mahadeo (Siva) kept them captive in a cave. Pahandi Kapar Lingal, a Gond hero, who received help from the goddess Jangu Bai, rescued them from the cave. They came out of the cave in four groups, thus laying the foundations of the basic fourfold division of Gond society.

The Gonds suffered a significant long-term handicap, though, one that goes to the heart of the Endangered Alphabets. Over the centuries, they fell from their earlier position of eminence and, crucially, had no script for their own language. The Gondi language is usually written in the Devanagari or Telugu scripts, but these mainstream writing systems neither convey an entirely accurate sense of how to pronounce Gondi words nor give the Gonds a sense of their collective identity – especially in India, where a language community without its own script is generally given less respect. It meant, in effect, that the Gonds had no control over the writing of their own history.

To try to address this identity vacuum, in 1918 (or 1928, depending on the source), Munshi Mangal Singh Masaram of Kochewada, Balaghat District, Madhya Pradesh, created a script that came to be known as Masaram Gondi. By some accounts, the script is actively used today for handwritten and printed materials. Fonts have been developed for the production of books. In 2011, the Akhil Gondwana Gondi Sahitya Parishad (Chandgad, Maharashtra) passed a resolution adopting Masaram's script as the official one of the Gondi language.

Unlike Sequoya's Cherokee (see page 212), though, Masaram Gondi does not seem to have had the desired effect of a custom script – to inspire people to use it. Literacy among the Gonds has remained low, even in their own writing system.

The next attempt involved not a new custom script but the revival – indeed, the rediscovery – of an old one in the tiny Gond village of Gunjala (population: under 1,000) in Adilabad district of Telangana. Around 2010, a collection of manuscripts >>

in Gondi were discovered, dating from around 1750, which included horoscopes, information on numbers and grammar, information about sixth–seventh-century trade relationships between the Pardhan community and civilizations in Myanmar; the origins of the Indravelli mandal; and the early eighteenth-century rebellions of the Chandrapur Gond kings against the British – in short, the very materials that granted the Gonds and their language a historical legitimacy. The script in which the documents were written (which apparently only four elders in the village could still read) became known as Gunjala Gondi in honour of the village.

Professor Jayadhir Tirumal Rao, who spearheaded the research and unveiling of the script, has been quoted as saying: 'Andhra Pradesh has thirty-four tribal communities and none of them has a script except the Gondi community. The script is their self-esteem and we took up the task of preserving it by reviving the language.'

Teaching materials have reportedly been produced in the script and it is being taught in a number of schools in villages with a high Gond population. In 2008, the Integrated Tribal Development Authority published a book originally written in the script by Pendur Lingu in 1942. A digitized font has been developed and a script primer has been created using the font. A presentation on the script and font was given by S. Sridhara Murthy and Jayadhir Tirumalrao at Typography Day 2014 in Pune, Maharashtra.

Meanwhile, Professor Prasanna Sree of Andhra University devised yet another writing system for Gondi, based on a graphic iconography based on Gond culture.

The common design feature in all the letters of this alphabet involves both spiritual beliefs and elements of the familiar landscape. Tribal people often worship family household gods, most frequently Siva in the form of a *linga*, or phallus. The upper part of each letter, then, represents the head of the phallus. (Another common shape is that of their headgear, or *gussadi*, made of peacock feathers.) The lower part of the common letterform represents both an animal face looking toward the sky and water flowing among hills through a valley, a characteristic feature of their terrain.

It isn't clear to what extent this new script is being used, but it illustrates a vital aspect of a script and its connection to its community: the script becomes a positive visual emblem of Gond culture, a manifestation of self-respect for a community that sorely needs it.

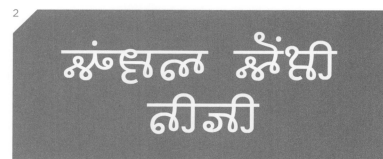

1 **Character grid:** examples of the Gondi script.

2 **Sample words:** the phrase *Gunjala Gondi lipi* – that is, the Gunjala Gondi script.

OL CHIKI

Origin:
India

The Ol Chiki script (the word *ol* means 'write' and *chiki* means 'script') was invented by Pandit Raghunath Murmu between 1925 and 1939 to write Santali, a language spoken in the Indian states of Jharkhand, Odisha, West Bengal, Assam and Tripura, and also in Nepal and Bangladesh.

As has happened a number of times in Asia, this was an act of cultural promotion – an effort to gain respect because in India a language that does not have its own script is often at a disadvantage, sometimes a vast disadvantage, politically, economically and in terms of respect. As a script, it's not only Indigenous but ingenious, created so as to make it easy to learn, using a series of built-in visual cues or mnemonics.

One letter, for example, represents a sickle used for cutting or reaping; others depict a vessel used for preparing food, a peak of an unusually high mountain, a mushroom. Some are a kind of visual onomatopoeia. A flying bee becomes the bee-letter, representing a buzzing sound.

Raghunath was honoured by the Orissa state government, and, more recently, his creation has benefited from an unusually far-sighted multilingual education programme that supports linguistic diversity in Jharkhand. The programme's full title is Mother-Tongue-based Active Language Learning, or M-TALL. They began in 2011 by conducting a statewide sociolinguistic survey that discovered – and this is hardly a surprise in India, with its affinity for 'official' languages but a vast diversity of Indigenous ones – that 96 per cent of children in Jharkhand spoke tribal and regional languages rather than Hindi at home or in the playground; and in fact, they had great difficulty understanding their teachers who spoke Hindi, and textbooks written in Hindi.

By 2014, the programme had developed bilingual picture dictionaries in nine tribal and regional languages, and began setting up language centres in multiple districts. By 2016, new textbooks were ready in sixteen languages, printed not only in the standard Devanagari script but also in Ol Chiki, for the Santali language, and Warang Chiti, for the Ho language.

As a result, the script is increasingly used by Santals, not only in Jharkhand but West Bengal, Odisha and Assam, and in neighbouring Bangladesh and Nepal.

Presently, in West Bengal, education is imparted in Santali from class one to Master's level using the Ol Chiki script. At North Odisha University, Bachelor's- and Master's-level education is provided in Santali language using Ol Chiki script. It has appeared on railway station signs in Santali-speaking areas of Jharkhand and on the governor's residence, and a Wikipedia edition in Santali has been launched, using downloadable Ol Chiki fonts, now an official script of Odisha.

SORA SOMPENG

Origin:
India

Sora Sompeng, which is used by a small minority of Soras to write Sora (or Savara), a language spoken by about 300,000 people mainly in Odisha and Andhra Pradesh in the east of India, has an extraordinary function: it acts as a bridge between the physical and the spirit worlds, and each of its individual letters is profoundly holy.

'In the 1970s they [Soras] held what may well be the most elaborate form of communication between the living and the dead documented anywhere on earth,' writes Piers Vitebsky in *Living Without the Dead*. 'Almost every day in every village, living people engaged in conversations with the dead, who would speak, one after another, through the mouth of a shaman … in trance. Together, living and dead would chat, weep or argue for hours at a time.'

This transcendental use of language was carried over into their script. According to tradition, on 18 June 1936, a Sora called Mallia 'received a dream showing him where to find a special Sora script magically inscribed on a mountaintop'. Not merely inscribed in a rock, say, but actually embodied in the spirit landscape: in Mallia's dream, each of the twenty-four *sonums*, or resident spirits, who populated and made up the Sora spirit world, changed into the letter that began their name.

'People thought he was crazy', Vitebsky writes, 'but "his standard of thinking was so high" that he remained without food on that mountain for twenty-one days.' Mallia's daughter married a man called Manggai, who propagated the script and turned it into a cult called the 'alphabet-worshippers'.

The alphabet-worshippers, Vitebsky explains, called themselves Marirenji, meaning the Pure, Alert or Clear-Sighted Ones.

Though this script is Sora, its main proponents, the alphabet-worshippers, use it almost entirely in oral performance, and in 2011, Vitebsky estimated, only a few hundred people could read the script at all: 'Since their texts are a limited homemade corpus locked up in almost unknown symbols, one could only worship this script as a mystery rather than use it as a tool for everyday purposes: literacy without literature.'

Nevertheless, in 2016, the Indian Institute of Technology created a Sompeng font as part of the Idital Project, named after the main deity of the Soras to whom their traditional mural paintings ('Italons') are dedicated. The first steps have been taken to introduce the script in primary education in parallel with the more mainstream Odia and Sora scripts, and Sompeng has been used by community members for textbooks, calendars and other printed documents.

Script:
Khema
—
The Gurung script is a perfect
example of a community
creating its own form of
writing as a means of acquiring
identity and self-respect. But
what happens when the same
community, scattered across
mountains and valleys, creates
two different scripts?

GURUNG SCRIPTS

Origin:
Nepal

One of the disadvantages of the remarkably deep allegiance a people may feel toward their writing system is – what if they have more than one? What if a widely scattered minority community supports or creates one writing system in one area and a different one in another?

Roughly half a million Gurungs live in Nepal and the surrounding region, of whom perhaps two-thirds speak Gurung. Gurung culture was traditionally oral and its language was generally written in the Devanagari or even the Latin alphabet until World War II.

In 1944, when Jagan Lal Gurung was fighting in Burma in a battalion composed primarily of Gurungs, he began to develop a Gurung script, today known as Khe Prih. When he returned to Nepal, he began teaching Khe Prih to the children in his village of Hyanjakot.

The current government strongly opposed Indigenous languages, and Jagan's life was threatened to the point where he fled his village and rejoined the army. He returned in 1965 and began lobbying for and teaching his script, but as with many Indigenously created scripts, its radius was limited. Nevertheless the Gurungs were starting to feel a sense of their cultural identity, and in 1977 a committee was formed to create a Gurung script. And as Khe Prih was barely even known, let alone widely adopted, Bal Narsingh Gurung,

under the supervision of Guru Pim Bahadur Gurung, was tasked with creating a Gurung script. Given this official genesis, it's hardly surprising that the result, called Khema (or Khema lipi, meaning 'script') overtook Khe Prih in popularity and usage. But that endorsement sounds more final than it actually is. Living in small villages in hilly regions, even in different countries, speaking different variants of their language, and lacking the unifying power of statehood, the Gurungs are in danger of cultural fragmentation. Resham Gurung, president of the Gurung cultural organization in Nepal, acknowledges that most of the young generation cannot speak the language and that makes it doubly important that the Gurung community rally around one script for their language:

'Our youths go to learn Japanese or Korean language because they know they will get a job after learning them. But what opportunities will they have after learning Gurung language? The significance of the language is just limited to cultural identity, which is why many youths do not bother.'

The Gurung community has recently decided to adopt Khema, which is now used in Nepal, India and Bhutan and is also listed as the official script of the Gurung language by the Nepal Language Commission. What will happen to usage of Khe Prih is unclear.

WARANG CHITI

Origin:
India

The Warang Chiti script (used for writing the Ho language, spoken by roughly a million people, largely in the state of Jharkhand in eastern India) may be the only script to begin with the letter Ong, or Om, the sound of the universe. It is also one of the few writing systems to have been chosen by committee.

Warang Chiti script is remarkable, in fact, for being profoundly rooted in Ho culture and spirituality. Each character has a mythology that relates its shape, sound or appearance to the unique Ho cultural context and world view.

Among these are a character meaning 'he/she', in the overall triangular shape of the hand when pointing at someone; another character, pointing in the opposite direction, means 'you'. A character meaning 'carry' is shaped like two people carrying something between them, and one meaning 'stork' is shaped like a stork with its one leg on the ground, another retracted. These graphic components also serve as a mnemonic when used in teaching the Ho syllabary.

Not surprisingly, the script has mystical and even mysterious roots. It was invented in the 1950s by Lako Bodra, a charismatic Ho community leader, as an alternative to the writing systems devised by Christian missionaries. He claimed that the alphabet was invented in the thirteenth century by Dhawan Turi, and that he rediscovered it in a shamanistic vision and modernized it.

Interestingly, Warang Chiti was not the only home-grown script created for the Ho language. In 1984, a social organization called Side Hora Susar Akhada held a conference in Odisha to choose the best writing system for the Ho language. Warang Chiti was selected as the best choice, and sportingly, the other script creators signed a legally binding document in which they promised not to propagate their creations.

Warang Chiti remains very much a minority script even among the Ho (who, as a Scheduled Tribe, are some of the poorest people in India), many of whom don't write their language in any form, while those that do may prefer the standard Devanagari script.

Currently, the Ho language and the Warang Chiti script exist online only in the form of informal chat and video songs, though computer fonts and a script converter are in development.

Offline, Ho is taught at university level in Jharkhand, despite the lack of teachers at earlier stages of education. Being primarily a spoken language, Ho is looked down upon by non-native and native speakers alike. Wealthier Ho usually switch to speaking Hindi, which is seen as the more prestigious language, but there is a lot of enthusiasm among Ho youth for the preservation of their language and culture. There have been rallies and protests in recent years demanding recognition of Ho language by the Indian government.

JENTICHA

Origin:
India

The Indian state of Sikkim, a model of multiculturalism and multilingualism, recognizes eleven official languages and scripts. Some are traditional scripts, centuries old; some are refugee scripts used by people who have been exiled from their homelands and some are emerging scripts, created recently for languages that do not have their own specific writing system.

The last category is especially important as displaced ethnic groups struggle to find ways to survive. To maintain one's dignity, integrity and identity in a foreign country is never easy, and all over the world, language – both spoken and written – is a vital factor in the face of feeling marginalized and despised.

One specific survival tactic, used by minority groups not only in Sikkim but elsewhere in India, is to demonstrate that they represent a disadvantaged and identifiable culture. (The terms used in Indian official circles are Scheduled Tribe, Other Backward Communities or Most Backward Communities.) Such a classification, if achieved, grants somewhat easier access to seats in the local political bodies, to places in universities, to certain jobs and, in some instances, financial loans. Needless to say, this leads to a politically charged and often acrimonious situation.

To receive that classification, émigré and refugee groups have had to prove that they have a distinct culture and language different from others, and one indication of such distinctness is to have their own script. Hence the particular importance of minority alphabets to the region.

Jenticha is one script that has had to go through this process of recognition. The script was developed in 1942 by Karna Bahadur Jenticha (also Karna Bahdur Sunuwar, 1926–91) to write the Kiranti-Kõits language (also called by the outsider name of Sunwar or Sunuwar), spoken in Sikkim and eastern Nepal.

Like most newly created scripts, Jenticha subsequently fell into disuse and died – but, again like many newly created scripts, it became a labour of love and ethnic commitment by one person. As part of his PhD work, Lal-Shyãkarelu Rãpacã wrote alphabet books, primer books and an elementary grammar for children, and the Kiranti-Kõits were successful in reviving the script and language in Sikkim.

A Sunuwar edition of the *Sikkim Herald* is produced in Jenticha, the first edition, in 2002, being handwritten by Lãl-Shyãkarelu Rãpacã himsef, though now the paper is printed in digitized type. The script is used in grammars of Sunuwar, proceedings of the Sikkim legislative assembly and anthologies of Sunuwar poetry.

PRASANNA SREE SCRIPTS

Origin:
India

It's a common observation that writing is a necessary characteristic of civilization. Unfortunately, in many parts of the world the converse is also held true – that any community that does not use writing, or does not have its own writing tradition, is uncivilized, primitive, even contemptible.

As the twenty-first century gets into its stride, dozens of linguists all over the world are working with language communities whose language either has never been written or has never been written in a script that conveys the full range of sounds used in everyday speech. In most cases, these tailored scripts consist of extensions of the Latin alphabet, the International Phonetic alphabet or a popular nearby script the users are likely to know, or need to know.

One Indian linguist takes a very different approach. Instead of creating scripts that are adapted from those of other cultures, she starts from the position that minority groups need writing systems that are proudly and uniquely their own, asserting their identity and history in the face of assimilation or marginalization.

Her name is Prasanna Sree. Based in Andhra Pradesh, to date she has visited, studied and created writing systems for nineteen rural minority groups in Andhra Pradesh, Odisha and some of the neighbouring states.

Aware of widespread prejudice against 'hill tribes', especially those who maintain an oral rather than a written tradition, Sree creates writing systems that not only adequately express all the sounds of the language but also incorporate a design feature (or features) that visually reflect some aspect of the culture. In this way, the script is not only uniquely theirs, but feels like an outgrowth or expression of the people themselves and their lives – a fascinating way to try to reinstate some degree of self-respect and sense of worth.

In some cases, the letterforms are based on tribal architecture:

The Bagatha construct domed or semi-circular huts, so all the letters in their alphabet are designed with the same dome shape as their homes.

The Goudu build their huts without a threshold or doorway, so entrance is gained by crawling. The common shape for the Goudu letters, then, is a triangle, imitating the shape of their dwellings; the lower vertical line represents a crowbar, which is one of their most common implements for agricultural and domestic use. Other letters are based on domestic implements – a sword, a mirror, a scythe.

The Jatapu are mainly cattle grazers. One feature of their culture is a type of parasol to shield them from the sun, and that forms the basis of the common design feature of the letters of their alphabet: the curved upper part represents the umbrella, made of palm leaves, and the vertical line beneath it is the shaft that supports the leaves.

Many of the cultures Sree works with have fallen, they believe, from a state of greater grace – as professional archers, blacksmiths, priests, members of a warrior caste or even gods – to their present state as subsistence farmers, basket makers, auto-rickshaw drivers or cattle grazers. To reconnect them with their sense of ancestral importance or purpose, some scripts are based in mythology, harking back to the tribes' roots and often recalling days of greater prosperity or higher status.

The Kupia script, created for the Valmiki people, is based on their belief that they are descended from the great sage Valmiki, the author of the Hindu epic, the *Ramayana*. According to legend, Ratna Kardah was a thief and a bird hunter. One day, he shot an arrow at two pigeons and one of the birds fell dead. The sight of the surviving pigeon in tears beside her dead partner made the thief regret his crime. He was so consumed by remorse that he did not notice a vast ant hill grow up around him. God appeared and instructed him to write the great Indian epic *Ramayana*. After his emergence from the ant hill, or *valmikam*, he was known as Valmiki. The language his descendants spoke was the Kupia language of the Valmiki tribe – so their script is designed around the form of a bow and arrow.

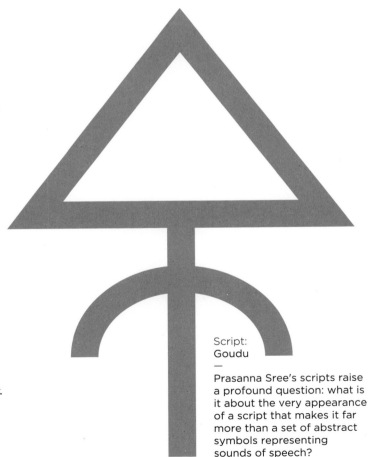

Script:
Goudu
—
Prasanna Sree's scripts raise a profound question: what is it about the very appearance of a script that makes it far more than a set of abstract symbols representing sounds of speech?

TOLONG SIKI

Origin:
India

The Tolong Siki alphabet was created over an eighteen-year period by Dr Narayan Oraon, a physician from Jharkhand, with assistance from Francis Ekka, the former director of the Central Institute of Indian Languages, Ramdayal Munda, the former vice chancellor of Ranchi University and Nirmal Minz.

In 1989, Dr Oraon decided to create a new script for his native language, Kurukh, which is usually written with the Devanagari alphabet. His alphabet was published on 15 May 1999 and introduced into some schools later that year. It was formally recognized by the government of Jharkhand in 2007, in a ceremony at Ranchi University.

A number of books and magazines have been published in the script, and at least six fonts have been created.

The script is being promoted by the Oraons, one of the two principal Kurukh tribes, even though acceptance is by no means universal. Tolong Siki is used and highlighted in half a dozen Oraon schools, though in government schools books are printed in the mainstream Devanagari script. Tolong Siki is also used in West Bengal, Odisha, Assam and nearby states.

As with other scripts, Tolong Siki's progress toward acceptance was helped by the creation of a digitized font, in this case created by Rewa Kislaya. He was approached around the year 2000 by Dr Narayan Oraon and his team, who requested help on the front of font making. At the time, Kislaya was primarily a journalist, publishing a weekly magazine on computer usage, and an IT hobbyist. Dr Narayan apologized for the fact that he could not afford to pay the high fees a professional type designer would charge.

'Finally, I decided to do the job free of cost for the Kurukh-speaking tribal community,' Kislaya said. 'My only request to them [was] that the font will carry the name of my only child, Kelly.'

Narayan agreed, and thus the first Tolong Siki font was, and is, KellyTolong.ttf.

WANCHO

Origin:
India

It's common to talk about writing in terms of an evolution from the pictographic to the purely symbolic – in fact, to think of pictographic writing as primitive or childish. This is not only perilously close to racism, it also undervalues visual symbolism in writing.

Consider Wancho, a language spoken by some 50,000 people in Longding District of Arunachal Pradesh in northeast India, plus others in the states of Arunachal Pradesh, Assam and Nagaland, and across the border in Myanmar. The language has usually been written in the Latin alphabet, but as is becoming increasingly common among minority languages in India, a purpose-built script has arisen from the Wancho community.

Its author is Banwang Losu, a teacher at a government middle school in his home village in Longding District, Arunachal Pradesh.

In 2001, when he was still in high school, he was working with some of his teachers on the socioeconomics of their culture. He tried to translate the material into Wancho using the Latin alphabet, but found the script could convey neither the tonal qualities of Wancho, nor certain sounds specific to the language.

He spent the next eleven years studying Wancho and phonology in general, and developing a script that is Indigenous in the most colourful sense.

Its forty-four letters, he explains, are based on 'human actions, birds, insects, trees, tattoos, traditional handicrafts' – in other words, familiar sights and customs.

In Wancho culture, the feathers of the hornbill have value and significance, and are worn in headgear for festivals and special occasions. One of Banwang Losu's letters is a stylized hornbill feather.

Other letters are likewise derived from familiar sights and customs: the initial letter for the Wancho word for 'light' is a stylized sun, the initial letter for the word for 'fire' is a stylized lamp, the initial for 'nose' is very clearly a nose in profile.

This obviously has mnemonic value, but it also makes the script distinctly Wancho; it is part of who they are and what they do. As such, it implies a message to an increasingly monolingual, or monolithically lingual, world. To learn Wancho is not simply to learn another spoken/written language; it is to learn another people.

S O U

E A S

A S I

T H -

T

T

A

INTRODUCTION

Southeast Asia, a vast promontory extending into the Andaman and South China Seas, might seem a safe and stable region where alphabets would flourish in the fine, fertile soil – such a rich agricultural area, in fact, that one of its ancient kingdoms was known as the Kingdom of a Million Rice Fields.

The northern part of the region, though, an upland massif recently termed 'Zomia', is entirely different; it is a remarkable and complex area that encompasses parts of China, India, Bangladesh, Myanmar, Thailand, Vietnam, Laos, Cambodia and Malaysia.

As it is remote from major population centres, Zomia has traditionally been ignored by the governments of the lowlands around it, and as a result, it has long been a region of refuge, where the dispossessed have formed their own micro-territories.

It's an area of perhaps unparalleled linguistic, political, religious and cultural diversity, where at least ten Indigenous writing systems have been created since the early nineteenth century, typically by radical, charismatic leaders who recognized that having their own script would unite their followers and give them an identity – not to mention a means of written communication their enemies could not read!

For more than a thousand years, this has been an area in flux, with migrants and refugees arriving from the north, fleeing from the great powers of China and Burma. Endangered alphabets are often the vestigial remains of lost kingdoms, and Southeast Asia is a region of ancient kingdoms overrun. Members of stable, literate communities have been reduced to small pockets of ethnic minorities, or, worse, to refugees in camps – stateless, homeless, unable to leave their ghastly and ramshackle circumstances.

As Ben Mitchell, who wanders the byways of the region researching scripts for type design, has said, 'There are whole swathes of uncharted territory in the scripts of Southeast Asia, even for languages with many hundreds of thousands of speakers.'

Members of a defeated minority are vulnerable in countless ways. When the Kingdom of Champa was overrun and destroyed by the nineteenth-century Vietnamese emperor, Minh Mang, the Cham who were Hindus were force-fed beef and the Cham Muslims were force-fed lizard and pig meat to degrade them and destroy their cultural identity.

History, as we've seen, is written by the winners in their own writing systems. The losers are forced to adapt, and adopt the scripts of their enemies, or to cling to writing systems whose meaning is simultaneously deep and functionally irrelevant. Or to remain exquisitely aware, for generation after generation, that they do not have, or no longer have, their own writing. Many cultures are so awed by the profound values of writing that they have writing-creation myths; in Southeast Asia, alas, writing-loss myths are as common.

Piers Kelly, an Australian anthropologist specializing in Indigenously-created scripts and one of the few linguists to do field research in emerging writing systems, writes: 'A tragic motif of lost writing resounds throughout the highland folklore of mainland Southeast Asia. In this vast region … the apparent absence of Indigenous literacy is lamented through tales in which writing was lost through profligacy, carelessness, treachery or acts of desperation. The Akha, it is said, kept their writing on buffalo skins but were forced to consume it while fleeing the invading Tai armies. The Wa wrote on oxhide that was eaten in hard times, while the Lahu wrote their letters on cakes that met the same fate. The writing of the Hmong was destroyed by the Chinese or eaten by horses, while Karen writing was variously stolen, eaten or left to rot. Similar stories of being cheated out of literacy and its presumed benefits are told by the Kachin, the Chin and the Khmu…'

Under these conditions, we see most clearly the relationship between culture, identity, mental health and writing. Every sight of a familiar script is a reminder of who their ancestors were, and who they themselves might be once again, a reminder that they are not marginalized and often despised outsiders, but people who belong.

For this very reason, sadly, many scripts are kept secret or abandoned – the memory too painful, or the political associations too radical, too dangerous – and a secret script is far more easily lost than one in general use.

Many opt for assimilation, so even within a language community there may be strong differences of opinion over which script to use. Can the old ways really be kept alive? By whom? At what cost?

So Southeast Asia is also a region of linguistic heroes, including three who invented, and then died for, their people's writing.

Script:
Lanna
—
This delightful cluster of
Tai Tham strokes would
translate into English as
'to grasp'. Not all scripts are
side-to-side sequential: many
abugidas in particular build
around a central character,
including above and below.
This is an initial consonant,
a vowel diacritic and a final
consonant subscript.

TAI SCRIPTS

Origin:
Myanmar

Those of us in Europe or the Americas instinctively think of writing in imperial terms: expanding with the armies, employed by the subsequent administration, obedient to a central authority, uniform. All letters lead from Rome.

Some scripts, such as Arabic, have expanded with a similar sense of central, uniform identity; others, like Brahmi, were more adaptable to local conditions and customs. But what about cultures without an army or an empire, or a popular religion? How would their script grow?

Like a bean sprout.

The Tai peoples are perhaps the most complex and far-flung family of Zomia (see page 142), living today in clusters in India, Vietnam, Myanmar, southwestern Yunnan Province of China, Thailand and Laos. Not surprisingly, this spread has led to variations in dress, cultural traditions and language.

And writing. Each of these related ethnolinguistic groups developed their own versions of a Tai script of (probably) common origin, adapting it under the influence of local circumstances, even individual local writers.

One of the earliest Tai scripts was Lik Tho Ngok, known as the 'bean-sprout' script, as many of the letters look like the first growing tendril emerging from a bean sprout. It probably originated somewhere along what today would be the border between China and Myanmar, morphing

from the Old Burmese or Mon some time before the fifteenth century. A descendant of this script is still used today by several of the Tai communities – the Tai Nuea in southwestern Yunnan Province, with variants used by the Tai Dehong and Tai Maw – but the seed, not carried by armies but usually fleeing from them, would sprout and pop up here and there throughout the unpromising soil of Zomia.

In northeastern India, for example, in one of those mysterious steps of evolution, possibly just by the style or preference of a single scribe, Tai Aiton and Tai Phake have the bean-sprout heart of the letter filled in as a solid dot rather than an empty circle. Tai Phake, moreover, seems to have two sub-versions, one with large dots, one with small dots.

In nearby Assam, the Tai Ahom script of Assam was once well established. The Tai Ahoms originally arrived from Yunnan province in China, possibly around 1200. The earliest inscription in the Ahom script, on a stone pillar, dates from the fifteenth century. The alphabet also appears on coins, brass plates and numerous manuscripts on cloth or on the bark of the sasi tree.

They ruled the Assam valley for six centuries, gradually converting from their own form of Buddhism to Hinduism, until their kingdom fell to the Burmese in 1819 and their ruling class was all but wiped out. Under British rule, the Assamese worked to assert their superiority over the Ahom

>>

Script:
Tai Dam, also known
as Tai Viet because
of its use in Vietnam.

people, whom they characterized as an unattractive, degenerate and stupid people.

By the end of the nineteenth century, conventional thinking held that Ahom culture and language were either dead or folded into Assamese, to the extent that there was no point in making a distinction. In 1931, the category 'Ahom' was no longer even included in the census. But Ahom was by no means dead.

The first Ahom typeface was created in 1920 for an Ahom–Assamese–English dictionary, compiled by Golap Chandra Barua. Although the accuracy of the dictionary itself was subsequently called into question, the font was used in a number of other influential publications and has since become an authoritative model.

In 1967, the Ahom petitioned the Indian government to recognize them as a separate community 'in which Ahom-Tais and the various other tribes would enjoy social recognition and all political rights'. The petition was turned down. Instead, the Ahom were forced to remain a subgroup of the Hindu Assamese – a 'backward community'.

A turning point was the publication of Padmeshwar Gogoi's *Tai and the Tai Kingdoms with a Fuller Treatment of the Tai-Ahom Kingdom in the Brahmaputra Valley* (1968), which gave the Ahom people a new name and a revived sense of historical legitimacy, not to mention a connection with the Tai people elsewhere in South and Southeast Asia.

The new term Tai Ahom was seized upon and the new Tai-Ahoms revived a religion, calling it Phra Lung, which emphasized the worship of ancestors, mainly heroic warriors.

'New prayers were written by the late Domboru Deodhai Phukan, the last of the Tai-Ahom ritual experts,' writes linguist Yasmin Saikia. 'Domboru

Deodhai explained to me the Phra Lung religion in these words. "Phra is a Buddha-like figure. Lung means the Sangha. Phra Lung means the community of the worshippers of Phra." Dietary habits were also changed to mark the departure from Hinduism. Beef, taboo among caste Hindus, was introduced in the Tai-Ahom diet, as [was] partaking of alcohol called haj or lau pani.'

As the century came to an end, a new Tai Language Academy was established at Patsaku, new Tai festivals and commemorative events were created and publicly celebrated and several conferences were organized in Assam and elsewhere. Recently, the Tai Ahom International Society has continued these efforts.

Yet those identifying as Ahom continue to be among the poorest in Assam, which is one of the poorest states in India. The future of the Tai Ahom language, script and culture remain in the balance.

'I think very few people speak Tai Ahom,' said Mrinalinee Khanikar, a Tai Ahom living in northeast India. 'It's an endangered language. In upper Assam a few villages have kept it alive in Tinsukia, Sivasagar.' Sivasagar, formerly known as Rangpur, was the capital of the Ahom Kingdom from 1699 to 1788. '[Most of us] all speak [the] mainstream Assamese language.'

In Vietnam, the Tai Dam people have their own script that is used by three Tai languages spoken primarily in northwestern Vietnam, northern Laos and central Thailand: Tai Dam (Black Tai), Tai Dón (White Tai or Tai Blanc) and Tai Song (Lao Song or Lao Song Dam). A fourth language, Tai Daeng (Red Tai or Tai Rouge), uses a closely related script.

The name 'Black Tai' originates from the traditional black skirts and headdresses worn by Tai Dam women, made of black silk embroidered with flowers and beautiful patterns. The health of the Tai Dam language >>

ଠ ໝ ຣ ຫ ຟ

and script varies considerably from country to country. In Thailand, where the Tai Dam are often referred to as Lao Song or Thai Song Dam and the script is called Lao Song, Tai Dam is now taught in schools in Tai Dam regions; Tai Dam can also own land, farm and travel freely.

At the other extreme, in northwestern Vietnam children are taught Vietnamese from a pre-kindergarten age, and although the government in theory backs mother-language education for ethnic minorities, no funding is available for teachers or textbooks. One scholarly estimate is that of the roughly 800,000 Tai Dam in Vietnam, there could be fewer than 1,000 who read and write the script fluently on an everyday basis.

Along the northern fringes of Zomia in China, where several Tai communities are still to be found, their script variants survived well enough, in their scrappy, local way, until the latter part of the twentieth century, when they drew the attention of the national government, with its tendencies toward centralization and uniformity and a history of official involvement in the development and revision of writing systems.

A version of Tai Tham, called New Tai Lue or Xishuangbanna Dai, was introduced in China in the 1950s and promoted by the government, but it did not prove popular. Tai Le, known in China as Dehong Dai, was revised in 1954 and again in 1988, but neither the reformed versions nor the traditional script is doing well.

'Dehong, like other Tai minority languages in China, is a dying language,' writes researcher John Hartmann. 'Traditional Dehong writing came with the spread of Buddhism and its revival depends on religious revival. The Cultural Revolution caused a cessation of the practice of Buddhism in China. Buddhism can now be practised again in China, but many traditions have been lost, including the transmission of literacy in Dehong.'

The script is still used to a small extent for signage, several Tai Le fonts have been created, and in theory, as the Chinese government has given the people of the region autonomous status as the Dehong Dai-Jingpo Autonomous Prefecture, Tai Le culture, including its script, should be protected. In practice, it would be optimistic to see anything ahead but steady cultural erosion and loss of traditional identity.

In this complex landscape of misfortune, one of the few bright sparks is Tai Tham, or Lanna, in northern Thailand. Tai Tham was the only Tai script developed specifically for sacred purposes, and partly as a result was – and is – the only Tai script to enter the twenty-first century with any degree of status and visibility.

The early LikTai scripts were developed for writing everyday language, but the arrival of Buddhism, with its strongly Indic flavour, necessitated a different approach and led to the development of Tai Tham (*tham* means 'scripture'), which for a while was used exclusively in a religious context.

It flourished especially in northern Thailand in the Lan Na or Lanna Kingdom, known as the Kingdom of a Million Rice Fields. The script became known as Lanna, keeping its strong religious roots but expanding for everyday use as well to write the Northern Thai (Kam Mu'ang), Tai Lue and Khün languages.

The kingdom of Lan Na flourished between 1259 and 1558, when it was conquered by Burma and later taken over by Siam. In 1920, the Kingdom of Siam annexed the Lan Na states into the present-day Thailand.

As with all scripts without a country of their own, Lanna devolved into regional status in northern Thailand and is now in the process of losing even that   >>

role, as the standard Thai language, with the force of official status and usage behind it, becomes the norm. Even though there are some 6 million speakers of Northern Thai, 500,000 speakers of Tai Lue and 100,000 speakers of Khün, only those born before about 1950 know and use the script.

Lanna is to some extent taught in monasteries and schools, and Chiang Mai University offers a graduate degree in Lanna Language and Literature, but it is gradually declining to a purely totemic status, used on temples and other culturally significant buildings in northern Thailand. A new generation is taking an interest in the script as a sign of their history and heritage, but whether Lanna will displace Thai on an everyday basis is doubtful.

Lanna is also one of the rare scripts that has an endangered number system, possibly even two. The first set, Lek Nai Tam, is reserved for special purposes, such as religious texts. The second set, Lek Hora, is the one usually used in everyday life. Its name (Hora) suggests that it is also used for astrology.

Lanna's decline is also in part because the script is an unusually difficult one to digitize. The sacred function of the script, especially for writing in Pali, means that the letters are combined on wood, metal, stone and even on skin in the form of tattoos, in rich, complex, even non-linear ways that give, in the words of one linguist, 'an extra dimension to the reader consciousness'.

In less academic terms, the decline of Lanna represents another loss: an aesthetic one. With its swirls and eddies of vowel and tone markers that may appear above, below or even around their accompanying consonant, Lanna is among the most ornate and alive in the world, with flourishes in every direction. A line of Lanna is like a pond full of koi.

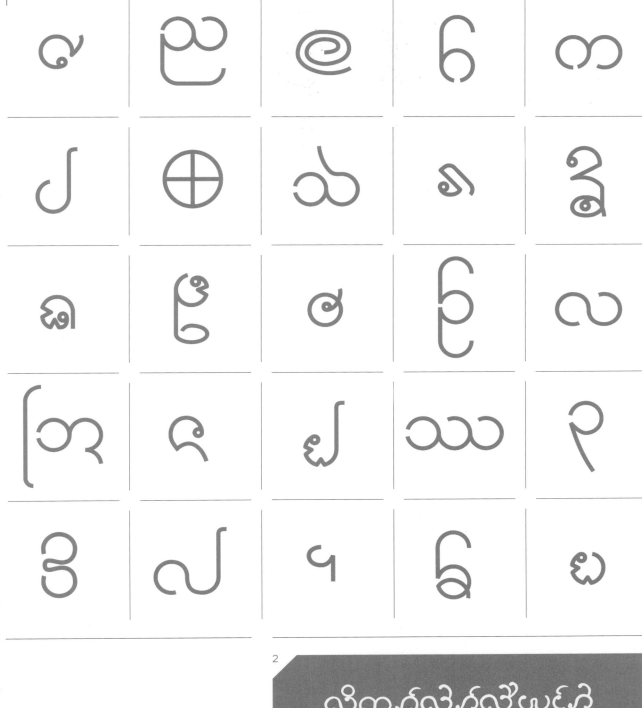

1 **Character grid:** examples of the Lanna script.

2 **Sample words:** part of a song by the Tai Phake, a tiny community of about 250 families living in Assam, India. It goes, 'If our books and writing slowly disappear, then we will regret it.'

Script:
Kayah Li
—
Kayah Li, the 'camp script'.

K A R E N   S C R I P T S

Origin:
Myanmar

The Karen people live mostly in Thailand and Myanmar, and, like other Zomian cultures, are all too aware of the importance of being a minority culture, lacking their own script and literacy tradition (see Introduction, page 6). In the 1820s, a Karen villager said, '[W]e have been an ignorant people, without books, without a king, without a government of our own, subject to other kings and other governments, we have been a nation of slaves, despised and kicked about, trodden underfoot by everybody like dogs.'

Their lack of a writing system has even permeated their mythology.

As Piers Kelly writes: 'In ancestral times, the legend goes, the Karen people were personified as the youngest (in some versions, the oldest) of seven brothers who were each gifted with divine writing by the supreme deity Ywa. A Chinese brother was given a book of paper, a Burmese brother a book of palm leaf and the Karen a book of animal skin or a book of gold. The other brothers looked after their books and studied them carefully. But because the Karen brother was busy tending his field, he entrusted the divine text to a "white" brother who assumed possession of it and carried it over the seas in the company of Ywa. To this day, the Karen await the return of the sacred book, Ywa and the white brother...

'In a variant narrative the Karen brother was distracted by his work and failed to give due importance to the gift. Thereupon he left the inscribed animal skin on a stump or at the base of a plantain tree where it was left to rot over the monsoon. When he came back to it he discovered to his great dismay that it was chewed up by dogs and pigs, and pecked at by chickens beyond all recognition. Since chickens had consumed the text, he supposed that chickens now embodied the wisdom and lost laws it had contained. For this reason, the descendants of the Karen brother initiated the practice of divination through chicken bones. Having thus lost the capacity to read and write, the Karen were easily dominated by the literate Burmese who expelled them from the lowland plains they had once inhabited.'

In response, the Karen have created their own scripts, which have flourished in a determined, hyper-local way, beyond the view, and certainly the use, of outsiders.

One of their earliest scripts is used by the Leke, a messianic Buddhist sect. According to tradition, the Leke religious movement and its script trace their history to the 1830s when Baptist missionaries set out to translate the Bible into Karen. The missionaries adapted the Burmese script for this purpose; another Mon-based script was already in use in Buddhist monasteries for transliterating Karen languages.

As these new scripts were being propagated in the region, a Karen man named Mahn Thaung Hlya objected to the choice   >>

between two scripts, neither of which represented the Karen people linguistically, historically, politically or spiritually.

In about 1844 or 1845, the story goes, he scaled Mount Zwegabin to begin a seven-day fast together with six companions. Mahn Thaung Hlya was the only one to complete the full week of fasting, and on the final day, he was rewarded with a vision of a figure dressed in white who asked him what he wanted. When Mahn Thaung Hlya replied that he wanted a native Karen script, the figure touched a flat rock with his staff and forty-seven symbols appeared, resembling the scratches left in the dirt by chickens.

When Mahn Thaung Hlya came down from the mountain, he searched for somebody to decipher the symbols. (Given that many visionary scripts occur to people in non-literate cultures, this two-person revelation-transcription partnership is actually not uncommon.) In Hnitya village he found Mahn Maw Yaing, a man who was known to have assisted Baptist missionaries in translating the Bible, who created glyphs for the twenty-five consonants, thirteen vowels and nine numerals that would become known as the *leit-hsan-wait*, or the 'chicken-scratch script'. Interestingly, this apparently scornful term was not coined by outsiders but by the Karen themselves, perhaps because it echoes the Karen myth.

In the early 1860s, according to tradition, divine messengers revealed a holy book written in the sacred Leke script to two men of Hnitya village. The book, which is said to exist to this day, became the foundational sacred text of the Leke.

Today's Leke leaders are strict vegetarians who wear topknots and white robes, and their followers dress in traditional Karen clothing. In 2011, it was estimated that there were about 200 leaders and over sixty places of worship in Karen State and the Karen refugee camps on the Thai border.

Another Karen script appeared under even more mysterious circumstances – as an ancestral metal plate, said to have been passed down since time immemorial, and on which writing had been engraved in a script that could no longer be read. This plate was inspected by missionary visitors in the mid-nineteenth century, by which time it had become the focal point of a cult that invested the plate with power over life and death and of producing famine or bounty. Every year in March a feast day was held in which people arrived from neighbouring villages with offerings of slaughtered livestock and money. By the 1870s the plate, still undeciphered, had vanished.

The tragic history of Karenic scripts continues to this day.

In March of 1962, a university-educated teacher in Kyebogyi village by the name of Htae Bu Phae spent the night inventing a new script that was to represent and unify the Karen languages of Myanmar. 'I thought of the possibility of a special alphabet for the Kayah peoples since my boyhood,' he later said.

Known today as the Kayah Li script, it was specifically created as an Indigenous alternative to both the Latin-based script that had been introduced by missionaries in the 1950s and was used only in Sunday schools, holiday programmes and literacy projects, and a Burmese-based script that had been adapted in the 1960s and had been received with encouragement by government authorities. Unique in appearance, Kayah Li nevertheless accommodated the various sound elements of all the family of Karen languages, and so epitomized Karen political unity.   >>

Script:
Kayah Li
—
What does it say about
the profound connection
between writing, culture
and identity that this script
flourishes in the grim
conditions of refugee camps?

Htae Bu Phae soon began teaching the Kayah Li script in his region, and by 1975 it had prompted the formation of the Kayah Literature Association, dedicated both to the promotion of the script and the documentation of local folklore. The following year, the separatist Karen National Progressive Party, of which Htae Bu Phae would rise to the rank of General Secretary, proclaimed the script as the official and national alphabet of Kayah State. In the 1980s, officials in Kayah State began to print and circulate schoolbooks, dictionaries and magazines in the script.

Little could Htae Bu Phae or any other Karen people have known that the cultural imperialism of Latin-based missionary scripts would be the least of their troubles.

In the early 1980s, the Burmese government policy of 'Four Cuts' resulted in the widespread destruction of communities and the decline of traditional cultures. Thousands of villages, especially in the Karen and Karenni States, were burned to the ground, including houses, religious buildings, schools, belongings and sometimes even domestic animals. In many areas, it became the norm for the villagers to live in constant fear of the Burmese military coming to their village, terrorizing the villagers, stealing their food, forcing them to become porters and mine sweepers, raping ethnic women and torturing and killing anyone suspected of having a connection with the ethnic armed opposition. While some villagers endured the abuse by developing warning systems and repeatedly fleeing to the jungle, others, who had heard about Thailand, decided to leave their village for good. Others still had no choice as their village was already in ashes.

When the first refugees arrived in Thailand in 1984, no one could have predicted that many of them would still be there thirty years later: by the end of 2014, nearly 100,000 had been resettled to third countries, but more than 110,000 were still in the camps.

Refugees live in harsher and more demeaning conditions than most non-refugees know, or can imagine – virtual prisons, in many cases. Forced to be nearly completely dependent on outside help for food, shelter, protection and other basic needs, their coping mechanisms are severely eroded. Travel and work restrictions have adverse psychological and social effects on the refugees, decreasing their self-sufficiency, camp morale and mental health.

A 2006 study cited by Human Rights Watch found that 50 per cent of adult camp residents suffer from mental-health problems and anti-depressants constituted one of the most common drug prescriptions for refugees.

Considering the often-traumatic backgrounds as well as the challenging circumstances that refugees face in Thailand, many people who visit the camps are impressed by the significant effort refugees make in order to maintain dignity and hope in the camp communities. As in prisons, anything that shores up identity, individual and collective, is vital. Despite severe restrictions and depressive realities, refugees strive to remain active and to maintain their cultural traditions through practices such as teaching traditional dances – and their own writing system.

As a result of its turbulent history, Kayah Li has two alternative labels: 'rebel literacy' on account of its origins within a separatist movement, and 'camp script'.

1

1 **Character grid:** examples of the Kayah Li script.

2 **Sample words:** a unique, indecipherable Karen script on a metal plate that may or may not still exist. Photo courtesy of Piers Kelly.

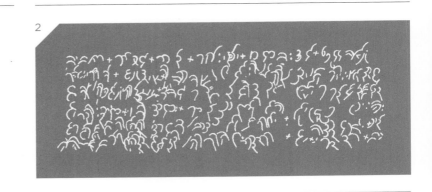

CHIN SCRIPTS

Origin:
Myanmar

The Chin people, who include several subgroups speaking a family of languages, are one of the complex patchwork of peoples occupying the highlands of northwest Myanmar and neighbouring Bangladesh and India. Like the Hmong and the Karen peoples, they have traditional tales that lament the lack of a writing system to call their own.

According to one tale, their ancestral mother laid 101 eggs, from which 101 brothers hatched. The youngest brother was the Chin, who wandered far from the nest. By the time he returned, the world had been divided up among his older brothers, but his mother gave him the mountains, along with elephants, horses and other livestock, and placed him under the tutelage of an elder Burmese brother, who was supposed to teach him to write. Instead, he tricked the Chin out of his livestock, leaving him landless and illiterate.

Again like the Hmong and the Karen, this bitter state of affairs eventually produced both a writing system and a messianic religion, created by a legendary prophet named Pau Cin Hau.

Pau Cin Hau was a prophetess's apprentice who, around 1900, began having prophetic visions that culminated in a series of instructions, apparently delivered by an envisioned Englishman, for the creation of a writing system. Interestingly, the deputy commissioner of the Chin Hills was so

impressed with this invention he encouraged Pau Cin Hau to publish it right away, but Pau Cin Hau kept revising it from a logographic system of more than 900 characters until its completion in 1931 as an alphabet of twenty-one consonants, seven vowels, nine coda symbols and twenty tone marks.

By then, he had received further dream instructions to abandon the traditional Chin animist religion and develop a new, Christian-inspired monotheism, worshipping one all-powerful god. This became the Laipian religion, which still thrives in the region, practising healing rituals that have a curious form of authority. Piers Kelly writes: 'The consecrated healers are known as paliki and wear official-style uniforms while ministering their services. If the illness does not yield to lower-ranking paliki, higher-ranking officers are called for until the patient recovers on the principle that bad characters are supposed to yield to law enforcement ... Indeed, the term paliki is derived from the English [word] police.'

As with other scattered peoples, the Chin have developed more than one writing system. Another of the Chin subgroups, the Zo, Zomi or Zou, also have a self-created script, developed by M. Siahzathang in 1952. It apparently took some time for the script to attract much interest, but the United Zou Organization adopted the script as its official writing system for the Zou language in 1976.

In the 1990s, literary organizations instituted working groups to manage the development and promotion of the script, publishing books to provide instruction in it, including the *Zou Script Self-Instructor* and the *Zou Script Primary Book*.

As with the Gurung (see page 132) and other scattered minorities, a multiplicity of scripts is not necessarily a helpful thing: the debate over whether to use one script to unite the different groups, and if so, which, serves mainly to emphasize the culture's marginalization, and its disadvantages.

Script:
Pau Cin Hau
—
In the West, where we use the same script for every purpose, the concept of a script created specifically for devotion lies beyond our comprehension.

Script:
Nyiakeng Puachue Hmong
—
We think of a script as having developed in the same place as the people who use it – but a surprising number of scripts have developed in the diaspora, where a community has even more need for a sense of identity.

HMONG SCRIPTS

Origin:
China

The Hmong languages hold at least three records in the endangered-alphabets field: the most scripts, most invented scripts and most different countries in which a script has been invented. They may also hold the record for number of writing-genesis stories and most script creators killed for trying to use writing to bring their people back to their former glory.

In part, this is because the Hmong themselves have traditionally been widely scattered over Southeast Asia and southern China. It's also because for much of their history their language communication has been oral rather than written. In addition, history has dispersed them across the globe, and in an effort to retain their cultural identity, groups of Hmong have created scripts for themselves in countries as far afield as Australia and the United States.

The Hmong have at least a dozen scripts for which there is some kind of historical evidence or hint.

Three that are unique to the Hmong, currently in minority use, and thus could qualify as endangered alphabets, are Nyiakeng Puachue Hmong, Pahawh Hmong and the Sayaboury Alphabet.

The Nyiakeng Puachue Hmong script is also called the Cher Vang Hmong script after its inventor, the Reverend Chervang Kong Vang, who created it in the United States in the 1980s for use within his church community. This script has been

used by members of the United Christians Liberty Evangelical church in America ever since, in printed material and videos. It is also used to write White Hmong and Green Hmong in Laos, Thailand, Vietnam, France, Australia and Canada.

Nyiakeng Puachue means 'genesis complete', but the script has other names including 'Hmong Blessing Script' and 'flower-cloth Hmong script', Hmong culture closely identifies writing with embroidery or decorative weaving.

One of the Hmong writing-genesis stories, in fact, tells that the Nanman, the ancestors of the Hmong, lived in central-east China, but after being defeated in battle by the Chinese, they had to flee southward. One version says that in crossing a river, the Hmong lost their books and thus their ancestral writing tradition. Another version says their writing was pre-served in the 'flower cloth', or embroidered clothing, of Hmong women.

Pahawh Hmong, meanwhile, is a sign of how potent writing is – how important and inspiring and threatening it can be to create an alphabet: its author was executed for producing a writing system for his people.

The Hmong people in Southeast Asia, remember, had no homeland, and no written language. In 1959, an unlettered Hmong farmer and basket maker named Shong Lue Yang announced that he had been inspired by God in a series of visions to create a written language for the Hmong, >>

ꕮ   ꕩ   ꕪ   ꕫ   ꖂ

and, like Sequoyah, set about converting first himself and then his people from non-literacy to literacy.

'The writing system presented the Hmong with a conception of themselves as united, sovereign and spiritually redeemed,' the linguist and rhetorician John Duffy writes in *Writing from These Roots: Literacy in a Hmong-American Community*. '[It] was more than a writing system for its users; it was, in addition, a guide to moral life and religious salvation.'

The effect of Shong Lue Yang's invention was rapid and radical. Almost at once he took on a messianic status for the Hmong: his followers called him 'Mother of Writing', and looked to him for ethical and religious teaching and advice.

At the time, he was living in Vietnam and the nationalist feelings he was stirring up in the Hmong minority made the government uneasy. His supporters helped him to avoid arrest and smuggled him into Laos, but the complex and interrelated wars throughout the region and the outsider status of the Hmong meant that wherever he went, he was accused by each side of aiding the other. Besides, no government in the region had any sympathy for a nationalist Hmong movement.

By 1971, his religious and cultural influence among the Hmong had grown simply too strong for the Laotian government's liking, and soldiers were sent to assassinate him.

After Yang's death, Pahawh Hmong was taken to northern Thailand refugee camps, and then moved with waves of immigrants to Minnesota and California in the United States, and to Australia, undergoing various developments as it went.

At least half a dozen of the Hmong scripts have been messianic, perhaps the most remarkable of which was first noticed in a United Nations' refugee camp in

Thailand during the Vietnam War in the form of a nine-volume text, reported to be 700-800 years old, in the possession of a refugee.

The text, apparently, had been passed from the Hmong deity La Bi Mi Nu, transcribed and preserved. The script that had been used, though, being intimately connected to Hmong beliefs about political, spiritual and ethnic identity, was as remarkable as the content. It has been named the Sayaboury Alphabet, after its region of origin in Laos.

John Duffy writes: 'As with other spiritual writing systems, the Sayaboury Alphabet was unique. For example, all words appear to be represented by only five letters, the first two always identical. Another unique element of the Sayaboury is that it includes characters representing nonspeech sounds, such as the intonation used for chanting, the sound for calling chickens, the sound for shooting chickens …'

Finally, I think it's important to document two Hmong scripts that have not survived. Both were rebel scripts; both became the visible tokens of messianic religious movements. Both ended tragically, but one has the world's most remarkable writing-revelation story, and the other receded into the mythological mists from which it came.

The first prophet to bring writing back to the Hmong was the rebel Pa Chay Vue who, in 1918, led a revolt against French rule in Laos during what the French called the *Guerre du Fou*, or War of the Insane. Pa Chay asserted himself as the Hmong equivalent of King Arthur, a leader who had returned from death and history to save his country. He claimed he had visited heaven, where he met four madmen who knew how to write and with whom he communicated by means of a single letter. It was this writing system, written with   >>

Script:
Pahawh Hmong

natural ink on processed bamboo bark and expanded to include other glyphs, that he later used to urge Hmong to rise up and join his movement. Pa Chay also distributed squares of cloth inscribed with his script as amulets for protection in battle. Despite this protection, Pa Chay Vue was assassinated in 1921.

Three years later, the French army in Indochina began to intercept insurgent correspondence coming from southern Laos and circulating as far as Vietnam and Cambodia. What distinguished these particular messages, over thousands of kilometres of upland terrain, was the unusual Khom script in which they were written.

Its creator was Ong Kommadam, one of perhaps a hundred self-styled messiahs who led rebellions against the French colonial state in the early twentieth century. His was another 'revealed' or trace script. According to Hmong stories, he would repeat a sound again and again until its corresponding symbol manifested itself on the bare skin of his chest, at which point a scribe would copy it down and wait for the next one.

Kommadam developed an aura of invulnerability, especially after he survived an assassination attempt when a French official, claiming to have been sent for peaceful negotiations, shot him in the chest with a pistol hidden in his pith helmet. This was too much for the French, who eventually mounted a land–air operation that used both bombers and elephants, in which Kommadam was killed. The French authorities collected and destroyed every document in his script they could find.

Like Arthur, though, his legend, along with his script, lived on. According to one Hmong narrative, his sons transcribed the characters from his tattooed back before he was buried; in another version, a man who may have been the immortal Kommadam had himself tattooed with the script, escaped to the Vat Phu temple and still lives there as a monk.

CHŨ-NÔM

Origin:
Vietnam

Vietnam was ruled by the Chinese for over a thousand years, from 111 BC to 938 AD. During this period, the official written language was Classical Chinese, or Chũ-Han. Sometime during the tenth century, though, the Vietnamese adapted the Chinese script to write their own language and called their script Chũ-nôm, or Southern Script.

After Vietnam escaped Chinese rule, Chũ-nôm remained in use, and from the late thirteenth century, it became the script for writing literature and poetry. Confucian intellectuals recorded folk stories and village entertainment in Chũ-nôm for posterity, while Chũ-han was retained as the script for business, politics, law and formal communication.

In particular, this period saw the flourishing of Vietnam's greatest classical poet, Hồ Xuân Hương, who, remarkably for her time and culture, was a woman. Though much of her poetry survives, it loses a host of shades of meaning when rendered out of Nôm and into the Latin alphabet.

This heritage is now nearly lost. With the seventeenth-century advent of Quốc Ngữ – the modern Roman-style script – Nôm literacy gradually died out. During the French colonial era, it was the Vietnam-ese intellectuals who exploited Quốc Ngữ to the full and in 1908, the Royal Court in Hue created the Ministry of Education which incorporated Quốc Ngữ into the

curriculum. In 1919, it was declared the national script and replaced both Chũ-han and Chũ-nôm.

Today, fewer than one hundred scholars worldwide can read Chũ-nôm. In other words, approximately a thousand years of Vietnamese cultural history is recorded in a system that now almost no Vietnamese can read.

In 1970, the Chũ-nôm Institute was established in Hanoi to find, store, translate and publish the Chũ-nôm heritage. To date it has collected 20,000 ancient books, most written in Chũ-nôm.

Courses in the Chũ-nôm script were available at Ho Chi Minh University until 1993, and the script is still studied and taught at the Hán-Nôm Institute in Hanoi, which has published a dictionary of all the Chũ-nôm characters. Nevertheless, much of Vietnam's vast written history is, in effect, inaccessible to the 80 million speakers of the language.

The Nguyen Du epic poem *The Tale of Kieu*, originally written in Chũ-nôm, is still considered important enough to be taught in secondary schools (and by some to be a feminist text) and is available in both Chũ-nôm and contemporary Vietnamese scripts. For many Vietnamese, though, the older text is hard to learn and, being based on Chinese characters, offends their strong sense of national identity.

In one area, though, the country's cultural history still comes together through writing. In the Classical Chinese period and the Chữ-nôm era, Vietnam saw a strong tradition of calligraphy, and over time, Vietnam developed a unique style of calligraphy called Nam tự – used first by the bureaucracy, but later for all writing purposes.

The custom of Hán and Nôm calligraphy during New Year still exists in north Vietnam, where Hanoi's Temple of Confucius hosts calligraphers of Latin, Hán and Nôm and showcases their works.

Script:
Chữ-nôm
—
This character translates as 'is', from the verb 'to be'.

Script:
Chữ-nôm
—
The Chinese influence on the
script can be seen clearly.
This is the character for 'sleep'.

Script:
Eastern Cham
—
The Homkar is the Cham
equivalent of the Om symbol.
It balances the universe, and
can be found in important
sacred contexts such as
funerals and burial grounds.

CHAM

Origin:
Vietnam

The Cham alphabet is yet another relic of a lost kingdom.

From the second century, the Cham people inhabited Champa, a region now occupied by central and southern Vietnam. One particularly charming origin myth holds that their culture was founded by Lady Po Nagar, who, with the help of spirits, floated on a log of sandalwood to China, where she married a prince and had two children. She eventually returned to Champa and did many good deeds, it is said, helping the sick and the poor.

More prosaically, the Cham people were defeated by King Minh Mang of Vietnam in 1832. They lost their status, their ownership, their land; many fled westward into the mountains along the border with Cambodia. It's a sign of the importance of their script, and of how powerfully written language evokes a sense of identity and history, that the current Cham script is based on the inscriptions on the Po Rome temple in Ninh Thuận province – the last Cham temple built before their defeat.

That defeat left the Cham uprooted and scattered. Most of those who have stayed in the region live in two major groups: the Western Cham of Cambodia and the Eastern Cham of Vietnam. Each has its own version of their script: Western Cham, also called Huruh Srak, is slightly more angular and Arabic in influence; Eastern Cham,

also called Akhar Thrah, is more rounded, more Indic, with influences from Brahmi.

Fragmentation is the dry rot of an alphabet – the loss of control, the loss of a critical mass. People find themselves in a dilemma repeated all over the world: to look forward or back? To stand out or fit in? To use the old writing or adopt a new script? A generational fissure opens up and widens.

The sense of the script's importance, however, goes so deep in Cham culture that, among some Eastern Cham, learning this script is a rite of passage in funerary ceremonies – for the person who has died. As part of a four-day cremation ceremony, one of the rituals that a priest will perform is to kneel down and teach the deceased how to read and write Cham. Only after the human spirit has acquired these skills may they be cremated and pass on to the afterlife. Even if Cham is struggling in this world, then, we can take comfort at the thought that it must be thriving in the next.

Script:
Eastern Cham
—
The beautiful,
sinuous letter E
in Eastern Cham.

M R O

Origin:
Bangladesh

The Krama script, created in the 1980s for the Mro people and their language, is in some ways a typical contemporary Zomian script: composed of strong, clear, simple characters by a charismatic leader for a minority upland community – and now highly endangered.

As such, it also provides a tragically clear illustration of the relationship between endangered alphabets and cultural genocide.

Perhaps 20,000 Mro (also pronounced/written as Mru or Mrung), most of whom are Buddhist, live in Bangladesh's Chittagong Hill Tracts (with others elsewhere in Bangladesh or across the border in India), but since the founding of Bangladesh in 1971–2 they have suffered from the national government's refusal to grant full citizen status to non-Bengalis, and a policy of granting tracts of land traditionally farmed by the Indigenous inhabitants of the region to Bengali settlers.

This resulted in a period of virtual civil war in the region, with the military siding mainly with the settlers. A substantial number of Mro have fled across the borders into Myanmar and India.

Studies conducted by Amnesty International and the United Nations High Commission on Refugees found that Mro people living in Myanmar were also affected by 'a campaign of widespread and systematic violence, including violence by state forces' in 2017 against the Rohingya.

Official education in the Hill Tracts is in Bangla, which for many of the region's Indigenous people is not even their second language. The result, coupled with the instability in the region, has been a catastrophic school dropout rate and steady cultural erosion among the Mro.

As elsewhere in Zomia, this sad state is fertile ground for the growth of script-loss mythologies and charismatic script creation. The Mro's narrative is that God offered them a religion and a script. They accepted, but the bitter twist so common to these tales is that the script was sent to them, written on banana leaves and carried by a cow – but the cow ate the banana leaves. In a ceremony commemorating their misfortune, the Mro punish a cow.

In 1984, a community member named Menlay Murang, also known as Manley Mro, created and introduced the familiar pairing of an alphabet and a religion, now known as Crama or Khrama.

As is common in the minority communities of the region, the future of the Mro community, its religion, language and script, are uncertain. Since 2017 the Bangladeshi government has reversed its policy and begun publishing schoolbooks in some of the country's Indigenous languages/scripts, but the Mro script was not included, and in any case, a lack of mother-tongue teachers has meant that these books are gathering dust.

HANIFI ROHINGYA

Origin:
Myanmar

*When I speak my own language,
I am free. When I hear someone else
speaking Rohingya, I feel like I am home*
– Rohingya refugee, via **Translators
Without Borders**

The relationship between language, freedom and home, is an especially poignant one for the Rohingya, who until 2016, were an Indigenous ethnic Muslim minority in Myanmar numbering roughly 1 million.

Descendants of the ancient kingdom of Arakan, the Rohingya have their own culture, language and script. In the past, Rohingya has been written in the Latin, Arabic, Urdu and Burmese scripts, but in the 1980s, looking to create a unique script that was their own and reflected their own culture, the Rohingya Language Committee completed that task under the guidance of Maulana Mohammad Hanif (hence the name 'Hanifi'). Its Arabic flavour reflects the Rohingya history – they say they are descendants of Arab traders and other groups who have been in the region for generations – and religion.

Most of the group's members have no legal documentation, effectively making them stateless. Myanmar's 1948 citizenship law was already exclusionary and the military junta, which seized power in 1962, introduced another law twenty years later that stripped the Rohingya of access to full citizenship. They were even excluded from the 2014 census, the government refusing to recognize them as a people and claiming they were illegal immigrants from Bangladesh.

Starting in late 2016, Myanmar's armed forces and police started a major assault on Rohingya people in Rakhine State in the country's northwestern region. Investigations by the United Nations found evidence the Burmese military had committed wide-scale human-rights violations, including extrajudicial killings, gang rapes, arson and infanticide. The United Nations described the military offensive in Rakhine, which provoked the exodus, as a 'textbook example of ethnic cleansing'. Hundreds of thousands of Rohingya fled the destruction of their homes and persecution for neighbouring Bangladesh.

As with the Karen and Karenni people thirty years earlier, the surviving Rohingya found themselves in refugee camps, and attempted to maintain a sense of dignity and community in part by preserving and teaching their language.

Mohammad Noor, creator of the Hanifi Rohingya font, reports that there are about fifty Rohingya community schools in Bangladesh refugee camps teaching the Hanifi script: 'We are estimating over 25,000 kids learning in these centres. In Malaysia and Saudi Arabia there about 2,000 kids learning in different centres. There are a number of school syllabus, general books, magazines and many other types of content already developed and we're developing more.'

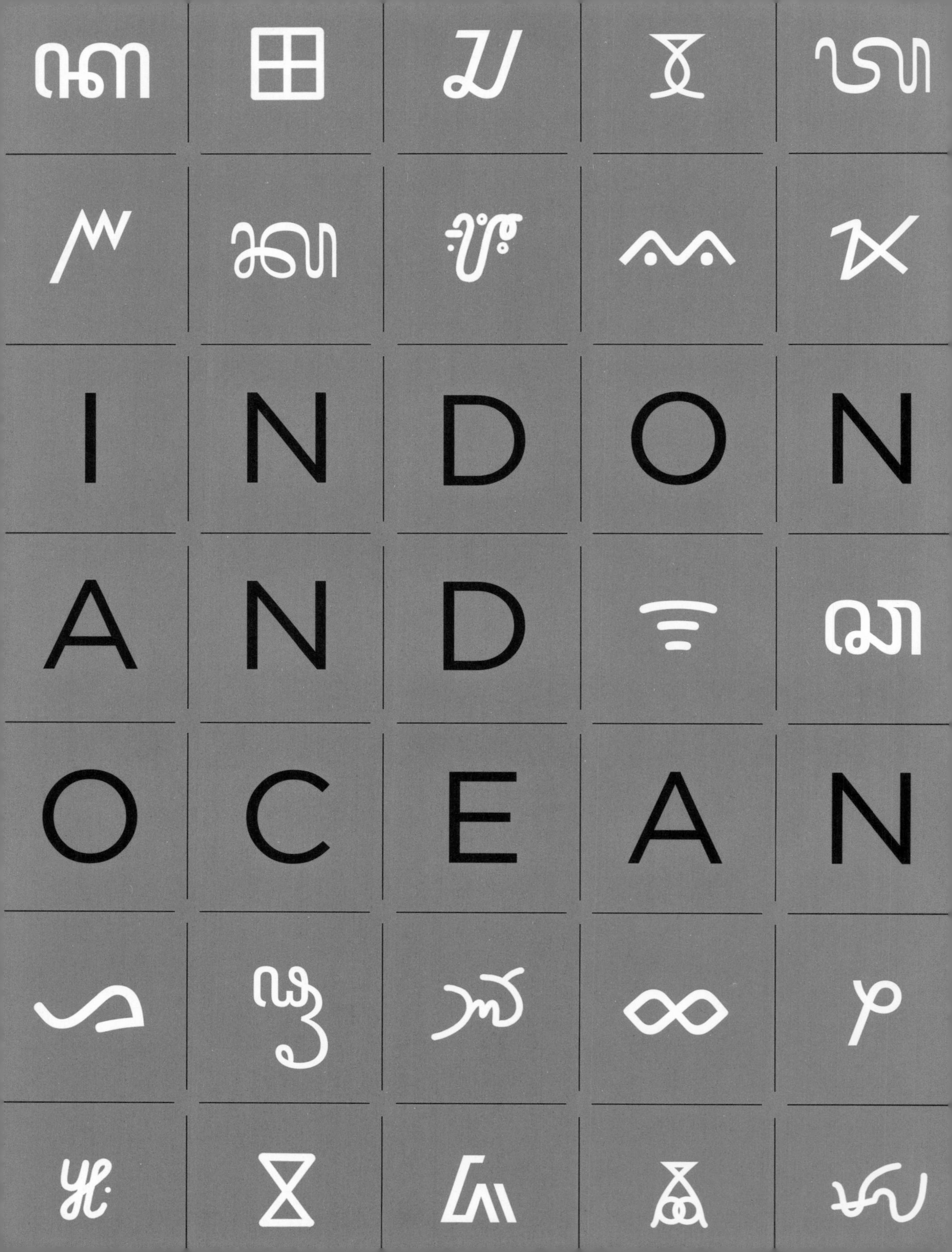
INDON
AND
OCEAN

E S I A

I A

INTRODUCTION

As much as 2,000 years ago, an active trading network connected China, Southeast Asia, India and the Middle East, and it seems likely that one of the exports to the islands now called Indonesia was writing.

Hinduism and Buddhism were also actively attracting converts throughout the region, and whether or not any Indigenous scripts existed at the time, the arrival of these Indian religions brought writing, like a wind, from the northwest.

The earliest Brahmi-descended inscriptions that have survived date to the third or fourth century AD; texts in Arabic script began to appear several centuries later.

The script that developed in Java was called Kawi: etched in stone and pottery, engraved on copperplate, painted on silk, written on paper, painted on bark, incised in bamboo. Almost all the scripts in the region grew out of it.

Like tortoises and finches on the Galapagos, writing in these islands adapted to and was adapted by local conditions: religions, cultural influences, writing materials, even climate, as differing forms of vegetation offered differing writing surfaces, and thus affected the way people shaped letters and even the way they held their writing implements.

Court writing, composed by professional scribes, was so prized that the manuscript became an object of reverence and an art form. One extraordinary example is a letter written in 1768, incised on gold in the shape of a palm-leaf manuscript, sent by two Balinese princes to the Dutch governor of Semarang, on the north coast of Java, in which they affirm their everlasting friendship with the Dutch, and agree not to allow enemies of the Dutch East India Company to pass through their territory without an official pass from the Company.

Outside the court, a rich and diverse range of religious writing was composed by priests and shamans on bone, palm leaf and bark. Writing was so revered that many documents have survived – indeed, one day a year is set aside for families to take out, clean and revere their *lontars*, or palm-leaf books, and public collective readings and translations take place.

At some point, possibly in the thirteenth or fourteenth century, writing sailed north to the islands we now call the Philippines, developing yet another set of island-by-island variations.

Even before the Portuguese, Dutch and Spanish arrived in the region, then, there was a wealth of writing in dozens of scripts. The European administrations, as usual, favoured some cultures over others, and the narrowing accelerated when the mid-nineteenth-century arrival of printing, as elsewhere, began to restrict the range of hitherto handwritten scripts in use. European and Chinese printers used the Latin alphabet to print in Dutch, and even the ornate and sacred calligraphy of the Arabic script was reproduced using lithography.

Ironically, while the end of colonialism ultimately may have opened a door to the revival of traditional writing systems elsewhere, it threatened the regional scripts of Indonesia.

Indonesia, the world's fourth-most populous country, consists of 17,508 islands, about 6,000 of which are inhabited by people of some 300 different ethnicities practising at least 6 different major religions and speaking more than 700 local languages and dialects.

With the withdrawal by the Japanese at the end of World War II and the almost immediate declaration of independence from the Dutch, Indonesia needed to establish some sense of coherence among an extraordinarily diverse population scattered over a vast area.

One of the means of bringing about national unity and identity was by creating a national language, Bahasa Indonesia, or Indonesian, and making it the language of education, government, business and the national media. Indonesian, unlike many of the languages local to individual islands,

is written with the Latin alphabet, which quickly became the medium of instruction in schools. As a result, within two generations all the region's unique and remarkable scripts had fallen out of general use.

Yet since the beginning of the twenty-first century, a tide seems to have turned: several of the provinces in Indonesia have begun to install signage in traditional scripts and offer them, albeit briefly, in schools. A group of Indonesian calligraphers are developing fonts that explore the graceful and expressive qualities of traditional scripts, even some that are no longer in use.

And the Philippines may be leading the world in legislation to preserve, protect and promote traditional writing systems.

Watch this space ...

Script:
Javanese
—
Javanese has the most
elaborate and beautiful
forms of punctuation, some
of which have functions
for which English has no
equivalent. This flower is
the equivalent of a closing
set of quotation marks.

JAVANESE

Origin:
Java, Indonesia

Looking at the Javanese script, it's almost impossible to believe, simply from an aesthetic point of view, that it is highly endangered.

Old Javanese inscriptions first appeared around 800 AD. One of the earliest surviving inscriptions is a legal document in which a king grants a freehold to a village official – but it is written in verse: twenty-nine four-line stanzas based in the Sanskrit tradition. This combination of the courtly and the mundane, the legal and the musical, would set the tone for one of the world's great creative and artistic scripts.

Over time, a second, simpler set of characters – called *ka-ga-nga* after the first three syllabic characters – emerged, spreading out through the islands, as far as the Philippines.

No other written tradition from the region created so many works on so many subjects, nor had such an astonishingly rich tradition of manuscripts that were in themselves works of art. Not everyone in Javanese society was literate, but writing held a position that was both exalted and central. Scribes and poets were held in esteem both in court and at large, writing epic poems, historical accounts, stories, ancient verses and divination guides, or *primbon*.

Primbon were calendars and almanacs, but in a deeper and more all-encompassing sense than contemporary Western farming guides. An extraordinarily complex interlocking cosmology was interpreted to explain omens, specify charms and healing techniques and reveal auspicious and inauspicious days and even hours for particular activities. One combination would reveal a day when sex would be highly inadvisable, at the risk of conceiving a damaged child. Another text warned that burglars should avoid a certain day or run the risk of being caught and even killed.

But this makes it sound as though this arena of writing was merely an exercise in superstition. In fact, writing was an intrinsic part of Javanese cosmology. Individual letters were, in a sense, points of spiritual nexus, like written chakras.

As T. E. Behrend writes in 'Textual Gateways: The Javanese Manuscript Tradition': 'As elsewhere in the Indonesian archipelago, writing and script in Java were not just so many arbitrary signs and characters. Rather, the alphabet as a whole and each of its letters were seen as occupying a special position at the meeting point of macrocosm and microcosm, and consequently as being invested with power. The widespread use of letters and writing in cures is evidence of this power, as is the popularity of letter-based forms of prophecy, interpretation, and graphomancy. Individual letters are said to have mystical significance, and there are strains of philosophy that locate each apsara in a certain part of the body.'

An illustration in the *Kridhaksara*, a nineteenth-century text on the mystical

>>

dimensions of orthography, shows each letter mapped out around the body, each associated with a vital organ.

Even what we would think of as a simple alphabet-teaching nursery rhyme can be recited as a poem about the legendary King Ajisaka, who is said to have introduced civilization and writing to Java.

With such a wealth of meaning invested in writing, not only as a content device but as a medium in itself, it's hardly surprising that secret scripts were often used. Around Yogyakarta in the second half of the nineteenth century, it was popular to write pieces of text or even entire books in code, with the result that for decades afterwards, books were published that contained, or claimed to contain, the keys to earlier books that had been encoded.

Manuscripts were frequently lent or even rented out to family, friends and neighbours, to such an extent that one text renter (by day a foreman at a brickworks) begged his customers, 'My request to those who wish to read this – forgive me for even mentioning it – is that you not read while chewing betel, lest spittle get on it, nor while smoking, to avoid burn marks or worse.'

The wide range of forms of Javanese script was reduced when the Dutch introduced printing, but worse was to come.

During World War II, when the Dutch East Indies were occupied by the Japanese, the use of many Indigenous scripts was banned – a sign of how deeply people tend to associate a script with its culture of origin. After the war, when Indonesia achieved independence, the official language became Indonesian, written in the Latin alphabet. Within two generations, the number of Javanese who read and write their traditional script has been decimated.

In recent years, as a preservation effort, the Indonesian government prescribed most elementary and junior-high schools in Javanese-speaking areas to teach the script as a compulsory subject, though that has not necessarily made the Javanese script popular among schoolchildren. The script is also reappearing in commercial signage, especially at establishments wanting to brand themselves as offering traditional products or services.

Yet the fact remains that complete revival of a script is a massive and daunting task. Only Meitei Mayek (see page 117) has in effect died and been reborn into daily usage. As yet we have no idea what a Javanese revival might look like.

1

1 **Character grid:** examples of the Javanese script.

2 **Sample words:** 'I love you' in Javanese. Note that the traditional Javanese script, like others of the region, often does not leave spaces between words.

Script:
Balinese
—
The Balinese script, like its close
Javanese cousin, also uses forms
of punctuation unknown in the
Latin alphabet. This symbol, the
pamada, indicates that the text
that follows is sacred.

BALINESE

Origin:
Bali, Indonesia

A number of cultures around the world are so aware of writing's extraordinary qualities that they view it as sacred, and/or of divine origin. In these cultures, writing is not simply a way to record speech: it has a power that is deeply intertwined with the values and cosmology of its users.

The Balinese have traditionally been such a culture. For a thousand years, writes Professor Raechelle Rubinstein, the palm-leaf or *lontar* manuscript has been an important and prized artifact, used for a remarkable range of purposes: '… personal records, village records (membership of village councils and members' duties), regulations about cockfighting, rice cultivation, irrigation; contracts between kings; letters; esoteric socialist lore, such as the vocational manuals of high priests, temple caretakers, Sudra exorcists, metaphysical treatises on *wayang*, artists' guides, guides for healers'. One set of texts deals with the characteristics of roosters and was consulted as a kind of betting-form guide at cockfights; another famous text deals with 'the philosophical foundations of alphabet mysticism'.

Rubinstein continues: 'Belief in the divine origin and the supernatural potency of writing has also produced a web of rituals that surround literate activity including writing, reading, discarding lontar texts, storing lontar texts and paying homage to the Goddess Saraswati, the patroness of literature, knowledge and eloquence.'

For example, mantra must be recited when carrying out the following activities: '… writing; requesting a boon to write; crossing out consonants (this must first be recited over the tip of the stylus); crossing out vowels, the mute symbol and numbers; opening exalted writings; reading; closing and storing lontar; absorbing knowledge quickly; burning lontar (damaged lontar cannot be just thrown away but must be cremated, like the human body); and "adorning" consonants with vowels. Failing to recite these mantra is said to result in dire consequences: a short life-span results should the letter named cecek be crossed out; blindness and headache are the consequences of crossing out the letter hulu (hulu means "head"); lameness arises should the letter suku (suku means "foot" and "leg") be crossed out; deafness and stomach ailments follow the crossing out of the letter taleng (talinga means "ear").'

Lontar need to be stored in wooden chests, woven baskets or cupboards, which, in turn, need to be in a sacred space within the house, according to the principles of geomancy.

On the day dedicated to the goddess Saraswati, which takes place once a (210-day) year, the entire day is scripted by ritual. During that day, nothing written may be destroyed, or even a letter crossed out for fear of punishment by the goddess Durga and malevolent spirits. All the *lontar* in a household are gathered and act as the representation of the goddess, to whom eighteen offerings are made, one for each of the letters of the Balinese alphabet. Each offering contains the symbol of the supreme god, made of fried rice dough.

Even the act of reading is traditionally ritualized as a public act called *pepaosan*. Poetry is sung, prose declaimed dramatically in an act that involves communal recitation and translation.

'The situation was similar to the one in a karaoke room,' writes Ida Bagus Adi Sudewa, a Balinese writer. 'Everyone is eager to take turns reading. In one turn, there were three people participating; one reading the Kawi text, one translating to Balinese, and the last one telling the description of the meaning or the moral story of the verse. Of course the singing part is the most exciting one that also requires the higher skills. Those sessions can take hours, even from dusk until dawn.'

Since Indonesian independence, though, the Balinese script has all but fallen from general use, and the Balinese language is written in the Latin alphabet.

All the same, the past five years have seen a growing sense of the importance of the Balinese script. To support community *lontar* curation, a group of specialists visits villages and discusses the manuscripts they own, providing support for the preservation and understanding of those collections. A new manuscript study centre offers a focus on palm-leaf book production.

The governor of Bali, Wayan Koster, declared that every Thursday be a Traditional Thursday, on which all Hindus working in government offices should wear traditional Balinese dress and speak Balinese.

There are reading, writing and speaking competitions in Balinese and Balinese script for school-age children, and a new law requires public signs to be in Balinese language and script as well as Indonesian.

'The aim is to preserve our cultural heritage, especially in relation to literacy, which is a cultural identity of Bali,' Koster said. 'I think Balinese letters, Balinese text is in our identity, a symbol of our civilization.'

1   **Character grid:** examples of the
    Balinese script.

2   **Sample words:** *Durusang ngajeng dumum,*
    the Balinese equivalent of 'Bon appetit'.

SUNDANESE

Origin:
Java, Indonesia

It's hard to know whether to call Sundanese an extinct script, a living script or an endangered one – or even all three.

Over the past 1,200 years, the island of Java has been a cultural and commercial crossroads, and the Sundanese language – the Sunda people occupy the western part of the island of Java and are a distinct culture from the Javanese – has been written in several scripts.

The last native script generally used in West Java was Aksara Sunda Kuna, or Old Sundanese, which flourished in the Sunda Kingdom from the fourteenth to the eighteenth century. From the seventeenth century, both the Javanese and Pegon (Arabic) scripts were used, and the founding of the new nation of Indonesia, of which the island of Java became part, brought with it the decision that the official national alphabet would be Latin.

In 1996, though, the government of West Java Province announced they were going to choose a script to call their own.

They had four criteria: it should be a script that would work well with the sounds of the Sundanese language; it should correspond to Sundanese culture, in terms of both period and area of usage; it should be as simple as feasible; and it should reflect the Sundanese identity.

This was no simple task, and the question was taken seriously. After much discussion, the script that seemed to best fit the criteria was the Old Sundanese script, hitherto to be renamed Aksara Sunda, or Sundanese script, or Sunda Baku (Official Sundanese).

One consideration was the relationship between the script itself and the tools and materials that had been used to write it. Given that, over the past millennium, Sundanese had been written using stone, metal, skin, leaves, knives, ink, pen and hammer, should the visual impact of any, some or all of those technologies be reflected in the design of the adopted script?

The outcome represents a very rare attempt by a government to adopt a writing system based on historical cultural identity rather than simplification or convenience.

To date, though, the script has been used more as a display type for commercial, artistic and touristic purposes rather than as the de-facto writing system of Sunda. So Sundanese has the strange distinction of being the only native Indonesian script without its own body of literature.

That may change. The *Jakarta Post* reports that the classic novel *The Little Prince* has just been translated into Sundanese by Syauqi Stya Lacksana with text in both the Latin and Sundanese scripts.

KULITAN

Origin:
Luzon, Philippines

Colonial powers often use a divide-and-conquer strategy, dealing only with Indigenous groups they see as familiar or friendly, resulting in a system of privileges and preferments that may be perpetuated for centuries.

A case in point is Kulitan, a script used for writing Kapampángan, a language spoken mainly in central Luzon. Like the other Filipino scripts discussed here, this is probably one of a family that arrived in the islands from South Asia or Indonesia, pre-dating the arrival of the Spanish.

Kapampángan cultural advocate Michael Raymon Pangilinan writes: 'Long before the idea of a Filipino nation was even conceived the Kapampángan, Butuanon, Tausug, Magindanau, Hiligaynon, Sugbuanon, Waray, Iloko, Sambal and many other ethnolinguistic groups within the archipelago, already existed as bangsâ or nations in their own right. Many of these nations formed their own states and principalities centuries before the Spaniards created the Philippines in the late sixteenth century.'

The Spanish tended to respect each Indigenous ethnic group as a nation in its own right. However, during their period of influence, the Americans created a new classification, dividing the Filipino population into two major groups: lowland Christian Filipinos and the unconquered tribes. They considered the lowland Christian groups to be one and the same people, hispanized

and no longer in possession of any cultural distinction, their separate languages treated as mere dialects. As the capital, Manila, was in southern Luzon, they created a de facto preferred status on the language of that region: Tagalog.

Tagalog flourished so well under colonial rule that it survived a switch in colonial occupation: under Manuel Quezon, president of the 1935 Philippine Commonwealth under US Occupation, the idea of a Filipino nation based on Tagalog was conceived. From then on, anything 'Filipino' and 'national' was understood to mean 'Tagalog'.

Tagalog gained official status under a third occupation: that of the Japanese. In 1943, the Japanese promoted its use over English so that the Filipinos would, as in the words of Prime Minister Tojo Hideki, 'forget their mistaken Americanism and return to their Great East Asian roots'.

The other languages and scripts of the islands languished, while Kulitan became a medium of protest. In 1989, a group of young writers led by Pangilinan and Edwin Camaya formed the Kapampángan National Liberation Movement, to promote the teaching and usage of Kulitan.

Pangilinan said: 'Currently, Kulitan is still used for heraldry, seals, logos, as well as for titles of public and private events and publications, and also for signatures and private diaries. We hope to remedy the dearth of literature in the near future. Only Kulitan is Kapampángan.'

Script:
Bugis
—

The letter *la* in the Buginese or
Lontara script, which features
the chevron or boomerang
shape appearing time and again,
in different configurations and
at different angles.

BUGIS

Origin:
Sulawesi, Indonesia

The Indonesian province of South Sulawesi has a writing tradition at least 300 years old, and its people, most of whom are Bugis or Makasar, share an Indigenous script, often called Lontara because of its use of the traditional *lontar* palm leaf. (A related and equally old second script, Makasarese, died out in the nineteenth century.)

The Bugis living along the coast were famous as boat builders and navigators (and, in some cases, as pirates), and the Bugis script found its way to the nearby islands of Sumbawa and Flores, where it was adapted to the local languages and referred to as Satera Jontal ('palm-leaf writing') and Lota Ende, respectively. It may also have sailed north and become the basis for some of the Indigenous scripts of the Philippines.

Historically, Bugis script was used to write formal documents such as chronicles of kingdoms, contracts, trade laws, treaties, maps and journals, or a combination of all of them: a single manuscript might be a compendium including an epic poem, some prayers or charms, an almanac, some business jottings and a drawing of a fort.

Manuscripts were both in Western book form and on palm leaves – but unlike the *lontar* book fashion of Java and Bali (see pages 174–181), the Bugis created a form that worked like an audio/video cassette or a microfilm reader.

A number of ribbons, usually about 2cm wide and 60cm long, were sewn together end to end, with each end being fastened to a wooden reel. The two reels were then mounted side by side within a device looking like a wooden tuning fork, and the manuscript was read as it unspooled from left to right.

One of the most visually striking uses of the Bugis script was in the widespread practice of keeping a daily record of events. Each day had its own page. When there was just too much to write about for one page, the scribe would invade other pages, continually rotating them as he wrote and ran out of space. The result is literally amazing: a well-filled page looks like the street-plan of a medieval city.

The history of the Bugis people and their script cannot be told without the story of Colliq Pujié, whose role in Bugis literature is even greater than that of any single figure in English – a fact that is all the more remarkable for her being a woman.

Colliq Pujié (or, to give her her full name, Retna Kencana Colliq Pujié Arung Pancana Toa Matinroé ri Tucaé) was the daughter of La Rumpang, king of Tanete, now the Barru Regency in South Sulawesi. Born in 1812, she grew up in a time when her island was still struggling against the Dutch to achieve autonomy. Her father entrusted her not only with an education but with the running of royal affairs. She did this with a possibly unique feat of linguistic >>

subversiveness: in order to communicate in secret with others in the Bugis resistance, she began incorporating Bilang-bilang characters into the Bugis script.

Bilang-bilang (the term means 'numbers' – specifically Arabic numbers) was an importation of one of the secret shorthand scripts used by Muslim travellers or the Gujarati merchants of northeast India, which had spread along trade routes into South Asia, Southeast Asia and Indonesia. Because these characters were numbers, which were not only incomprehensible to the Dutch but appeared to have no meaning when embedded in a text, they had a fascinating hidden-in-plain-sight quality, and became woven into the Bugis–Makasar script.

Linguist, historian, classicist, resistance fighter, editor, poet, diplomat, Colliq Pujié eventually died in the process of writing out and editing *La Galigo*, the great 6,000-page, twelve-volume epic poem of Bugis literature – one of the longest epics in the world. The text, by the way, is not merely an epic or mythic poem, but each volume is thought to contain the spirits of the characters: before it is opened and read aloud, it must be preceded by ritual that may include the burning of incense and the sacrifice of a chicken or goat.

Nowadays the Bugis script is used only for printing traditional literature, and for specialized, handwritten items such as wedding documents and personal notes and letters. It can also be seen on some street signs, and a number of Indonesian typographers and graphic designers are bringing it back, to some degree, into the public eye.

Bugis also illustrates a truth that runs throughout the Endangered Alphabets project – that in representing how we think and talk, words are saturated with common understanding.

For example: one fascinating feature of Bugi language and culture is that it recognizes five separate genders that are necessary to keep the world in balance and harmony: *makkunrai* (feminine woman), *calabai* (feminine man), *calalai* (masculine female), *oroané* (masculine man) and *bissu* (a gender that embodies both male and female energies, and is thus revered as mystical and wise). Lacking those words in English, we find it almost impossible to think like the Buginese.

The absence or loss of a word, then, can literally make an important concept or belief unthinkable.

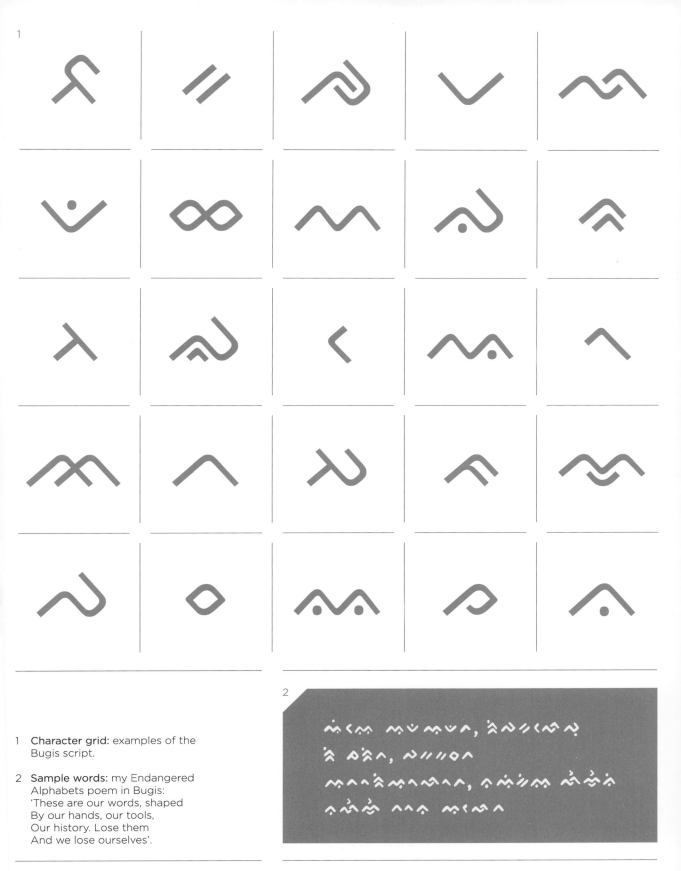

1   **Character grid:** examples of the
    Bugis script.

2   **Sample words:** my Endangered
    Alphabets poem in Bugis:
    'These are our words, shaped
    By our hands, our tools,
    Our history. Lose them
    And we lose ourselves'.

Script:
Batak
—
The Batak letter *ma*. Batak
folding books made of bark,
often used for divination, are
among the most fascinating
documents of the region.

BATAK

Origin:
Sumatra, Indonesia

Aksara Batak, or Batak writing, is a group of scripts used to write the Batak languages of North Sumatra, Indonesia. Batak writing grew out of the Pallava script, a writing system in South India at least as early as the fourth century AD. By the 1700s, Batak writing had already developed into a number of regional variants – not surprisingly, as each Batak language is spoken by groups of people with distinct histories, social organization and ethnic identities.

Each *surat*, or script, consists of nineteen to twenty-one radicals called *ina ni surat*, or 'mother of the script', and six to eight diacritical marks called *anak ni surat*, or 'children of the script'. 'Mother' and 'child' in these cases stand in for 'big' and 'small', and these big and small letters combine to form syllables.

Traditionally, Batak culture wrote on bamboo, water-buffalo bones or tree bark. In the first two cases, the writing was incised using the point of a knife and then soot was rubbed into the cut letters so they could be read more easily.

Early Batak writing is unusual in many ways, one of which is that it included an entire genre of threatening letters. The writer would use a short piece of bamboo to write down his demands and accompany it with tiny bamboo weapons to drive home the point – rifles, spears and lances, for example, or a flint, which meant, in the case of European plantation owners, 'I'm going to burn your tobacco barns down'.

Anyone in Batak society, wealthy or poor, could learn to write, and young men in particular wrote love letters. A German visitor observed in 1847: 'The children are not instructed in anything and the only thing they learn by imitation is writing, that is, scratching characters with the point of their knife onto bamboo and reading what was thus written down. This art of written communication is the only scientific art which they have; it is, however-er, widespread among them, especially in [Toba], where young men scarcely fourteen years old usually begin their first literary efforts by sending love letters to young girls, scratched on pieces of bamboo …'

Writing on bamboo tubes and buffalo bones included proverbs and sayings, called *umpama* and *umpasa*, and lamentations used during funeral-rites, called *hata ni andung*.

Perhaps the most famous media were books made of folded bark called *pustaha*. According to Batak mythology, there was once a bark book (called *Tumbaga Holing*) so rich and compendious it held all the knowledge possessed by humankind; but many Batak believe the Dutch stole this marvellous book and took it back to Holland.

Writing a *pustaha* was a specialized skill, though, practised only by the *datu*, the Batak magicians and healers, and professional scribes. >>

INDONESIA AND OCEANIA   189

The ink alone, of resin soot and tree sap, had its own spiritual potency and took considerable care to make, as one *pustaha* directs: 'When the oil is added to the other ingredients, the following signs should be observed … If the oil separates out in the middle, this is a bad omen. There will be unrest. Since this is unavoidable, one should stop the preparation of the ink.'

In addition to the materials, the *datu* needed to know the *hata poda*, or secret language of instruction – an archaic southern Batak dialect mixed with a dose of Malay and only learned through apprenticeship to another *datu*.

This rich tradition was ended by a twofold assault: by incoming Muslim warriors in the 1830s and Protestant missionaries in the 1850s. The missionaries saw the Batak writings as being all too similar to the magic books of the Jews and the Greeks and thus, in the words of one missionary, 'ripe to be burned'.

Yet the missionaries supported the script, if not the literature, recognizing the Batak language and its script as vital to the culture. They created typefaces and printed a variety of books in Batak until the end of World War I. When they stopped, it was for a reason all too common in colonial cultures: the traditional writing system had come to seem insufficiently sophisticated compared to those of the Europeans.

The Batak script is taught a little in North Sumatran elementary schools as a feature of Batak heritage, as a cultural artifact rather than as a day-to-day writing system for spoken Batak language, for which the Latin alphabet is generally used.

As of 2020, several font packages are available for use on Windows, Linux and Mac operating systems. This has made the teaching and writing of Batak script easier for students of Batak language, and institutions of higher education in North Sumatra, such as the University of North Sumatra, incorporate regional Batak language and literature into their curricula.

Out in public, the script is now, to some extent, used for display and decorative purposes, in the signage of shops and governmental institutions, on street signs and in the universal art of the T-shirt.

1 **Character grid:** examples of the Batak script.

2 **Sample words:** the Batak carving from my exhibition for International Mother Language Day, each of which displayed the phrase 'Mother tongue'.

BAYBAYIN

Origin:
Luzon, Philippines

When the Spanish arrived in the islands they named after King Philip in 1543, they discovered to their surprise that the people of those islands already used their own family of scripts. The one most commonly used to write Tagalog was called Baybayin, a term that more or less means 'alphabet', from the root *baybay*, meaning 'spell'.

According to an anonymous Spanish report in 1590: 'When they write, it is on some tablets made of the bamboos which they have in those islands, on the bark. In using such a tablet, which is four fingers wide, they do not write with ink, but with some scribers [the tip of a knife, or a sharp piece of iron] with which they cut the surface and bark of the bamboo, and make the letters.'

As with other scripts in the region, once the letters had been cut, the writer took a handful of ash and rubbed it into the thinly incised letters to make them stand out more clearly. Interestingly, the very way in which the letters were formed meant that Western observers were thoroughly confused: in which direction was the Baybayin written, and in which should it be read? Some thought the text should be read vertically from bottom to top in columns progressing from left to right because that was how the ancient Filipinos carved it. This writing process, though, had nothing to do with linguistics – the script is actually the familiar left-to-right, top-to-bottom – and

everything to do with occupational safety. Given that they were carving with a sharp tool on an irregular and non-flat surface, they carved away from their bodies. This actually gave them the unusual ability to read and write in different directions and from different angles.

Once the Spanish arrived, though, Baybayin was doomed to the long, slow decline of a minority writing system.

Filipinos found being able to use the Latin alphabet helped them to get ahead in life under the Spanish regime, working in relatively prestigious jobs as clerks, scribes and secretaries. Printing presses were set up and Filipinos adopted the use of pen, paper and ink, so the technological basis for their written language, and thus its very look, was lost.

All the same, Baybayin never quite died out, and today a variety of people are doing what they can to revive it.

Baybayin tattoos are returning as signs of cultural pride and overall cool. One artist, Kristian Kabuay, has expanded his repertoire to include calligraphy, graffiti and custom artwork – a panorama of Baybayin. Meanwhile, the Philippine government has added Baybayin symbols to the country's peso banknotes as an anti-counterfeiting measure. In fact, the Philippine government has shown global leadership in this arena. Writing that 'the importance of writing in general and the alphabet in particular for the preservation and progress of civilization

is incalculable', in April 2018, the House of Representatives proposed an act mandating the inclusion of the traditional Philippine writing systems in the basic and higher education curricula, local government signage, and newspaper and magazine publishing. It is very, very unusual for any government to view its own Indigenous writing systems with such respect. The legislation is still a long way from being enacted, but the Philippines may be showing the world the way ahead.

Script:
Baybayin
—

The Baybayin script was almost certainly developed from the Bugis script, and though the two look quite different, in many cases the letterforms are basically the same – but incised in bamboo instead of written on a palm leaf, making them more slender, more curved.

Sample characters based
on a collection by Piers Kelly

ESKAYAN

Origin:
Bohol, Philippines

Eskayan, from the Philippine island of Bohol, is one of the world's more mysterious writing systems, created to write one of the world's more mysterious languages.

The script is made up of over a thousand alphabetic, syllabic and alphasyllabic symbols, many of which have additional curlicues that are apparently entirely decorative, even whimsical. Several hundred seem to be superfluous or redundant, and thirty-seven characters represent sounds that never even appear in Eskayan words.

This makes no sense if one starts from the assumption that writing is developed by a culture as a means to represent its spoken language. This may not be the case with Eskayan, however. One theory is that the script was originally intended to transliterate Spanish and Visayan, the language spoken throughout the Visayas region of the Philippines, including Bohol. According to this line of thinking, the script was retrofitted as a vehicle for spoken Eskayan, a utopian language used by some 550 people and also known as Bisayan Declarado.

The Eskayan language is also something of a mystery, as it has no clear relationship to other languages in its vicinity and appears to be a conlang – a deliberately constructed language – but its exact origins remain unclear.

Eskayan is also one of a number of fascinating scripts that have their own writing-creation myth. Eskayan speakers say the script, and its language, was invented by an ancestral figure called Pope Pinay, who was instructed by Jesus to create a writing system based on parts of the human body. According to the same legend, Eskayan was later carved on wooden tablets and stored in a cave to preserve it from destruction.

The language was then apparently pushed into extinction by Visayan and later Spanish, but then 'rediscovered' by Mariano Datahan, a charismatic rebel leader who founded a utopian Indigenous community in southeast Bohol in the aftermath of the Philippine–American War. Datahan used the Eskayan language and script as an embodiment and expression of his movement.

Even though the script is not yet fully digitized, numerous handwritten books exist in Eskayan. It is taught in several traditional schools on Bohol and in at least one public school. The Bohol Division of the Department of Education and Eskayan tribal leaders have begun to establish a language school, but as is often the case in revitalization efforts, a shortage of active speakers means a shortage of teachers. According to one of the tribal leaders, few Eskayans are still using the language, spoken or written, at home.

Nevertheless, Piers Kelly says: 'The sheer size, complexity and irregularity of the hybrid Eskaya script is unparalleled among the world's writing systems.'

AVOIULI

Origin:
Pentecost Island,
Vanuatu

Many scripts have been produced by individuals, and many of these have been created specifically as an alternative to Western or colonial alphabets, but few have been developed as recently, or in such a spirit of resolute independence, as the Avoiuli script of the northern part of Pentecost Island, part of the Pacific Island nation of Vanuata. Plus, it has its own bank.

Drawing inspiration from traditional sand drawings (arguably, a form of endangered writing system in themselves), Chief Viraleo Boborenvanua of the Turaga Indigenous movement spent fourteen years developing the script for the Raga language (the word 'avoiuli' comes from the Raga words *avoi*, or 'talk about', and *uli*, 'draw' or 'paint') as part of the movement's aim to reduce the island's dependence on and therefore vulnerability to outside influences.

The script is also remarkable in its resolutely cursive nature: like the culture's sand drawings, letters are designed so words can be executed in a single stroke; and as such, it opposes the current digital trend of dividing words into individual key strokes.

The way the script is taught and learned is also a unique example of one way in which an Indigenous culture tries to resist the forces of globalization, recognizing that a culture's language has value, both intangible and tangible.

Anyone wanting to learn the script has to do so – and must pay to do so in pigs' tusks and mats – at Turaga's 'school of custom' at Lavatmanggemu in northeastern Pentecost. In Lavatmanggemu, Avoiuli is used rather than the Latin alphabet (which is the standard on most of Pentecost), and can be seen on posters, schoolwork, financial records, carved stones and even graffiti.

As if these qualities aren't unusual enough, Avoiuli letters are so close to being symmetrical that the script can be written from left to right or right to left, and from top to bottom or bottom to top.

The script is also used for record keeping by the Tangbunia Bank, which operates in a similarly Indigenous and autonomous spirit: instead of dealing in Western currency it uses local items of value such as hand-woven mats, shells and pigs' tusks. Its very name comes from the word for large baskets traditionally used for storing items of value.

Script:
Hanunuo
—
Many of the scripts of the
islands bear the characteristic
shapes resulting from being
incised into bamboo tubes.

NATIONAL CULTURAL TREASURE SCRIPTS OF THE PHILIPPINES

Origin:
Philippines

The Philippines may be unique in identifying traditional writing systems and making efforts to research, protect and teach them.

Four scripts were declared to be National Cultural Treasures by the National Museum of the Philippines: Surat Mangyan, Surat Buhid, Surat Pala'wan and Surat Tagbanwa. All four have also been inscribed into UNESCO's Memory of the World Register.

Mindoro Island is home to two closely related, incised-in-bamboo traditional alphabets – Hanunuo, in the southern part of the island, and Buhid, further north, in the central highlands. Surat Buhid has two known varieties: the northern variety used in Bansud, and the southern variety used in Roxas and Bongabong.

In Mindoro, the challenge of incising letters into bamboo tubes led to cultural and regional differences in traditional writing styles. This difference may be aesthetic, but it is also rooted in the technical.

'The rounded *garagbutan* style', researcher Christopher Ray Miller explains, 'is made with the tip of a bolo knife whereas the *dakdahulan* (big or bold style) is made with the blade … leading to the contrast between thin verticals and thick horizontals.'

Surat Buhid is written and read horizontally from left to right. However, when writing on live bamboos (the traditional medium used by the Buhid), Surat Buhid is written from bottom to top, vertically

upward, away from their bodies, to avoid injuries. Using the cylindrical bamboo tubes leads to characters that are more angular rather than wavy compared to other Philippine scripts.

The script is mostly used to write forms of Buhid traditional literature, such as *fangasay* or riddles, and *ambahan* and *urukay*, which are poems with seven- and eight-syllable lines respectively, but only about a hundred elders or culture bearers are considered expert in Surat Buhid. Buhid children are all too often the targets of discrimination and bullying from their lowland peers, and their allegiance to their cultural traditions has suffered – a challenge made harder by the fact that they are exposed to an education system that uses the Latin script and is taught mainly in English and Filipino.

Surat Mangyan, commonly referred to as the Hanunuo script or Surat Hanunuo Mangyan, is the Indigenous writing system used by Hanunuo Mangyans to write their language.

Historically, young Hanunuo men and women learned the Hanunuo script in order to write each other love poems. The goal was to learn as many as possible, and using the script to write them facilitated this process. Nowadays, they are more apt to use digital devices, which are unlikely to support the Hanunuo script.

An example of the traditional seven-syllable *ambahan* poetry of the Hanunuo

>>

Mangyans of Mindoro, Central Philippines:

So, you will be going now,
Starting on a journey far!
Your eyes will enjoy the trip
Many things you will behold.
But I, who will stay behind,
Here within this four-walled room,
What thoughts could I entertain?
Just looking up at the roof,
Just looking down at the floor.

The Mangyan Heritage Center has started teaching the Hanunuo Mangyan Syllabic Script in Mangyan public elementary and secondary schools, partnering with the Department of Education to give a one-hour once-a-week schedule for each class in selected schools.

The centre has developed and published materials on Mangyan literature, cultures and scripts. The *Primer to Mangyan Script*, first published in 1986 and currently being revised for its third iteration, is one of the materials used to teach the script. Additional primers for the various Buhid scripts and a localized version of the Hanunuo primer for communities in the Occidental region are also being developed. Another publication, *Bamboo Whispers*, is an anthology of a hundred Mangyan poems in two scripts and four languages.

Surat Palawan and the closely related Surat Tagbanwa were developed on the island of Palawan, by the Tagbanwa and Palawano peoples respectively. Very little is known about the current status of either script, but both are among the most endangered in the world.

A School of Living Tradition teaching Surat Tagbanwa was started in October 2019, but its activities were stopped by the COVID-19 pandemic. Currently, one of the elders who still practises Surat Tagbanwa is trying to teach it to her relatives.

1   **Character grid:** examples of the
    Hanunuo script.

2   **Sample words:** from the poem
    quoted on the opposite page from
    the Mangyan Heritage Center.

Script:
Rejang
—
Similarly to the Philippine island
scripts (see page 196), the
shape of the upstream scripts
of Sumatra result from being
incised into bamboo tubes.

SURAT ULU SCRIPTS

Origin:
Sumatra, Indonesia

The Surat Ulu (the term means 'upstream') scripts are a family of closely related Sumatran writing systems that include the variants of Incung, Rejang, Lampung, Bengkulu, Lembak, Lintang, Lebong and Serawai.

Lampung is spoken in Lampung province in southern Sumatra, one of the major islands of Indonesia. It has been written for perhaps a thousand years with its own script, known as Aksara Lampung or Had Lampung, and related to other scripts of the region, such as Rejang and Kerinci.

The Lampung script was used to write spells, letters, traditional laws, religious works and courtship poems. It was written on bark, palm leaf, metal plates, animal skin, horn, stone and bamboo. Its simple, strong, clear, curving lines developed from their Indic roots, becoming more angular than curved, to suit incising on bamboo or horn with the point of a knife.

Aksara Rejang (that is, the Rejang script), which has been used in the highlands of Bengkulu Province for perhaps 300 years to write both Malay and the Rejang language, has also been called Kaganga, a term invented by the twentieth-century British anthropologist Mervyn A. Jaspan, after the sounds of the first three letters in the writing system, ka-ga-nga.

The Rejang script flourished until the arrival of Islam, but it was not well suited to the phonetic needs of reciting the Qur'an, and gradually was replaced by Jawi, the regional version of Arabic.

In time, both the script and the language suffered the stigma of being unsophisticated, according to Fikri Ansori, a historian from Rejang. 'Due to derogatory terms that are often used to label us when we speak Rejang, I was very careful not to speak it and I didn't even want to have an accent in Malay or Indonesian.'

Aksara Incung is used by the Kerinci people of the Jambi highlands. Incung literally means 'slanting' or 'cursive': the script is written on a slant of about 45 degrees, giving it a truncated, foreshortened look. Historically, it was used to document ancestral history, for literature, and for incantations, blessings and spells.

Tembo, or traditional historiography or clan stories, were mostly written on buffalo or goat horn; *karang mindu*, or poetic lamentations, were usually written on bamboo or palm leaf.

Almost all villagers in Sungai Penuh and Kerinci keep heirlooms decorated with Incung scripts, though these are rarely seen by outsiders: village elders must first deliberate whether the heirlooms can be seen or not, and without the proper deliberation and ceremony, it is believed the daughters of the household will experience misfortunes.

All the Surat Ulu scripts could be considered endangered, but in the last few years, the tide has been showing signs of turning. >>

First, the provincial government of Lampung established that street signs in the city of Bandar Lampung should be in the Lampung script as well as Latin, and that the Lampung language and script should be taught first in primary and now in secondary schools. Likewise, in Sungai Penuh and Kerinci, Incung has been used for street names and regional government signage, and the local education board has reintroduced the Rejang script, making it mandatory teaching from the third to fifth year of primary school.

An urban clothing line has adopted the Lampung script as a motif for products such as T-shirts, skirts and bags. And native Lampung speaker Indra Gunawan has taken it on himself to create, at his own expense, with help from friends and crowdsourcing, a Lampung–Indonesian–English dictionary.

The project, he explains, began when he was still in college: 'I started this project because I want to contribute for my local language preservation. There have been many Lampung dictionaries in Indonesia, yet I haven't found the three-language version and therefore I had this idea.

'I have also tried to manually input it into a dictionary software, suggested by my friend who is an alumni of a master degree program in University of Indonesia, which enabled me to input all of my dictionary content into a more tidy style like a printed dictionary as the output of the software.

'I still update my dictionary manually. The methods I use are varied: crowdsourcing in social media; adding vocabulary whenever I think that it has not been input yet into my dictionary; asking my friends, and families who I know are native speakers of Lampung language; and recording the conversation between my friends in Lampung language; and every day I always bring a small notebook which I usually use to write down some additional vocabulary words for my dictionary.'

He has received support from an unexpected source: Google Earth. The platform, he reports, 'has launched a local language series … which involved me as a collaborator, and I see that as good progress'.

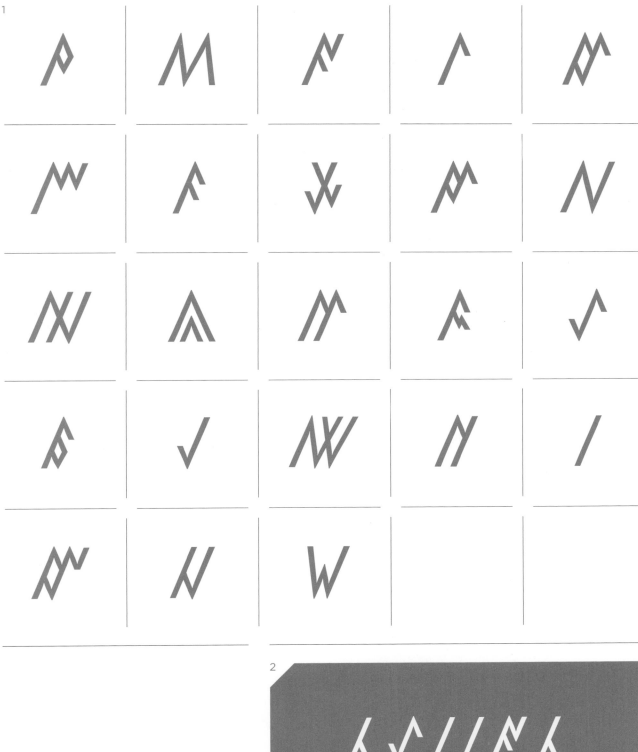

1 **Character grid:** examples of the
   Rejang script.

2 **Sample words:** 'Mother tongue'
   in the Rejang script of Sumatra.

Script:
Iban Dunging
—
Surely nobody who invented
a script also invented as many
other things as Dunging Gunggu.

IBAN DUNGING

Origin:
Sarawak, Malaysia

Authors of writing systems need to be as creative as they are linguistically knowledgeable. A little self-promotion helps, and a lot of perseverance is vital. Of all the script creators we know about, though, nobody was as inventive as Dunging Anak (son of) Gunggu, creator of the Iban script that now bears his name.

The Iban is the largest Indigenous group in Malaysia with a population of more than 1 million, most of whom live in the state of Sarawak. The Iban language is spoken by almost 2 million people in Malaysia, Brunei and Kalimantan, Indonesia. In Sarawak, Iban language is a *lingua franca* in most rural towns among speakers of different ethnic backgrounds. Iban is the only Indigenous language that is officially taught in Sarawak schools, using the Latin alphabet.

Born in 1904, when education was almost non-existent in rural Sarawak, Dunging taught himself how to read and write Malay and Iban in Latin and Jawi scripts. He invented the first Iban alphabet in 1947, teaching it to his nephews and, briefly, at a local school, but at the time he was better known for other inventions.

By the age of twenty-one, he had already shown his skills in Iban traditional *ukir* designs, making utensils such as plates and bowls from *tapang* hardwood, and various Iban traditional musical instruments from wood, bamboo, gourd and palm leaves.

Dunging's *bilik* (apartment) of the longhouse was designed and decorated so it looked like a small museum. On the door, Dunging had written, in his own script, 'Raja Menua Sarawak' – King of Sarawak.

During one grand festive celebration, Festival of the Departed (*Gawai Antu*), he cooled this home/gallery/workshop with a fan of his own invention, powered by a bicycle, which was so strong it blew the traditional Iban headgear off the heads of passers-by.

One of his original creations was the *rebab* musical instrument made out of a coconut shell cut in half. He also made bamboo flutes and created a two-string (out of rattan) wooden *nyakun* that he played to entertain himself.

He planted his own cotton and spun it into thread, which was used by a substantial number of women weavers around the Rimbas, Layar, Paku and Padeh basins.

He also made hats from the light *empalaie* wood and the *kerupuk* palm, which were popular and said to be quite durable and comfortable. He experimented with making hats, trousers and jackets from the bark of the *tekalung* tree that he flattened by pounding, tailoring the items on himself and walking around as his own model to sell his creations.

Valentine Tawie Salok, a writer with the *New Sarawak Tribune*, wrote: 'I remember when encountering him in Sarikei in 1982, he used an orange outfit made out   >>

of the tree bark, including the hat. In fact he looked resplendent in the outfit with matching orange *tekalung* footwear, then possibly the one and only pair of such kind in the world.'

Another invention was his own brand of perfume, created by gathering local wildflowers, including wild orchids, boiling them and then filtering the liquid. He enjoyed brisk sales, but ran out of the raw materials and abandoned the project – as he also abandoned his plans to mass-manufacture bicycles made out of local plant materials, which unfortunately turned out to be too bumpy, unsafe and uncomfortable.

More successful were a hydro-powered rice mill he designed and built himself, and his use of the local rubber plantations to invent a laundry mangle (to press water out of newly washed clothes) made of rubber and the hardwood *tapang* tree. These were lighter and cheaper than the usual metal mangles, and he donated many to his employees and to the local community.

This colourful context suggests he saw writing – specifically, an Indigenously created writing system – as more than a linguistic exercise, but as part of a broader range of efforts to contribute to and improve the lives of those in his community.

His most lasting legacy was his alphabet, though that might have gone the way of the tree-bark outfit were it not for the efforts of his grand-nephew, Dr Bromeley Philip, an associate professor of applied linguistics and ethnolinguistics at the Academy of Language Studies, Universiti Teknologi MARA (UiTM) Sarawak.

In 2010, extending Dunging's work, Philip developed computer fonts for the Iban alphabet, called LaserIban, using which he launched a course called the 'Training Unto LaserIban System', or TULIS Program. (*Tulis* means 'writing' in Iban.) 'The ultimate purpose of the course is to help revive the otherwise disappearing Iban alphabet,' he explained.

Philip is now transliterating three Iban folk tales into the Iban alphabet as part of an effort to transcribe as many Iban language materials as possible. He is also building an Iban alphabet dictionary for use as a reference for the Iban spelling system.

'Most Iban [whether], old or young, are by now aware that the Iban language has its own alphabet that can be used to accurately translate the Iban's spoken language into a written language,' Philip says. He has run Iban alphabet training courses at UiTM Sarawak campus, promoted the script on radio and television, and written *Urup Iban*, a primer and workbook to teach the alphabet, which he described as 'a must-buy item for each and every Iban who loves the language and sense of identity'.

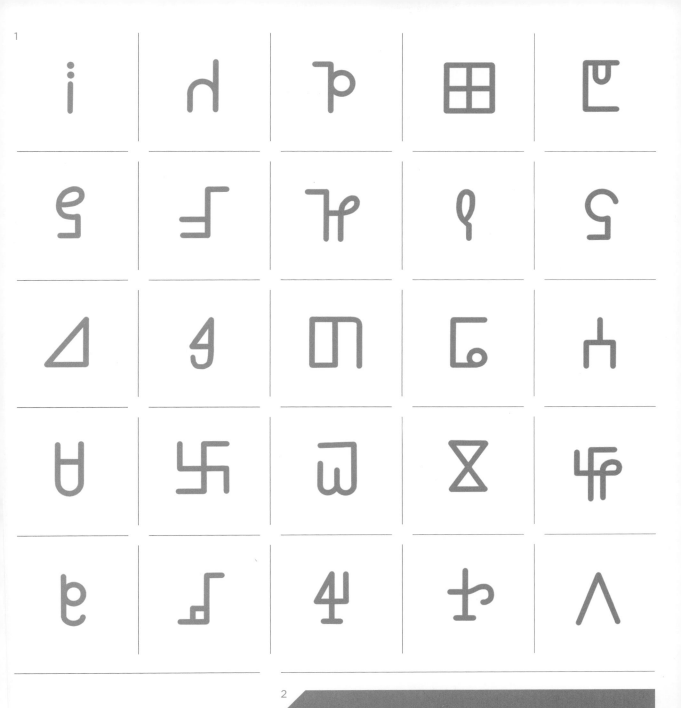

1 **Character grid:** examples of the Iban Dunging script.

2 **Sample words:** part of a poem that describes the suffering of the Dayak people, the loss of their script in a great flood and the hope that someone would rediscover it.

THE AMER

I C A S

INTRODUCTION

Central America is one of a handful of places in the world where writing developed independently – that is, it was invented rather than learned or adapted from some other culture.

More than a dozen Mesoamerican symbol systems have been identified, dating back as much as 3,000 years, most of them still undeciphered. The most complex of the writing systems that emerged there, building on earlier systems, was Mayan.

Perhaps 2,200 years old, the extraordinary Mayan glyphs, which still stare out at visitors from vast architectural formations such as the ruined city in Tikal, have still only been partially deciphered. We now believe they are a combination of logograms – signs indicating words or phrases, such as shorthand symbols, or numbers – and phonetic symbols, much like modern Japanese writing. We now know, for example, the spoken word *b'alam*, meaning 'jaguar', could be written: as a single logogram, B'ALAM; a logogram with syllable additions, as *ba*-B'ALAM, or B'ALAM-*ma*, or *b'a*-B'ALAM-*ma*; or completely phonetically in syllables as *b'a-la-ma*.

Further south in the Andes, the Inca developed a system of *quipu*, so innovative that it was often not recognized as writing at all: each *quipu* was a bundle of between a handful and a thousand knotted fibre strings, with the knots encoding records, tax obligations, census records and calendars.

Other, less phonetic systems, such as the Mixtec and Aztec, emerged after the Maya, but none would survive the invasion by the Latin alphabet. When the Spanish arrived in South America, they equated Roman Christianity with the Latin alphabet, and, conversely, they saw local writing forms as manifestations of unchristian beliefs.

In more than fifty cases around the world, we know the names of the people who created writing systems. South America represents one of the few cases where we know the name of the person who destroyed them.

As part of his campaign to eradicate pagan rites, Bishop Diego de Landa ordered written Maya works to be destroyed. Only four Maya codices are known to have survived the conquistadors, and the Mayan writing system was functionally extinct within fifty years.

In North America, though, the story was a little different. Petroglyphs were created throughout the continent, the oldest being carved into boulders northeast of Reno, Nevada, more than 10,000 and perhaps 15,000 years ago. Sites in New England depicted hands, the sun, the moon in various phases, people or spirits, anthropomorphic beings, various native animals, markings similar to the letters 'E', 'M', 'X' and 'I', slashes, crosses, circles that may represent planetary figures, trees, river courses and figures from shamanic tradition like giants, thunderbirds and horned serpents.

Many Indigenous peoples used dendroglyphs – that is, symbols carved into trees and logs. Some served as boundary markers between tribes, some thanked local spirits in the wake of a successful hunt, some served mapping functions. The Lenape of Pennsylvania and New Jersey, for example, carved animals and etchings on to trees when they camped, some of which recorded their tribe, region or village. The Abenaki of northern New England used dendroglyphs to mark paths, or drew beaver huts and ponds to mark their trapping areas.

In Canada, the Mi'kmaq, a First Nations people of the east coast, developed a symbol system that they called *komqwejwi'kasikl*, or 'sucker-fish writings', because the glyphs looked like the tracks the sucker fish leaves on the muddy river bottom.

In North America, though, the tactic of the incoming Christians was to co-opt rather than to eradicate Indigenous symbol systems. A number of birch scrolls containing Mi'kmaq writings were destroyed by missionaries, but before long the writing system was adapted to help convert Native peoples.

Father Le Clercq, a Roman Catholic missionary on the Gaspé Peninsula in New France from 1675, claimed that he had seen some Mi'kmaq children impressing symbols on birchbark using porcupine quills. Le Clercq adapted those symbols, adding ones of his own invention, until he had a visual vocabulary he could use for writing prayers, a system that was still in use in the nineteenth century. Another priest, Pierre Maillard, independently created a different set of hieroglyphics to transcribe Mi'kmaq words, which he used for the principal prayers and responses in the catechism. This symbol set was used among the Mi'kmaq into the twentieth century.

Compared to most other continents, the Americas have almost no endangered alphabets in the usual sense: most scripts of the twin continents are either imported and in robust health or altogether extinct.

But the Americas are the continent of rebirth, of invention and reinvention, and it's all the more remarkable that in the face of this tide of invasion, infection, conversion and destruction, two writing systems emerged that were, for their time, astonishingly successful.

Sequoyah, with no training in European-style writing systems (his own people

suspecting them of being a form of witchcraft) had the astonishing intellectual imagination and the perseverance to invent a form of writing for the Cherokee language, in the process becoming the first person in history (as far as we know) to enable his people to convert to verbal literacy by doing so himself.

Given the tradition of Christian priests and missionaries destroying anything smacking of paganism, and learning local languages primarily to convert Native peoples, it's all the more remarkable that James Evans should have created a syllabary for the Cree that they could make their own.

Today, the United States is the principal engine that drives the globalization of the English language and of the Latin alphabet, and, as such, it threatens to overwhelm less powerful cultures and their languages, scripts and collective identities; yet it is also home to many of the companies and organizations that digitize minority scripts and enable people to text each other in an expanding range of mother tongues.

This greater array of fonts, plus advances in what is known as machine translation, or MT, open the fascinating and radical possibility that anyone will be able to communicate in writing with anyone else, regardless of their language background.

Script:
Cherokee
—
The Cherokee syllable *ma*
clearly shows the script's
double origin: the curly, cursive
lower half is very much how
the characters were originally
designed by Sequoyah; the
upper half with its serif is a relic
of the Reverend Worcester's
adaptation of the syllabary into
a European-style typeface.

CHEROKEE

Origin:
United States

The Cherokee script is the work of one of the great acts of intellectual imagination in human history; and its astonishing creation, remarkable growth, near annihilation and current struggle for revival illustrate all the issues in this book.

The Cherokee, who at the beginning of the eighteenth century numbered perhaps 17,000, originally lived in a region that probably extended from present-day Virginia down into present-day Georgia. Their situation, rarely a stable one thanks to a constant series of tribal wars, became more difficult with the arrival of the colonial powers. In 1738, a smallpox epidemic, brought to the Carolinas by the slave ships, killed thousands of Cherokee, and a series of shifting alliances with the British, French and Spanish turned them into pawns in the colonial game. Many of them were driven westward, taking their unwritten language with them.

At the beginning of the nineteenth century, though, the Cherokee language was changed in a unique way by an utterly remarkable man. His English name was George Gist, or Guess. His Cherokee name was Sequoyah. He was the first person we know of to become literate by inventing his own writing system – and in the process, brought literacy to an entire people.

He was born around 1770 in the former Cherokee village of Tuskegee on the Little Tennessee River. He was one of the Cherokee who moved west, and around the turn of the century, while living in Arkansas, he became increasingly aware of the fact that the whites could provide organized opposition over great distances by communicating using marks on paper. Why should the Cherokee not do the same?

His own people ridiculed him at first, pointing out that no Indian language had ever been written down (and in fact, writing was considered to be witchcraft by many Native peoples), but first by scratching marks with a nail and later using pen and paper, Sequoyah created a remarkably effective and suitable written version of his language. Rejecting the idea of coming up with a notation for every single word, which would require thousands of symbols, he broke words down into the most common syllabic sounds, and created a set of symbols that would represent each of these syllables – a task made easier by the fact that every syllable in Cherokee ends with a vowel.

He went through many trials and errors, working with such single-mindedness and in the face of such ridicule that his wife is said to have burned his cabin, or at least his papers, to try to get him to give up his linguistic labours. When he gave his first public demonstration to the tribal council in 1821, people suspected he was just remembering random marks he had made. To prove his claims, he and his daughter Ahyoka were placed out of earshot of each   >>

other and separately given dictation, then asked to read each other's messages. When the test was successful, and Sequoyah had subsequently taught a number of boys to read and write his new script, the Cherokee acquired literacy at a speed and with an eagerness possibly unmatched in history. By 1830, 70–90 per cent of Cherokee could read and write their own language. It's possible that in some areas of the United States, the literacy rate among Cherokee was higher than among their white neighbours.

Sequoyah's efforts were helped by Samuel Worcester, a white missionary, and Elias Boudinot, a Cherokee Christian convert, along with other Cherokee, including George Lowrey and Charles Hicks. Worcester organized Cherokee into an alphabetical order, adapted some of Sequoyah's curly characters to look a little more like conventional Latin letters, and had them type cast and set up a printing press. Boudinot became the first editor, in 1828, of the *Cherokee Phoenix*, the first American-Indian newspaper, with articles in Cherokee and English. At one point, the newspaper's circulation may have reached the astonishing figure of 3,000 and was read as far away as London.

But the Indian Removal Act of 1830 made it legal for Indian nations to be forcibly removed from their homelands and resettled further west. The editor and staff of the *Cherokee Phoenix* tried to move the printing press to Tennessee, but the Georgia Guard raided its offices, removed the press, set fire to the building and stamped the soft lead type into the red Georgia clay with their feet, effectively silencing the voice of the Cherokee Nation.

In 1838, some 7,000 militia and volunteers herded 13,000 Cherokee into what may have been the world's first concentration camps, and then forced them to march a thousand miles west, in winter, to Oklahoma. Thousands died of disease, exposure and starvation.

The survivors were settled around Tahlequah. The Cherokee language and script declined, especially as many schools punished children for speaking Cherokee. The syllabary survived, perhaps ironically, almost exclusively in bibles and other Christian materials intended to 'civilize' the Cherokee.

The Cherokee revival of the late twentieth century saw increasing numbers of Cherokee, both the eastern band in North Carolina and the western band in Oklahoma, relearning their language and syllabary, reviving the *Cherokee Phoenix* with articles in both English and Cherokee, establishing immersion-language classes for young children, setting up language committees to adapt the Cherokee language to modern needs and uniquely incorporating the characters of the syllabary into the visual arts.

Courses in Cherokee language, history and culture are now offered at colleges and universities, especially in Oklahoma, and some of the public signage in Tahlequah is in both English and Cherokee.

ᏂᎦᏓ ᎠᏂᏴᏫ ᏂᎨᎫᏓᎸᎾ ᎠᎴ ᎤᏂᎬᏩᎵ ᎤᎾᏕᏗ ᏚᏳᎧᏛ ᏂᎬᎢ · ᏂᎳᏅᎳ ᎤᏅᏔᏂᏓᏍᏗ ᎠᎴ ᎤᏓᏅᏖᏗ ᎠᎴ ᏓᏓ ᏂᎵ ᏗᎳᏛᏒᏌᏗᏂᏏ ᏓᏂᎵᎪᏗ ᎠᏕᎶᏆ ᎠᏕᎶᏗᏇ Ᏹ ᎦᏃ ·

1 **Character grid:** examples of the Cherokee script.

2 **Sample words:** Article One of the Universal Declaration of Human Rights in Cherokee.

Script:
Ojibwe
—
The Syllabics are one of the few writing systems in the world in which the pronunciation of a letter is based on the direction in which its symbol is facing.

UNIFIED CANADIAN
ABORIGINAL SYLLABICS

Origin:
Canada

There are several people who can be said to have revolutionized the act of writing, and there are even a few who created writing systems that today are used by not just one language culture but many. It's hard to think of anyone who so fully achieved both, but at such a personal cost, as James Evans.

James Evans was born in England in 1801, and went into the grocery business, where he learned shorthand. In 1822, he followed his parents to Canada, where he worked as a teacher. He underwent conversion to Methodism, and in 1828, he was sent by his superiors to a school for Indian children at Rice Lake, where he discovered he had a flair for languages, and, just as importantly, an interest in and a fondness for the Indigenous people he met. He picked up Ojibwe quickly, and began work on a radical document: a dictionary of Indian words. By 1837, he had translated hymns and scripture, and published his *Speller and interpreter, in Indian and English, for the use of the mission schools.*

He also seems to have recognized that the Indian languages were highly rhythmic and syllabic. He created a script for Ojibwe that may have been inspired by the Devanagari script of India and the shorthands that were emerging in the early nineteenth century, but he added, literally, a twist. Instead of creating a large number of letterforms for each of the possible consonant-vowel combinations, he used a small number of simple, easy-to-recognize, almost mathematical shapes to denote consonants, and then turned them through 90 or 180 degrees to indicate the vowel that followed. Thus, an L-shape might represent *ma*, but an upside-down L might represent *mi*.

Over the next half a dozen years, Evans continued developing an Ojibwe syllabary and began work on a writing system for another Algonkian language: Cree. Using that pioneer spirit of improvisation, he even printed a number of works using type cast from the lead linings of tea chests. He taught writing using soot as his medium and birch bark as his surface, and became known among the Cree as 'the man who made birch bark talk'.

Like the Cherokee, the Cree became not only remarkably rapid learners of writing but also teachers, especially given their solitary and mobile ways of life.

'Thousands of people who met in family grouping only a few times a year, with none of the usual supports such as schools, teachers, or libraries, became fluently literate,' writes researcher John Stewart Murdoch. 'In one year alone, the skill travelled from … Lake Winnipeg over a thousand miles to the mouth of the Moose River on James Bay.'

Creating a new writing system may seem like a harmless, even beneficial intellectual exercise, but it can be seen as challenging tradition and authority, and has led to backlash, imprisonment and even murder. >>

In Evans's case, his friendship with and advocacy for the Indians in his flock led him into trouble on two fronts – one secular, one sacred.

On the secular front, trade in Upper Canada was dominated by the Hudson's Bay Company (HBC), which owned a total monopoly on every aspect of commerce. Even churches operated at HBC's behest. Evans infuriated the HBC by defending the right of Indians to exchange furs – a practice that Indians saw as gift-giving but the HBC saw as trading, and thus an infringement on the company's monopoly. In retaliation, the HBC demanded the Methodist church remove Evans from its territory.

The Methodist leadership, meanwhile, was itself also turning against Evans. When any of his Indigenous flock fell ill, he sometimes cared for them in his own house, and as his patients sometimes included girls, rumours of sexual misconduct sprang up. Evans was investigated and found innocent, but the mere fact that he had cared for a sick girl in his home was deemed improper behaviour for a man of his church.

The two-pronged attack resulted in Evans being summoned back to England. He had been suffering from heart problems and kidney infections for some time, and even though he was once again found innocent, by now the stress on him was too great: he died without ever returning to Canada.

After his death, Evans's work was developed and adapted for the various Cree languages all across Canada, and in the far north another missionary, Edmund Peck, promoted the use of the modified Evans syllabary across the Canadian Arctic.

The ambiguous role of the Church in Indigenous languages, however, led to the development of Christian 'residential schools', where First Nations children were forbidden to speak their mother languages and underwent a programme of conversion and cultural erasure.

The health and usage of the syllabics varies greatly across Canada and across the languages that use it. A very general rule of thumb is that traditional languages and scripts survive in the most remote places: mountains, deserts, forests and the far north. Thus, the syllabics can still be seen in use a little for Ojibwe, more for Cree, with the healthiest usage being further north, for Inuktitut.

In Canada, there is now talk in national and local government about supporting Indigenous cultures and languages, though less about scripts. A rare lighthouse of hope is the twin company Inhabit Media/Inhabit Education, based in Nunavut, which publishes a wide range of storybooks and educational materials in English and Inuktitut, much of it in the syllabics.

'I'm more optimistic now that study materials are being published in their own language, culture and tradition,' said Monica Ittusardjuat, a translator and editor at Inhabit Media and Inhabit Education. 'When children see classwork as relevant and connected to their own experience,' she went on, 'they learn faster than before.'

1 **Character grid:** examples of the Ojibwe script.

2 **Sample words:** the Syllabics have been adapted for a range of First Nation languages. This reads *Anishinaabemowin*, or 'Our language'. The Anishinaabe are a group of culturally related Indigenous peoples of in the Great Lakes region of Canada and the United States, including the Ojibwe, Odawa, Potawatomi, Mississaugas, Nipissing and Algonquin peoples.

Script:
Afáka
—
The letter *fei* in the Afáka
script. Afáka stands in
notable isolation: it is the
only modern Indigenous
writing system of South
America still (barely) in use.

AFÁKA

Origin:
Suriname

Afáka stands in notable isolation: it is the only Indigenous writing system of South America still (barely) in use.

The Afáka script was created around 1908–10 by Afáka Atumisi – hence the name of the script – to write the Okanisi or Ndyuku language, a Surinamese Afro–English (Creole) currently spoken by about 23,000 people in Suriname and French Guyana.

Afáka's script came to the attention of the wider world in 1915 when Brother Bernard, a Catholic missionary in Suriname, observed a man reading a book full of unknown symbols. The man was Afáka's nephew Abena, one of about thirty people to whom Afáka had taught the script. Abena asked Br Bernard to dictate a number of liturgical Catholic prayers in the Ndyuku language, which he then recorded in the script. Much of what is known about the script is attributed to Br Bernard's colleague, Father Morssink, who went to considerable lengths to study and propagate the script, with limited success.

The number of current users at one point fell to a low of about twenty, but has been increasing due to the activities of André R. M. Pakosie, who lives in the Netherlands. He writes: 'Because of the Afáka script the Okanisi Maroons are the only Creole-speaking people, at least in the Americas, who own their own script.

'This script was designed by da Usa Atumisi Afáka, an Okanisi Maroon.

'According to da Afáka's story, he received in dreams, one by one, the characters which he wrote on paper the next day. He eventually came to 56 characters, with which he could convert thoughts into written stories.

'Da Afáka taught a few people in his immediate vicinity the script so they could read and write. Within a few years, a dozen of the Okanisi could use the Afáka script – men, women and children.

'One of the first people da Afáka taught the script to, was his nephew da Abena. In turn da Abena taught his son Alufaisi, in those days still a child, the script. Alufaisi also learned the Afáka script directly from da Afáka. At a later age, Alufaisi became the third *Edebukuman*, or head teacher of the script.'

After the death of da Alufaisi in 1993, Pakosie became the Edebukuman. 'This means that I do my utmost to ensure that the script is widely known among the Okanisi and other interested people, and is passed on to the next generation.'

The script has been used in artwork by the well-known Okanisi painter and sculptor Marcel Pinas, which has been its main means of survival during the twenty-first century.

Script:
Osage
—
The Osage letters were
deliberately designed to walk
a fascinating and fine line: to
be similar enough to Latin
letters so as not to seem hard
to learn, yet sufficiently new
that they are uniquely Osage.

OSAGE

Origin:
United States

The Osage people suffered a familiar degradation in the nineteenth and twentieth centuries: subjugation and forced resettlement from Missouri, Arkansas and Kansas to Oklahoma. Osages who were born after 1906 were sent off to boarding schools, where they were forced to abandon Osage and speak English. Most Osages born after 1940, even if they heard Osage spoken around them, spoke English as their first language.

'I grew up hearing Osage spoken all around me,' said Herman Mongrain Lookout, '[but] it never dawned on me to try to learn it.' By the end of the twentieth century, there were perhaps only two dozen elderly second-language speakers of Osage. His uncle told him, 'Don't learn Osage. It's dead. Let it go. Go learn Spanish or French, something that's going to do you some good.'

Yet Lookout – known as 'Mogri' – decided to commit to it. He could pray in Osage, as he had done so with his father, learning the words by rote, and with work, he could pick up conversational Osage. The biggest obstacle was not in the spoken language, but the written: 'When I first started trying to write down some of those sounds, I ran into problems with it, because every class I went to they never had an orthography … they would say, "Write it down the way you hear it."

'Well, I wrote it down all kinds of ways, but when I got home, I couldn't read it.

I never could really nail it using letters of the [Latin] alphabet, because they're dedicated to the English sound system. So then I said, I'm going to have to create [a new set of symbols] dedicated to the sound of Osage.'

In 2004, the 31st Council of the Osage Nation passed a resolution initiating the Osage Language Program. Soon after, Lookout was hired as the director, and was afforded office space in downtown Pawhuska, Oklahoma. At first, he tried to do what most Native nations have done – to take the Latin alphabet and adapt it with a variety of diacritical marks to represent the sounds of their own language. It worked to some degree, he explained, but it wasn't consistent. By using the English alphabet as his basic template, he inherited some of its problems: 'In English, you have two different kinds of "th" – in Osage you have three!' This approach also requires a kind of reprogramming of the reader's mind – not unlike the Cherokee syllabary, in which some glyphs are, in fact, identical to English upper-case letters, but have entirely different sound values. The familiar letters are mis-leading precisely because they are familiar.

'Having your own orthography,' explains Joshua Hinson, Chickasaw Nation language advocate, 'particularly one that doesn't particularly look like your Roman alphabet is pragmatically nice because you don't have to fight against what your learners [already] know about the English alphabet.'

>>

Lookout began developing a series of symbols unique to Osage, but in doing so, he faced a paradox that is central to the notion of developing a new script: if you create entirely new symbols, you have a unique script that gives a culture's writing its own identity, but new readers have to memorize them from scratch – a challenge that is bound to create a certain amount of difficulty and resistance.

He resolved to address this problem by an interesting hybrid approach: he would use symbols that were close enough to English not to seem too alien, but distinctive enough that they would have their own identity.

'I didn't want them to have to learn a bunch of symbols all at once,' he said. 'I tried to make it look a bit like the English alphabet, but enough like Osage.' He described his new version of the letter A, for example, as being 'like a tipi'.

Even as he was working on his orthography, the Osage Language Education Program faced a particular problem: many of those learning the script were also learning the language, so any time the sounds of the spoken word did not have a direct and unambiguous correlation with the letters of the script, the exceptions would need to be explained one by one.

So Lookout, now Master Teacher of the Osage Language Program, started with 578 sentences in the new script, believing that learning this basic core and repeating it would imprint the symbols and their sounds on the new learners. 'And it did.'

The new Osage orthography was taken up with alacrity by students and teachers, and has been consistently and regularly used throughout the Osage Nation since 2006.

Kiowa Tribe of Oklahoma language advocate Warren Queton says: 'I think the most important thing about creating an orthography is reclaiming your own identity as people, in terms of the sovereignty of your nation. An orthography brings back all these ideas about how important language is, saying, "We're going to do it our own way, whatever our community expects. We're going to make our own way in the language world." That's pretty significant.'

'When you see Cherokee, you know it's Cherokee,' Hinson says. 'When you see Osage, you know it's Osage.'

Weekly Osage language classes are currently offered at beginner and intermediate levels in Tulsa, Skiatook and Bartlesville, as well as online. According to the Osage Nation website, there are now five advanced students and approximately 300 currently enrolled in the tribal programme classes.

'To have an orthography', Queton says, 'is one more tool to say, as Osage people, "This is who we are. This is our identity. This is our language. We made this. We accepted it. We reclaimed it. Now we're going to carry it on to the future."'

1 **Character grid:** examples of the Osage script.

2 **Sample words:** part of a three-part carving I did for International Mother Language Day that read 'The right to speak, the right to read, the right to write' in three different endangered alphabets. This is 'The right to speak' in Osage.

N D

A B E T

INTRODUCTION

The writing systems in this atlas are not, of course, all alphabets. Some are not, in the strictest sense, even writing. Here's a curious thing: it's clear what is and is not an alphabet. What is less clear is what is and is not writing. In that respect, the Endangered Alphabets challenge our assumptions in every direction imaginable.

A conventional view asserts that writing consists of a series of signs or marks that represent the individual sounds of spoken language in such a way that if someone who speaks that language, and can read and write, sees these marks, they can a) read them out loud and b) understand what the writer intended.

For centuries, we in the West have believed that writing 'evolved' from pictures of objects or people in the real world, drawn by peoples who were too primitive to think in terms of using abstract symbols that represented sounds. Over time, the argument went, more civilized peoples moved to a phonetic system, reaching a mathematically satisfying conclusion: one symbol equals one sound.

There's no denying that these changes are connected to both efficiency and accuracy. Drawing a sacred jackal takes time and skill, and it could mean several different things, depending on its context, and a pictographic or ideographic system requires learning hundreds or even thousands of symbols. Clarity of expression using easy-to-execute phonetic symbols certainly has its advantages.

Ten years of working on the Endangered Alphabets Project, though, have led me to question this 'evolution', and have made me think of writing as something broader, richer and more ambitious than simply a set of phonetic symbols.

The notion that writing 'evolves' is, in fact, a Victorian, even a Darwinian one, and it implies a series of judgments about 'primitive' societies and their writing systems, and 'civilized' societies and theirs.

In *Ancient Society* (1877), Lewis Henry Morgan argued that writing, especially the written alphabet, was the sole innovation that marked the passage of humankind from what he called the 'Upper Status of Barbarism' to the final and consummate 'Status of Civilization'.

At roughly the same time, this general passage was broken down into linguistic stages by one of the earliest and most influential cultural anthropologists, who argued that as a culture evolved, its writing system did too. Morgan's contemporary Edward Burnett Tylor in *Researches into the Early History of Mankind and the Development of Civilization* (1865), proposed that writing progressed from 'ideograms' through to 'verbal', 'syllabic' and, finally, 'alphabetic' glyphs, each step denoting the intellectual and social progress of that society toward, presumably, an Anglo-Victorian ideal.

But the subtext of this view was that oral societies and societies that used graphic symbol systems were barbaric, exhibiting a kind of childishness: after all, Victorian children began by scribbling and drawing until they were schooled into good handwriting, logical argument and the visible trappings of adult thought, so the same must be true in terms of cultural evolution.

In short, there's an element of colonialism, even racism, in this paradigm of linguistic evolution. There's also the undeniable fact that some of today's most successful writing systems – Korean, Chinese and Japanese, for example – are not purely phonetic alphabets.

The scripts I discovered in my work on the Endangered Alphabets Project invite a different view of writing, one that stands apart from both the 'evolutionary' argument and the belief that the phonetic alphabet is the best of all possible written worlds – a view summed up in a simple question: What is it we want writing to do? Do we want writing to encode information?

Yes, certainly. But is that all we want it to do? How much more can writing convey than just a set of sounds bound up into symbols on the page?

If this all sounds abstract, consider one of the biggest changes to writing in many people's lives in very recent times: emoji. Within the last few years, emoji have taken off, first as stand-alone elements, then as graphic elements seamlessly incorporated into a text-and-graphic mélange. In doing so, they were also implicitly acknowledging that the austere abstraction of phonetic text was too narrow: it had lost the playfulness, the visual vividness and the emotional immediacy of the graphic. Writing is beginning to represent who we are and what we want to say in new ways.

All of which brings us back to the view that writing 'evolves' from the 'primitive' or 'childish' graphic toward the 'sophisticated' phonetic. Instead of an evolution, it seems more like a narrowing of purpose, accompanied by a narrowing of definition.

'We think it is improper and wrong to perpetuate the myth that phonetic writing is superior to other systems of signs,' writes Simon Battestini in *African Writing and Text* (2000). The mélange of forms we are starting to see in the West, he points out, already exists in Africa. 'All the so-called historical stages of the development of writing are present in contemporary Africa and some different scripts have been extant side by side for a long time or are used alternately for the same language.'

Since founding the Endangered Alphabets Project in 2010, I've come to believe our definition of writing may limit us, and that we can escape those limits by looking at marginalized and minority writing systems, many of which have ambitions for their writing that we have not considered, or we have forgotten.

This section, then, is dedicated to forms that extend the definitions of writing beyond the rigidly alphabetic or the purely phonetic. Many challenge the distinction we typically make between writing and art. All of them encode and offer to transmit knowledge, but some are not linear. Some are not static, but performed.

Some were never intended to be read by everyone, even everyone within their language culture. Shamanic systems were intended to be read only by trained priests and their initiates; Nsibidi symbols were the product of a secret society-within-a-society. Besieged and embattled minority groups had every reason to develop systems that could keep their accumulated knowledge and beliefs safe from their oppressors.

The symbol systems used for communication between the material and immaterial worlds in particular imply the question, How do we write about the things for which we have no words? When talking, we try to convey the inexpressible with words and hand gestures and facial expressions and body language and all kinds of multimodal hubbub such as grunts, whistles or oral sound effects. The fact that we have no corresponding resources in writing is another reminder that in conceiving writing as crisp, precise, rigorous, we may exclude some of the very dimensions we might want to convey.

Finally, some of the world's oldest surviving scripts were, and in some cases are, deeply connected to ritual magic, and that in itself suggests something unusual about writing – that one of its root uses was to create symbols that could be influenced and manipulated, and thus by extension manipulate and influence the physical world. In such uses, a symbol or picture is an extension of the world of ideas or, if you prefer, the world of spirit.

Dear readers, I give you the Endangered Non-Alphabets.

Script:
Shuishu
—

The Shuishu script is ideographic
– that is, each symbol represents
not a letter or a sound but an idea,
and is therefore open to a certain
degree of interpretation based on
context. No prizes for guessing
what this symbol represents.

SHUISHU

Origin:
China

There are many theories about the origin of writing – which, indeed, may have many origins. One starting point that is rarely discussed is magic.

Some of the world's oldest symbol systems are associated with divination, communication with the spirit world, spells or charms. In some cases, these symbols are prompts for shamans to guide them through ceremonies; in others, the symbols themselves have a totemic power by representing a person, object or deity. In this sense, a symbol is not only a form of representation but a focusing of intent, and as such, is not unlike prayer. Not unlike writing, too, in fact.

We think of writing and drawing as two different activities, and in fact, we don't really have a word that indicates both things are going on at the same time: 'sign' and 'symbol' have acquired their own specific meanings. Yet the Greeks used the same word – *graphos* – for both, and especially when only an elite minority practised reading skills, reading in itself was a form of divination. If that sounds odd, it is because we are accustomed to letters and words that have been updated and cleansed of their spiritual potency, existing only as phonetic signposts toward intellectual procedures, but such is a relatively modern view of writing, even an impoverished one.

Consider Shuishu, the writing system for the Southern Chinese Sui language,

and one of only a handful of pictogram systems still in use.

According to tradition, the Shuishu characters, which are undoubtedly very old, were created by Lù Duógōng, who seems to be more of a mythical figure than an actual historical personage.

One legend holds that an ancestor named Lù Duógōng spent six years creating a Sui script, at which point the emperor sent orders to burn his house, so from then on he memorized the characters so they could not be destroyed. Another legend says the script was created by six immortals including Lù Duógōng who recorded the script using bamboo and cloth. When one of them was murdered, Lù Duógōng decided to keep the script secret by reversing some of the characters and deliberately distorting others, thereby creating a coded script that has been passed down to the present day.

There are at least 500 different Sui characters in the Sui language – probably far more, as there are as many as thirty different variants for a single word. The script may also hold the world record for the most consonants at no fewer than seventy.

The script, like some other ancient ones, was originally used for divination and other ceremonial purposes; these practices were passed down orally or recorded in scrolls or books called 'water books'.

The word *sui* means 'water', and the Sui refer to their language as 'the water

language' and themselves as 'the water people'.
The word for the Sui people collectively translates,
fascinatingly, as 'the aquarium'. The aquarium numbers
some 400,000 people in China and Vietnam.

According to the Chinese Intangible Cultural
Heritage website: 'The ancient script of the aquarium
is called the water book. The water book is a unique
text summed up by the industrious and intelligent
aquarium ancestors in the long-term production and
life practice. It is an ancient text symbol similar to
Oracle and Jinwen. The water language refers to the
water book as "泐睢", which means "the words of
the water house" or "the book of the water house".
The water book records the ancient astronomy, geography, folklore, ethics, philosophy, aesthetics, law, religion
and other cultural information of the aquarium.'

Water books, of which some 6,000 exist, are collectively a combination of bible, encyclopaedia, history,
law book, calendar and book of spells – the *I Ching* of
the Sui people. According to the *South China News* site:
'In recent years, with its unique charm and high research value, Shuishu has attracted the attention of the
world linguistics community, [drawing] more and more
domestic and foreign experts and scholars to study
water books … Experts believe that the "Water Book"
is equivalent to the Han Dynasty's "Book of Changes".'

The oldest were written in bamboo-tip ink, the
more recent with a brush. They are not written with an
explicit character-to-meaning correspondence, so they
can only be read by someone knowledgeable in the subject – as was always the intention with Shuishu. Very
few shamans still continue teaching young successors.

Other Sui texts include Ruyi divination cards, the
Sui equivalent of Tarot, and a water-painted scroll,
apparently written during the Guangxu period of the

Qing Dynasty. The book has fifty-nine pages, with
five kinds of colours, painted figures, buildings, cattle,
horses, dragons, snakes, birds and beasts. The illustrations are realistic, vivid and familiar, reflecting the
ancient aquarium's pursuit of a better life and of
beautiful culture and art.

In 2006, Shuishu was included in China's first
archives of documentary heritage protection and
the country's first intangible cultural-heritage
protection list.

1 **Character grid:** examples of the
   Shuishu script.

2 **Sample words:** my Endangered
   Alphabets poem in Shuishu:
   'These are our words, shaped
   By our hands, our tools,
   Our history. Lose them
   And we lose ourselves'.

Script:
Naxi Dongba
—
Because the Dongba symbols
are used solely by Bon priests,
and taught only to their
apprentices, each character
is highly idiosyncratic. One
idea may be represented with
different characters by different
priests; conversely, the same
character may be interpreted
or used by different priests to
express different meanings.

NAXI DONGBA AND NAXI GEBA

Origin:
China

The Naxi people of Yunnan province in China have, astonishingly, not one but two endangered alphabets.

One of them, Dongba, has the distinction (along with Shuishu) of being one of the few pictographic writing systems still in use.

According to tradition, the Dongba script was created by Tönpa Shenrab, the founder of the Bön religious tradition of Tibet. The Dongba – the term refers to the script and also to those who use it – are Bön priests, who play a major role in Naxi culture, preaching harmony between people and Nature. Their costumes show strong Tibetan influence, and pictures of Bön gods can be seen on their headgear. Tibetan prayer flags and Taoist offerings are involved in their rituals. From Chinese historical documents, it is clear that Dongba was used as early as the seventh century, and by the tenth century, Dongba was widely used by the Naxi.

The script was, and is, used exclusively by the Dongba. They originally wrote with bamboo pens and black ink made of ash, as an aid to the recitation of ritual texts during religious ceremonies and shamanistic rituals, of which about a thousand have been set out in Dongba manuscripts. Instead of being a literal text like a prayer book, the Dongba characters serve as a prompt, and as such, only key words or ideas are written. This creates a highly subjective script, and

means a single pictograph may be recited as different phrases: likewise, different authors may use the same characters to convey different things.

Both the Naxi language and the Dongba script have been caught up in China's turbulent examination and prescription of its own cultural identity. After the Communist victory in 1949 they were discouraged, and during the Cultural Revolution both the Naxi shamanistic practices and their accompanying language were suppressed and many manuscripts were destroyed, some being boiled down into paste to use in building houses. In the 1980s, there were official attempts to revive the script in both newspapers and books, but by the end of the decade, it was phased out again.

In 2003, UNESCO admitted the Naxi Dongba manuscripts into its Memory of the World Register, commenting: 'As a result of the impact of other powerful cultures, Dongba culture is becoming dispersed and is slowly dying out. There are only a few masters left who can read the scriptures. The Dongba literature, except for that which is already collected and stored, is on the brink of disappearing. In addition, being written on handmade paper and bound by hand, the literature cannot withstand the natural aging and the incessant handling. Under such circumstances, the problem of how to safeguard this rare and irreproducible heritage of mankind has become an agenda for the world.'

>>

Yet Dongba has a life of its own, even to those who can't read it. It has become part of the visual identity of Lijiang, a city in the northwest part of China's Yunnan province, where it appears on souvenirs, buses and signage, and some Naxi people write phrases in Dongba on their houses as decorations.

Touristic usage is more common. The signage outside the Lijiang Starbucks, for example, is in Latin, Chinese and what might be called simplified faux-Dongba: the Dongba character for 'star', followed (as there is no character for 'bucks') by a flower character pronounced as 'bbaq' and the dog character pronounced as 'kee' – the whole combination thus approximating to 'star-bucks'.

Today there are about sixty Dongba priests who can read and write the Dongba script. Most are over seventy, though at least three are under thirty. In an effort to revive the script, the younger Dongbas frequently visit local schools in the Lijiang region to teach classes on it – quite a challenge, as there is no universal standard for the script, and to learn all its roughly 1,400 symbols is said to take fifteen years of study.

The second endangered Naxi script, the Geba syllabary, may be the only endangered writing system primarily used to transcribe or annotate another endangered writing system. It might even be called an endangered rubric.

While Naxi Dongba script is largely a series of pictograms, the Geba script that accompanies it is a syllabary. As some of the symbols seem to be adapted from the Yi script, and others from standard Chinese characters, it ought to be easier to understand and translate than the Dongba script, but the secondary nature of Geba works against this.

As it is used only to transcribe mantras and annotate Dongba pictographs, rather than existing in full stand-alone texts, it is like trying to understand a script by reading only marginal jottings.

It's a strange paradox: while the Dongba script enjoys an emerging iconic status in the city of Lijiang even though few people can actually read it, the Geba script – intended to improve comprehension of a Dongba text – is both failing in its traditional duty and falling further away from daily use and value.

1 **Character grid:** examples of the Naxi Geba script.

2 **Sample words:** my Endangered Alphabets poem in Naxi Dongba: 'These are our words, shaped By our hands, our tools, Our history. Lose them And we lose ourselves.'

Script:
Ersu Shaba
—
Like many shamanic
scripts, Ersu Shaba invites
outsiders to make simplistic
interpretations of its symbols,
which may have a potency
and depth of meaning we miss
entirely. This symbol is said to
mean 'a tray with food', but
what does *that* mean?

ERSU SHABA

Origin:
China; Tibet

Ersu Shaba, a divination script used by the *shaba*, or religious practitioners of the Ersu people of Tibet and southern Sichuan province, is highly unusual, and in two respects almost unique: it is one of the last surviving pictographic writing systems; and it is one of at most two scripts that use a quality we think of as being only whimsical: colour. Some Mayan glyphs used shading to suggest meaning, and the Ditema tsa Dioko script can use colour for expressiveness, but in Ersu Shaba, the colour of ink used can directly affect the meaning of the symbol.

Nobody knows how old the script is. Some Ersu say it is ten generations old, others much older. One account says Zhu Liang, a political and military figure of the Three Kingdoms era (*c.*184-280) carried books written in the script into battle with him, and when he lost the battle, he scattered them and only a few survived. Analysis suggests Ersu Shaba developed around the same time as another Chinese pictographic script, Dongba (see page 234).

Ersu Shaba is neither an alphabet nor even a conventional writing system: its glyphs do not correspond with spoken sounds, and the roughly 200 single-formed words that have been identified, most representing objects, are not intended to carry the entire range of the Ersu language. Most Ersu cannot read or write it; only the *shaba* themselves understand it.

Yet it is by no means arbitrary or wholly subjective. Individual pictograms may be executed in more or fewer strokes in any order, but their basic form and meaning remain constant. In fact, even though *shaba* rarely meet, books found in different counties look similar, and are pronounced and interpreted almost identically. Nor does it lack complexity: a single scripture may contain several hundred composite diagrams, each made up of single-formed words.

One such diagram is interpreted by author Wu Da of Minzu University, China, thus: 'The ninth day of the first lunar month, a dog day, will be a fire day. In the morning there will be fog under the earth. Before sunrise, clouds will appear in the sky. A ritual sword and a religious implement will appear afterwards. This means that the morning will be a good morning. After midday, two stars will die, only one of the three will still be shining and the sun will be in an abnormal condition. One can surmise that there is a deity under the earth; it is better not to move earth that day.'

The script is written by hand, usually with a bamboo brush or animal hairs dipped into red, yellow, blue, white, black and green inks, and the colour may affect the meaning of the symbol. The researcher Sun Hongkai reported seeing the pictograph 'stars and moon' written in black to mean 'dim' or 'not brilliant', whereas when written in white it meant 'shining', and was thought to be auspicious.

Script:
Adinkra
—
'Aya', the fern, a symbol of
resilience and resourcefulness.

A D I N K R A

Origin:
Ghana

West Africa's Adinkra symbols, like pictograms and emoji, exist in a broad hinterland of writing forms that lies beyond the clear, organized, well-defined street maps of alphabets. Likewise, their use goes well beyond the page or the computer screen, and they flourish in woodcuts, screen prints, architectural design, clothing fabrics, gold weights, jewellery and even furniture.

However, Adinkra are not simply visual designs or patterns. Individual Adinkra represent concepts, sayings or proverbs and, as such, are bearers of traditional wisdom. Such writing systems were once called 'primitive', in theory because they don't have the one-letter-one-sound correspondence of 'true' alphabets; in practice because colonial authorities were instinctively predisposed to think their own languages and writing systems were unquestionably superior because they were, after all, the ones doing the colonizing.

But pictograms and ideograms have significant advantages, especially in areas where multiple languages are spoken: the very fact that the symbols don't indicate sounds enables them to travel beyond the borders of specific language groups, like passports of meaning. This is why Europe has universal traffic signs that display symbols rather than verbal instructions.

Adinkra symbols are thought to have originated among the Ashantis during the wealthy, pre-colonial Asante Empire of present-day Ghana and Ivory Coast. The empire was founded in 1670, its capital Kumasi standing at a strategic crossroads of the Trans-Saharan trade routes. Ashanti oral tradition holds that Adinkra may be even older, originating in Gyaman, a state that existed for some four centuries before being subjugated by the Ashanti in the nineteenth century. According to tradition, Gyaman King Nana Kwadwo Agyemang Adinkra originally created or designed these symbols and named them after himself.

The oldest known Adinkra symbols were printed on a piece of cloth collected by an Englishman, Thomas Edward Bowdich, in Kumase in 1817. The patterns feature fifteen stamped symbols, including *nsroma* (stars), *dono ntoasuo* (double Dono drums) and diamonds, printed using carved calabash stamps and a vegetable-based dye.

Many writing systems were originally used by a specific minority within their culture, and Adinkra is no exception, albeit a different kind of exception. Adinkra-printed clothing was traditionally only worn by royalty and spiritual leaders for funerals and other very special occasions.

Over time, their use broadened, as did their background: where once they were typically hand printed on undyed, red, dark brown or black hand-woven cotton fabric, depending on the occasion and the wearer's role, they are now frequently mass-produced on brighter-coloured fabrics, literally >>

woven into the fabric of their society. The Ga (or Ga-Dangme) people of Ghana use a similar set of symbols, called Samai.

Each symbol represents a characteristic or a piece of traditional wisdom, and as such the design chosen for each traditional robe would illustrate the virtues of the wearer. Aya, the fern (see page 240), for example, stands for resourcefulness and resilience, as the fern can grow almost anywhere.

Ananse Ntontan is a stylized spider's web, representing the need for all members of a community to join together and cooperate if it is to thrive.

The most famous symbol, Sankofa, is of a stylized bird that appears to be walking forward while looking back over its shoulder. It means 'go back and get it' – a reminder to remember the past in moving forward toward the future.

1   **Character grid:** examples of the
    Adinkra script.

2   **Sample symbol:** Siamese Crocodiles
    (Funtunfunefu Denkyemfunefu). The
    crocodiles share the same stomach, yet they
    fight over food. This symbol warns against
    the dangers of infighting and tribalism.

N S I B I D I

Origin:
Nigeria

Nsibidi is not an alphabet but something more compressed, more graphic – more poetic, in a sense. Technically, it is an ideographic writing system, whose more than a thousand symbols (drawn in the air as gestures, drawn on the ground, drawn on skin as tattoos, or on calabashes, swords, masks and textiles) don't correspond to a single language but refer to concepts, actions or things that can be understood by people speaking a variety of different languages.

The roots of Nsibidi are in the Cross River region of southeastern Nigeria. Its oldest symbols were discovered on pottery found in the Calabar region, and have been dated back to the fourth century. Nsibidi was extensively used by the various fraternal secret societies of the Cross River region. In the era before these societies, Nsibidi was more broadly used, but has since declined following the introduction of the Latin script in the nineteenth and twentieth centuries.

According to 'Some Notes on Nsibidi' by Reverend J. K. Macgregor in the *Journal of the Royal Anthropological Institute of Great Britain and Ireland*: '[Nsibidi] originated among the great Ibo tribe which is said to number 4,000,000 people ... They are a great artisan tribe, and their smiths are to be met in every village in this part of the country, and wherever a smith goes he carries with him the knowledge of nsibidi. The system of writing is really the property of a

secret society, the nsibidi society, into which men are regularly initiated after undergoing a period of preparation. Some of the signs of the nsibidi are known to outsiders, but the vast majority are known only to the initiated. To the uninitiated they are mysterious and therefore magical, capable of doing harm because of the "medicine" that may have been used in making them ...'

When Macgregor himself investigated rumours of Nsibidi in 1905, he said: 'People smiled when I asked for information and declared that they knew nothing about it. The reason for this is that in Efik nsibidi is used almost only to express love, and this term covers such a multitude of most abominable sins that no self-respecting Efik person will confess that he knows anything about the writing of it.'

Of course, it's also more than possible that his interviewees hadn't been initiated into what was, to a considerable degree, a secret writing system – or that they were indeed initiates, and as such were pledged not to admit outsiders.

Like a number of writing systems, Nsibidi has its own creation myth. Macgregor writes: 'The native tradition of its origin is that it comes from the Uguakima section of the Ibo tribe. The Uguakima dwell between Ikorana on the Cross River and Uwet on the Calabar River, and seem to be the people known among the Efik people as the Uyanga. By them it was taught to the people round about. The way in which the Uguakima say

Script:
Nsibidi
—
This is the Nsibidi
symbol for Nsibidi itself.

that they learned Nsibidi is this. In the forests of their country live many large baboons called idiok. If a man is staying in the bush all night and makes a big fire to warm himself or to frighten away wild animals, the idiok will come down from the trees and sit round the fire just like men. When the idiok did this, all men were frightened and ran away, but the Uguakima were not frightened. Thus there sprang up a friendship between the idiok and the Uguakima. After a time the idiok began to write signs on the ground which the Uguakima did not understand. At last it was seen that when an idiok traced a sign on the ground and then acted in pantomime, the sign on the ground meant the act performed. These signs the Uguakima called nsibidi which is derived from an Ibo word *sibidi*, meaning to play, for they had learned these things through the playing of the idiok.'

The Nsibidi symbols are remarkable for many reasons, not least of which is their ability to compress complex ideas into simple characters. Macgregor points to a symbol like an elongated 'S' that means 'a man who makes trouble between two people'. Another, rather like a capital 'K', means 'a man who practises a bad habit' – any bad habit. More complex signs are compounds that imply an entire story.

In some instances, Nsibidi symbols were used like hobo signs in the United States and Europe – to pass on messages (which were in effect coded) to others in the know. Some might be used as signs of danger, others

that a chief welcomed people to his house. Nsibidi is also thought to have been transported to Cuba and Haiti via the Atlantic slave trade, where it developed into the *anaforuana* and *veve* symbols.

In 2010, a Neo-Nsibidi project was started with the aim of converting Nsibidi symbols into characters that might be used for a number of languages in this region, supported by additional characters called Akagu.

At the same time, Nsibidi characters are increasingly being included in artwork and textile design by artists of the region. Nsibidi was the inspiration for the Wakandan writing system shown in the 2018 film *Black Panther*, since when an increasing number of new Nsibidi symbols and new ways of communication using Nsibidi are being devised.

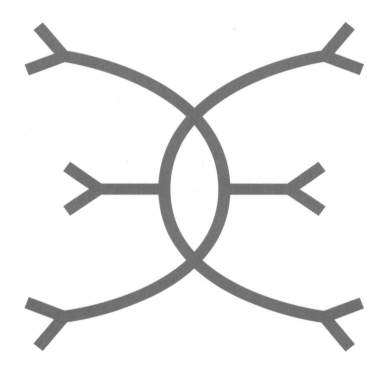

Script:
Nsibidi
—
This translates as 'Love, unity' in
Nsibidi. Individually, the forked-
stick figures represent individuals;
here they are interwoven,
implying unity or love.

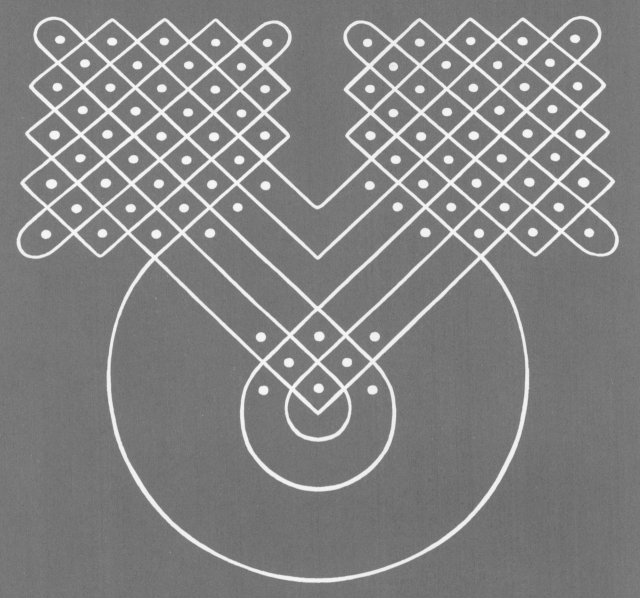

Script:
Sona
—

Though I've never heard a practitioner explain this figure, which translates as 'The house of a man and two women', the meaning seems clear: the two larger clusters represent the women, perhaps a wife and mother-in-law, while the man is smaller, almost trapped within the house. Their communication goes through him rather than directly to each other, forcing him to mediate and try to keep the peace.

S O N A

Origin:
Angola

If we define writing simply as an organized series of visual symbols that represent the basic sounds of a language, the Sona-sand designs of the Lunda-Tchokwe group of the Bantu people in eastern Angola (plus northeast Zambia, parts of the Democratic Republic of the Congo and parts of the Republic of the Congo) push that definition so far it finds itself utterly out of its depth.

Each design combines art, performance, narrative and even mathematics in such a way that even to represent it as a stationary image robs it of its startling, delightful impact and meaning. Yet the Sona may be part of a visual tradition over 2,000 years old.

Paulus Gerdes, who might best be described as an ethnomathematician, and the person who first studied and taught the Sona in terms of their mathematical qualities, wrote: 'The Tchokwe people (or Quiocos), with a population of about one million, predominantly inhabit the northeast of Angola, the Lunda region. Traditionally they are hunters, but since the middle of the 17th century they have dedicated themselves also to agriculture. The Tchokwe are well known for their beautiful decorative art, ranging from the ornamentation of plaited mats and baskets, iron work, ceramics, engraved calabash fruits and tattooings, to paintings on house walls and sand drawings.

'When the Tchokwe meet at their central village places or at their hunting camps, they are used, sitting around a fire or in the shadow of leafy trees, to spend their time in conversations that are illustrated by drawings (*lusona*, pl. *sona*) on the ground. Most of these drawings belong to a long tradition. They refer to proverbs, fables, games, riddles, animals, etc. and play an important role in the transmission of knowledge and wisdom from one generation to the next.'

To call them 'drawings', though, undersells the element of performance. The *akwa kuta sona* (drawing expert) begins by cleaning and smoothing the sand or dust, and then uses his fingertips to create a matrix pattern of equidistant dots. (This pattern actually has a series of inherent algorithms that mathematicians and IT experts have explored with what can only be described as glee.) The dots may represent trees, features of the landscape, people, animals or points along a journey.

He then begins his narrative, tracing a pattern that winds among and around the dots, never taking his fingers from the ground, never retracing the drawn path. Sometimes the pattern is symmetrical and predictable, sometimes not. The drawn line may represent a river, a fence, a wall, a journey or even more intangible forms of connectivity, and sometimes the dots themselves are enlarged or altered, becoming characters in the story. The effect is spellbinding.

'The designs have to be executed smoothly and continuously,' Gerdes explains, 'as any hesitation or stopping on the part of the drawer is interpreted by the audience as an imperfection and lack of knowledge, and assented to with an ironic smile.'

Under the influence of colonialism, according to ethnologist Gerhard Kubik, the Sona tradition has been vanishing: 'What we find today is probably only the remnant, becoming more and more obsolete, of a once amazingly rich and varied repertoire of symbols.'

Is this writing? Not in the standard linear, alphabetical sense. But it is certainly one form of inscribing meaning. What it lacks in the precision and avoidance of ambiguity we hope to achieve by writing sentences, and we call 'saying what I mean', it gains in visual impact and drama, and in doing so surely impresses its narrative on the mind more memorably than a line of standard text. In a sense, it is writing that goes beyond writing.

An interesting postscript: the mathematical community has seized on Sona as an excellent illustration of symmetry groups, mirror curves and Eulerian cycles. Only certain rectangular arrays of dots can produce a single, uninterrupted line forming a circuit, and the Tchokwe artists display such a strong understanding of the patterns involved that Sona are used in lectures and on videos as not only beautiful but technical illustrations.

Script:
Sona
—
The storyteller recounts the tale of the creation of the world as he traces a line in the sand around the pattern of dots.

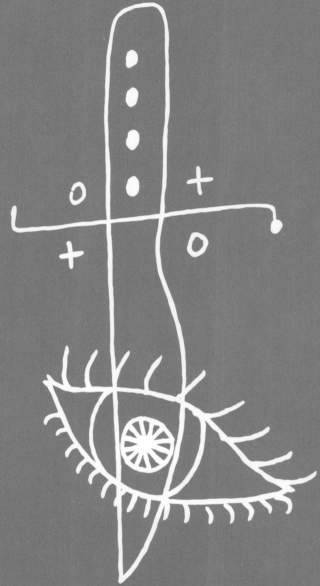

Script:
Firmas
—

Firmas are not so much what
we think of as a script – not
phonetic, not linear – but
more a constellation of
symbols that can be read in
terms not only of their own
meanings, but of their spatial
relationships to each other.

FIRMAS

Origin:
Central Africa;
Cuba

Firmas – the word means 'signatures' in Spanish – are a form of Afro-Cuban graphic writing, straddling and combining the forms that otherwise might be called diagrams, maps, writing and performance, used by priests of Palo Monte in Cuba.

Descended from the Bidimbu and Bisinsu symbols developed by the Bakongo people of Central Africa, Firmas are one of the world's most complex and visual symbol systems. They are also one of the forms of graphic writing that most clearly shows the full potential of the written or drawn symbol – the distinction here is meaningless – for conveying communications that go far beyond our narrow alphabetic/phonetic notions of writing.

Each of the Firmas is made up of a combination of written elements called *sellos* in Spanish, meaning 'stamps' or 'seals' – that is, units that officially mark something and send information. Each stamp represents not a letter but a concept – an action, an object, a place, an idea, a feeling, a means of attracting a force, a focus for meditation.

Firmas are used ritually, combining communication, divination and decoration on walls and doors of houses. And though there is a certain universality of meaning to the individual *sellos*, each signature is highly personal – that is, it is an expression of the energy and the personality of the person making it. As such, they also bridge the gap between writing, which we think of as

having more or less the same meaning to everyone who reads it, and art, which we allow to be expressive of the creator and open to multiple interpretations by the perceiver.

Barbaro Martinez-Ruiz explains in *Kongo Graphic Writing and Other Narratives of the Sign*: 'Although Firmas are widely used within Afro-Cuban culture, relatively few people can actually read and write this form of graphic writing. Their rarity is in part a result of the system's complexity, which demands a professional religious education; close work with a [priest] to learn the range of symbols, the syntax and structural components; and many years of practice.'

One *sello* in the shape of a knife crossing an eye, explains Martinez-Ruiz, and part of a larger and more complex Firma: 'must be made at the entrance of a cave, which is represented by a convex half-circle, and is used to control destructive forces known as "bad winds" that represent illnesses, ghosts, fierce animals, social discord and hallucinations. The eye represents the action of visualizing the divine powers through the *vititi messo* (divination mirror). The vititi MENSO is represented by the cross formed by the vertical line of the blade, the horizontal line representing the hilt of the blade, and the combination of the two crosses and two diagonal circles. The crosses also signify sacrifice, death and birth (in a dialectic sense) of all initiates into the religion.'

>>

By being non-linear, Firmas are particularly good at expressing relationships, connections and forces; they combine an implied narrative with an overall gestalt of meaning and power, as Martinez-Ruiz explains: 'Firmas are … used to depict and call forth spiritual forces, communicate with ancestral spirits and facilitate divination … [T]he signatures function as a type of map or electrical circuit whereby the electricity and force of God, like the cosmic vibrations manifested through religious objects, circulate and materialize. Signatures are used to convey feelings, intentions and desires to spiritual forces and serve as a means for a practitioner to visualize and communicate with the powers of the spirits. Like a text that conveys holy scripture, signatures enable both aesthetic and conceptual understandings of religious values.'

Through this explanation, Firmas offer a different way of understanding other visual/shamanic systems such as Dongba, Ersu Shaba and Shuishu, all of which have been dismissed as simple memory aids. The view that the symbols are mere mnemonics to organize the practitioner's thinking and remind him of the content and sequence of a particular ritual may be the paradigm of a Post-it age; but in context, the individual images may be far more meaningful and powerful. The act of drawing/writing them, especially among other such symbols, may be one of not just representing the forces involved but of summoning, participating in, harnessing and orchestrating them through the spiritual skill of the practitioner.

'Signatures are also used to energize people with the forces summoned by the signature,' says Martinez-Ruiz. 'When the people supplement the motion of the firma through dance and gesture, the result is a graphic in motion that becomes a perfect symbol of God as a unifying and active spirit. Similarly, Firmas are used for healing and meditation and for the facilitation of mutual transactions of energy between priests, practitioners and God or the forces relevant to a particular religious experience. Firmas are also used to teach practitioners religious values … and to provide … instruction in the organization of time and the sequencing of ritual components within the religious ceremony.'

Script:
Firmas
—
The combination of symbols has
almost more in common with
a cosmological map than what
we would think of as a text.
—
Source:
Barbaro Martinez-Ruiz

ACKNOWLEDGMENTS

Thanks to everyone who has contributed, in many different ways, to this atlas:

Bri Alexander
Ardwan Alsabti
Herdimas Anggara
Aimee Ansari
Deborah Anderson
Erik Archambault
Abhinav Amar Aaryan
Peter Austin
Zouhir Az
Siang Bacthi
Jargal Badagarov
Sammi Barch
Abdoulaye Barry
Ibrahima Barry
Aditya Bayu
Kristi Longworth Brennan
Roy Boney
Dörte Borchers
David Bradley
Savr Budschalow
Nigel Calcutt
Darren Cameron
Isvan Campa
Bivuti Chakma
Eric Cooper
Termy Cornall
Craig Cornelius
David Crystal
Andrew Cunningham
Sunita Dangol

Norman de los Santos
Mark Dingemanse
Eijun Eidson
Brian Emory
Jay Enage
Michael Everson
Mark DeFillo
Hans de Wolf
Cole DiGangi
Amdy Diop
John Duffy
Pia Flamand
Marco Franceschini
Elisa Freschi
Tapiwanashe S. Garikayi
Randy Gilliland
Surya Gnaneswar
Arpanjyoti Gogoi
Maggie Gordon
Jerry Greenfield
Julia Grunewald
Indra Gunawan
Sachitra Gurung
Chuck Häberl
Handoko Handoko
Chow Nagen Hazarika
Henry Onyekachi Ibekwe
Monica Ittusardjuat
Emily Jacklin
Alexander Joulakh

Alec Julien
Olivier Kaiser
Pule kaJanolintshi
Abba Karnga
Jerry Kelly
Piers Kelly
Jeffrey Kesselman
Mrinalinee Khanikar
Shaun Kindred
Bill Kinzie
Maria Konoshenko
Uli Kozok
Daniel Krausse
Devina Kaul Krishna
Prem Kumar
Ferry Kurniawan
Charles Kuzmech
Govardanan Laguduva
Ewen Lee
Charles J. Lippert
Joseph Lo Bianco
Mogri Lookout
Banwang Losu
Sari Lovyra
Richard Lowe
Ryan Mackey
Madghis Madi
Saki Mafunikwa
Hannah Majewski
Ashira Malka

A special thanks to Simon Ager, whose site Omniglot.com was the inspiration and original source of information for the Endangered Alphabets Project back in 2009. He has continued to maintain and update Omniglot ever since, almost singlehandedly.

Karthik Malli
Barbaro Martinez-Ruiz
Ridwan Maulana
Gary McCone
Miranda Metheny
Christopher Ray Miller
Nora Miller
So Miyagawa
Stephen Morey
Sagir Ahmed Msa
Yukti Mukdawijitra
André Müller
Hercules Singh Munda
Stan Murai
Vaishnavi Murthy
Nolence Mwangwego
Bill Myers
David Myers
Kylie Naig
Robert Wazi Nandefo
David Nathan-Maister
Paul New
Chiadikobi Nwaubani
Maung Nyeu
Roy Nolan
Vincent W.J. van Gerven Oei
Kefa Ombewa
André Pakosie
Ishita Panda
Anshuman Pandey

Mike Pangilinan
Donna Parrish
Binay Pattanayak
Dave Paulson
Earvin Pelagio
Mindaugas Peleckis
Bromeley Philip
Tochi Precious
Sanjibon Purkayastha
Mangu Purty
Farouk Azim Abd Rahman
Margaret Ransdell-Green
Lal Rapacha
Carlene Raper
Martin Raymond
Charles Riley
Andrij Rovenchak
Alsadig Sadig
Abdul Salek
Walter T. Sano
Ann Louise Santos
Ar Savedra
Adrienne Schatz
Zachary Quinn Scheuren
Omprakash Sharma
Sudarshan Shetty
Michael Shiver
Paul Sidandi
Sally Sillence
Samar Sinha

Greg Smith
Ann Sprayregen
Prasanna Sree
Dalsianpau Suantak
Paul Sutherland
Momen Talosh
David Tereschuk
Marie Thaut
John Tollefsen
Rahat Bari Tooheen
Jordan Toy
Alexandros Tsakos
Dukhia Tudu
Ramjit Tudu
Mark Turin
Val Turner
Enoabasi Urua
Olgierd Uziemblo
Jack Vernon
Ragasudha Vinjamuri
Erik Vogt
Artemis Walsh
Paul Walsh
Aubrey Wang
Naoki Watanabe
Robert Nandefo Wazi
Chelsy Jiayi Wu

ABOUT THE AUTHOR

Tim Brookes was born and educated in England. Before founding the Endangered Alphabets Project in 2010 he worked as a guitarist/singer/songwriter, football coach, tour guide, newspaper-delivery driver, waiter, English teacher, freelance writer and editor and tobacco picker. Since 1980, he has lived in Vermont, which is generally not quite part of the United States.

Every effort has been made to source the best reference material for the sample letters, characters, symbols and words featured in this book, to ensure as high an accuracy as possible when creating the artworks. The sources include Noto Sans fonts, the author's website and carvings, and other online sources. We would like to apologize should any errors have occurred in this process, and would be pleased to make corrections in any later editions.

First published in Great Britain in 2024 by

Quercus Editions Ltd
Carmelite House, 50 Victoria Embankment, London EC4Y 0DZ
An Hachette UK company

Text © 2024 Tim Brookes
Illustrations by Sarah Greeno
Illustrations © Quercus Editions Limited
The moral right of Tim Brookes to be identified as the author of this work has been asserted in accordance with the Copyright, Designs and Patents Act, 1988.

A CIP catalogue record for this book is available from the British Library

HB ISBN 978 1 52940 824 9
eBook ISBN 978 1 52940 825 6

10 9 8 7 6 5 4 3 2 1

Design by Sarah Greeno

Printed in Dubai